S0-ADR-669

Bob & Kendra Green

Books by John White

Church Discipline That Heals (with Ken Blue)
Daring to Draw Near
Eros Defiled
Excellence in Leadership
The Fight
Flirting with the World
Greater Than Riches
The Magnificent Obsession
The Masks of Melancholy
Money Isn't God
Parables (LifeGuide® Bible Study)
Parents in Pain
Putting the Soul Back in Psychology
The Race
When the Spirit Comes with Power

The Archives of Anthropos by John White

The Tower of Geburah
The Iron Sceptre
The Sword Bearer
Gaal the Conqueror

Booklets by John White

Bible Study
Prayer

EROS
REDEEMED

Breaking the
Stranglehold
of Sexual
Sin

JOHN WHITE

INTERVARSITY PRESS
DOWNERS GROVE, ILLINOIS 60515

© *1993 by John White*

All rights reserved. No part of this book may be reproduced in any form without written permission from InterVarsity Press, P.O. Box 1400, Downers Grove, Illinois 60515.

InterVarsity Press® is the book-publishing division of InterVarsity Christian Fellowship®, a student movement active on campus at hundreds of universities, colleges and schools of nursing in the United States of America, and a member movement of the International Fellowship of Evangelical Students. For information about local and regional activities, write Public Relations Dept., InterVarsity Christian Fellowship, 6400 Schroeder Rd., P.O. Box 7895, Madison, WI 53707-7895.

All Scripture quotations, unless otherwise indicated, are taken from the HOLY BIBLE, NEW INTERNATIONAL VERSION®. NIV®. Copyright © 1973, 1978, 1984 International Bible Society. Used by permission of Zondervan Publishing House. All rights reserved.

Cover illustration: Brad Purse

ISBN 0-8308-1659-3 (hdbk.)
ISBN 0-8308-1697-6 (pbk.)

Printed in the United States of America ∞

Library of Congress Cataloging-in-Publication Data

White, John, 1924 Mar. 5-
   Eros redeemed: breaking the stranglehold of sexual sin/John White.
     p.   cm.
   Includes bibliographical references.
   ISBN 0-8308-1659-3.—ISBN 0-8308-1697-6 (pbk.)
   1. Lust—Religious aspects—Christianity.   2. Sex—Religious
aspects—Christianity.   3. Sex addiction—Religious aspects—
Christianity.   4. Forgiveness of sin.   5. Spiritual healing.
6. White, John, 1924 Mar. 5-   I. Title.   II. Title: Sexual sin.
BV4627.L8W55   1993
241′.66—dc20   *93-36197*
                                                            CIP

17	16	15	14	13	12	11	10	9	8	7	6	5	4	3	2	1
07	06	05	04	03	02	01	00	99	98	97	96	95	94	93		

Prologue

Let me begin by saying what this book is not. It makes no attempt to be a classification of sexual sins, however important that might be. Nor is it a compendium of remedies specific to individual sexual sins. Neither is it primarily a statement of a Christian view of sexuality, though some of that is included. Other books emphasize what I only mention briefly; that is, the positive perspective of what the Bible has to say about godly sexuality.

Rather, and in a popular fashion, this book attempts to show the strategy of Satan, and of the ancient so-called gods, in relation to sexual sin. In the light of this objective, I wish to display God's principles of redemption from any and every type of sexual sin. The approach of science, while helpful, is too expensive, too piecemeal and not effective enough. To be changed we will need to get back to Scripture as our prime source of information.

The book has three parts, the first indicating the spiritual roots of the problem, the second, issues of gender and sex, and the third, the means through which God graciously comes to our rescue.

Eros Redeemed has been a surprisingly difficult book to write. I have been amazed not only at the strange way in which time after time things have gone wrong, but also at the bizarre manner in which they did so. Slowly and reluctantly I came to the conclusion that not only is spiritual warfare a reality—I personally had become an object of attack. We learned of voodoo and witchcraft attempts to "get at" me, but in the mercy of God we needed to have no fear.

I am more grateful than I can say for a band of faithful intercessors, organized by Susan Frizzo of the Surrey Vineyard, which came to my aid many times in effective intercession. My family, including the families of some of my children, experienced the same sort of bewildering and bizarre events, often simultaneously. I am profoundly grateful for their unflagging and cheerful support.

Shirley McNutt, my secretary, coped with fax messages, answered telephone calls and kept my workload ticking over while I gave more attention to the book. Andy Le Peau and others at InterVarsity Press supplied me with helpful material in addition to my own research, while Jim Waldron in California dug up very helpful information about war, crime and violent trends. Many other people prayed effectively on my behalf. My gratitude goes to all of them, though I must accept full responsibility for the opinions I express.

PART I
Eros Enslaved &
in Chains

Part one has seven chapters. In the first I explain how I came to write another *Eros* book, focusing on changes in the world, in the church and in myself. In chapter two I examine how those changes began at the dawn of our history. Chapters three and four are devoted to an understanding of Paul's implication (in 1 Cor 6) that sexual sin is unique, different from other sins. I ask what exactly he implies, and what makes him think as he does. In chapter five I try to show the relationship that has always existed between sex and violence, both in Scripture and in world history, and the extent to which this has now brought both the world and the church to a state of near chaos.

Throughout the book (just as throughout Scripture) I am deeply aware of the conflicts in the heavenlies, between the powers of darkness and angelic forces, and the playing out of such battles on earth. Always in human society there have been men and women who are conscious agents acting in full awareness of their opposition to our God. The Scripture talks about them, always in association with idolatry. Chapters six and seven examine the satanic strategy in relation to sexuality and witchcraft, the latter being an invariable accompaniment to either the fertility religions themselves or the worship of sexuality in the Old and New Testaments.

Part two looks at the interaction of science and Scripture, especially in relation to issues of gender and sex. Part three is devoted to those means of sanctifying grace by which healing from sexual sin becomes ours.

CHAPTER 1

A Sin-Stained Church in a Sex-Sated Society

We are half-hearted creatures, fooling about
with drink and sex and ambition when infinite joy
is offered us. . . . We are far too easily pleased.[1]
C. S. LEWIS

The modern talk about sex being free like any
other sense, about the body being beautiful like
any tree or flower, is either a description of the
Garden of Eden or a piece of thoroughly bad psychology,
of which the world grew weary two thousand years ago.[2]
MALCOLM MUGGERIDGE

Years ago I wrote a book called *Eros Defiled.* I sent it to a well-known Christian publisher, and after some months received the sort of letter many would-be writers receive, a refusal letter, and one that filled me with disgust. It told me my book was not the sort of book the Christian public needed. What was called for was not one dealing with morality, but one coaching Christian couples into more satisfying sex, teaching them how to have more bedtime fun.

The writer did not express himself quite so crudely, but my summary of his letter's thrust is accurate. Not that pleasure, even the erotic variety, is wrong. God gave it to us. Pleasure was God's idea. The manufacturer always knows how the machinery will operate best, and our Maker has left instructions. God plans piercing joys for all of us. As Lewis says, we opt for too *little* pleasure by following the world's wisdom—not too *much*.

The age of Christian hedonism was dawning when I struggled to write that book, which may have explained the publisher's attitude. I had written because I was receiving in my psychiatric practice an endless stream of would-be patients with "a sexual problem." Their Christian doctors had sent them to me, having advised them not to tell their pastors about their *problem*. (It is generally held that when you consult a psychiatrist or a psychologist— or even a Christian counselor—your sin may legitimately be referred to as a "problem.") I quickly came to the conclusion that while technical problems of one sort or another surround all types of sin, most sexual sins can and should be handled by churches.

Certain knowledge and experience will be needed to help individuals with their sin problems. Churches can have and can use that knowledge, and they should play a vastly more important role in the restoration of sexual sinners than they do at present. God is revealing to the church in these days a more profound understanding of sexual sin and how it should be dealt with than he has ever revealed to the human sciences. I want to show how.

As for my first manuscript, I threw it into a drawer in disgust, cursing myself for being such an idiot as to presume to write for God. A long time elapsed before I looked at it again.

It might never have been published at all, and my life might never have been changed, but for one or two casual remarks at supper in a restaurant. A year or so later my wife, Lorrie, and I entertained a well-known Christian leader and his wife. In the course of conversation the issue of sexual sin among evangelical Christians came up. I mentioned my disgust at the response to my book. At that time I had no writing ambitions. I felt I lacked the ability. I had attempted to write because I felt I had a message. If the message was there, surely editors could look after the forms of expression. All I wanted to do was to cry out about wrongs in the church, wrongs against the very sinners we should have been restoring. However, I had no voice with which to cry.

My guest suggested I send what I had written to InterVarsity Press. A short time later, my introduction to their editors during an hour or so of interview at O'Hare Airport in Chicago changed the course of my life. They discussed the manuscript. More importantly, they suggested that I write two more books, one about sacrifice and another about ordinary Christian living. Two *more* books?

Lights seemed to switch on inside my skull. Wonderful! Why had I never before discovered—never known—that this was what I really wanted to do with my life? I felt with sudden amazement the built-up pressure, the dammed-back flood of thoughts and words. I wrote two books rapidly. They were published before *Eros Defiled* ever came to light. Nevertheless, in 1977 it reached the bookstores and seems to have been a help to many people. I'm glad, now, that I wrote it.

Many changes affecting our sexual lives have taken place since I wrote *Eros Defiled*. The world has changed. It is a very different one from the world in which I then wrote. There have also been changes in the church, a sliding downhill in sexual standards. And I have changed too. I am not the same person as when I wrote my first book. Let me begin, then, by commenting successively on changes in the world, in the church and in myself.

Changes in the World

Knowledge of every kind has increased exponentially. Philosophies have changed. The Western world and all the cities around the globe are influenced by the changes and are openly sex-crazed. Public and private morality have both changed profoundly.

Feminism, gay liberation and now a growing men's movement have advanced in influence and power. The commercial interests behind pornographic literature and videos are in superb financial health, in spite of many efforts opposing pornography. Public standards of morality slide rapidly downhill toward a precipice. Legislative changes are creating a world around us that is more hostile to Christianity's view of sexuality. As I write, the battle over the rights of women vs. the rights of the unborn is still at its height. Sex crimes increase—and the increase is real, not merely a fabrication of news and publicity. AIDS is with us. Initial optimism about the disease eroded rapidly. In some parts of the world where it was not taken seriously until too late, it is already an epidemic. World conferences on AIDS now issue increasingly worrying reports.

Legislation struggles ineffectively to adapt to the changed sexual standards; problems multiply far more quickly than legislated answers. New inheritance problems spring into existence with the acceptance of "test-tube" babies. International organizations and civil forces of law and order cannot cope adequately with complaints related to prostitution and other sex crimes.

Rape increases. The increase seems to be real, not merely the result of recent trends for women to report rapes to the police. Violent sex crimes are so common that as news items we ignore them—but we start looking over our shoulders on dark nights.

Hard-core porn and even kiddie porn are with us. Adult-child sex has become *de rigueur* in certain circles. Acts of brutality are enacted on videotapes, commonly acts against women—beatings, rape, strangulation, mutilation, implements inserted into body orifices, murders—all designed to inflame the watcher with perverse passion.

Recently I watched the video of James Dobson's interview with Ted Bundy. Bundy was considered to be nothing if not a con artist, but on that particular tape I found his sincerity impressive. The interview took place only hours before his execution. Gone was the smooth, manipulative con artist who had played games with the press. Accepting full responsibility for the murders he had committed and aware of the horrendous suffering he had caused, he quietly discussed the road that eventually led him to rape and murder—a growing addiction to pornography, followed by graduation to hard-core porn. Bundy is the product of a Christian home.

We live in a society showing distinct signs of disintegration. Every month the abuse of women increases, as does the number of single mothers. In particular, change threatens the lives of children. Appalled, we wake up to the fact that sexually damaged children often grow up into sexually molesting adults, so that another generation of molesters is now growing up. And in a radically changed and sexually charged environment. Many children are damaged and many destroyed—by abortion, by abuse in the home, by sexual abuse, by parental abandonment, by satanic ritual abuse, by the horrors and hungers of street life in large cities, by death squads in Rio. In larger cities in North America, at least one boy in six and one girl in four are now molested during childhood, usually by a family member. And some statistical surveys give much higher figures than these.

The Changing Church
Throughout the period since World War II the church has been following the world, but following it at a respectable (though steadily decreasing) distance. By this I mean that changes have been taking place in the church, in its attitude and its situation.

The church knows more now than it did then about sex and shows a distinct tendency to talk about it more. But it does not talk about it anything like enough. Liberal churches pose as more enlightened than the rest of us, adjusting the categories of sin under the delusional lure of being theologically *avant garde*. Sadly, many conservative and many fundamentalist churches either remain silent on the topic of sex or else condemn sexual sins publicly but practice them secretly. Charismatic and noncharismatic churches seem equally vulnerable. We quarrel about the existence of charismatic gifts, but neither side displays (in the sexual area) the sanctifying graces.

The world is not fooled. Embarrassing disclosures of the sexual failings of prominent Christians add to the world's cynicism, not just cynicism about God's church—which would be bad enough—but about the gospel his church preaches, which is far worse. Underlying our failures is the subtle but widespread acceptance by church members of many of the world's views and sexual standards. That is not to say that the church agrees with the world. But the church reads the world's newspapers and magazines and watches the world's TV programs. Inevitably, the world's views impact the private feelings of church members. And it is the secret feelings of ordinary members that matter and that determine their behavior, not public statements of official bodies. As for public statements, a number of churches have now sold out to the world.

We both flounder and founder in a sexual morass. God gave us sexuality as a refreshing lake of joy. It offers us communion—and not just to the married, since all human beings (and thus all human relationships) arise out of the fact of sex. The thrill of a grandchild's hand holding mine is not in the least erotic, yet it is a thrill arising from the procreative aspect of sex that resulted in my grandchild's existence. Had I never enjoyed sex with my wife, and had my son never enjoyed sex with his wife, this child would not be here. And now this amazing act of God's creativity clings to me. It is a wonder and delight!

Unhappily, ever since humanity fell, the lake of joy has been bordered by a fetid swamp, threaded by trails of guilt-laden pleasure. In this evil-smelling place, this place of brooding darkness and death, the church is now sinking. Church members, even church leaders, are drawn by its malign allure in increasing numbers.

A number of years ago the research department of *Christianity Today* conducted two surveys among its readers. One had to do with pastors' sexual habits and the other with the sexual failures of lay readers of the magazine. The research department mailed out nearly two thousand questionnaires, divided equally between the two groups. Only about thirty percent of the recipients responded. One wonders why. The results confirm what some of us already knew. How would the statistics have changed, one wonders, had everybody replied? Some may have refused because they were too busy to fuss with questionnaires. Many others, I feel sure, found the material too threatening to face.

Twelve percent of the pastors responding to the survey admitted sexual intercourse with people they related to in their pastoral work. Under the same circumstances eighteen percent admitted to passionate kissing, fondling, mutual masturbation and so on. Such pastors regret and are troubled to make their admissions, but commonly they have nowhere to turn for help and counsel.

The *Christianity Today* statistics show that sexual failure in the pew is yet more common than that in the pulpit. The report continues, "Incidences of immorality [among the laity] were nearly double: 45% indicated having done something sexually inappropriate, 23% said they had had extramarital intercourse, and 28% said they had engaged in other forms of extramarital sexual conduct."[1]

Some professing Christians copulate for fun with whom they will. Our teenagers are "sexually active." Lonely and love-starved people snatch comfort where they can. Having bought the values of secular psychology, we claim to "take our sexuality seriously." We have joined the ranks of the pompously and self-righteously deceived. Slowly, looking around, we are becoming aware that along the route we have chosen we have lost our way. Church members, priests and pastors are increasingly found defending themselves against molestation charges in court.

The world at present influences the church more than the church influences the world. That is why we tumble into the morass. The fall of Christian leaders, whether local or national, once shocked and appalled us. Slowly we are beginning to take such a state of affairs for granted. We turn from them with boredom to think of more pleasant topics. We no longer want to know which leader is into what form of kinky sex. Yet we need to face up to our swamp-mired condition and ask ourselves what the solution is.

Francis Frangipane, a charismatic leader in the U.S., comments, "There are respectable men who love God and seek to serve Him, yet secretly in their hearts they are prisoners of Jezebel. Even now they are deeply ashamed of their bondage to pornography; and they can barely control their desires for women. Ask them to pray and their spirits are awash with guilt and shame. Their prayers are but the whimpers of Jezebel's eunuchs."[2]

I Too Have Changed

Since I wrote *Eros Defiled* the church has changed, the world has changed and, along with many in my generation, I have changed. I wrote as a psychiatrist, as the pastor of a church and as the father of a young family. I now write as a grandfather and as an unofficial pastor to many younger pastors. I have seen vastly more of life as well as of sexual strugglers since I wrote *Eros Defiled*.

Many older speakers and writers avoid talking about themselves. I intend to talk about myself a lot. I respect the older writers for their deliberate avoidance of self-centeredness. But there are two sides to the self issue. As Thoreau, himself an older writer, wrote in *Walden,* "I should not talk so much about myself if there were anybody else I knew as well."[3] Sam Keen writes, "We are most likely to touch something universal when each of us speaks personally and witnesses to the sliver of truth we have refined from our individual experience."[4]

My views remain the same on almost everything I wrote in *Eros Defiled,* but in one or two matters they have changed. Though I was then aware that homosexual behavior was wrong behavior, I did not know God had a glorious answer for the struggler, a liberation from the torture of inversion. I discuss the roots of inversion in chapters ten and eleven. Curiously, the discovery of God's ability to deliver men and women from overwhelming physical attraction to members of their own sex has brought new joys and triumphs for some gays, while other Christian gays oppose with bitter ferocity the very idea that change is possible. My views on masturbation have also undergone a significant shift. In *Eros Defiled* I described it as subnormal sexual behavior. I now see masturbation as both sinful and psychologically damaging. I explain why in chapter nine.

My own sexual experience has changed. When I wrote the book I had no reason to suppose that, as a sexual being, I had anything practical to learn. If one is capable of writing a book—however elementary—surely one's self-awareness must be more than adequate. Had you challenged me I would, of course, have smiled modestly and acknowledged that there is always more to learn.

I was naive. I little knew all that God had in store for me. During the past few years God has gone through every aspect of my life with a fine-toothed comb. I asked him to do so, but I never expected him to take me at my word to quite the degree that he did. My financial affairs, my relationships with others and, above all, my sexuality seemed to demand inordinate amounts of his time and patience. And I am still learning. Therefore, I write from my heart, from my own "sliver of experience" as well as from my head.

Most significant of all, I see sexual sin as far more important than I did at first. I had not fully realized its relationship to what Christians are now calling spiritual warfare or to the increasing violence in society. Sexual sin in the church may be the single greatest obstacle to the church's evangelistic impact on the world. Certainly our sexual enslavement is a prime goal of Satan's—a goal in which he currently enjoys enormous success.

Our evangelism is impoverished because we are under judgment. The church, believe it or not, is under judgment already. I do not speak of future judgment; I am declaring that *we are now in the midst of judgment.*

The Evolution of Judgment

The fact that the church flounders in a sexual morass and individual men and women struggle hopelessly against sexual sin is both the evidence for and a part of divine judgment. *God's principles of judgment are applied to his own people in the same way that they are applied to the world.* Ananias and Sapphira did not escape judgment. Nor did the church in Corinth. Five of the seven churches in Asia Minor were threatened with judgment unless they repented.

There is an evolution of judgment, whether in the world or among God's own people. It has always been so. Paul explains the principles in Romans 1. I discuss them in *Money Isn't God* and will do so again here.

Judgment begins long before earthquakes and "wars and rumors of wars." Let me express the gist of Paul's argument in Romans 1:18-32. Judgment comes in phases. One phase succeeds another. First comes intellectual and spiritual blindness, then idolatry and superstition, then loss of protection from sexual temptation of every variety, then sexual diseases, and finally a descent into total social disintegration. Only then do final judgments fall.

Phase 1 of Divine Judgment: Spiritual Blindness. If you believe a lie you come under its power. When we fail to live according to truth, a "judicial blindness" falls on us. It is both self-imposed and God-imposed. Divine judgment begins by *giving men and women over, Christian and unbeliever alike, to whatever folly they choose.* "For although they knew God, they neither glorified him as God nor gave thanks to him, but their thinking became futile and their foolish hearts were darkened. Although they claimed to be wise, they became fools" (Rom 1:21-22).

The sin? Knowing God but failing to glorify him. Knowing him but living lives empty of profound gratitude for the gift of life. Knowing him but accepting standards alien to Scripture, honoring ourselves and pursuing our own interests before his.

The result? The result is intellectual and spiritual blindness, the blindness of thinking we know so much, while we know nothing at all. Jesus, quoting Isaiah, affirms the phenomenon of "judicial blindness."

Though seeing, they do not see; though hearing, they do not hear or understand. In them is fulfilled the prophecy of Isaiah: "You will be ever hearing but never understanding; you will be ever seeing but never perceiving. For this people's heart has become calloused; they hardly hear with their ears, and they have closed their eyes. Otherwise they might see with their eyes, hear with their ears, understand with their hearts and turn, and I would heal them." (Mt 13:13-15)

The terrible part of the judgment is that the spiritually blind always assume that they can see.

Phase 2: Idol Worship Is Born. The next stage is the worship of false gods. Just like the world, his own people also became fools and "exchanged the glory of the immortal God for images made to look like mortal man and birds and animals and reptiles" (Rom 1:23).

We are not superstitious and do not bow down to idols. Instead we worship the demonic forces behind the idols directly. Our behavior indicates that we worship money, sex and power. Therefore we have become the playthings of the gods we adore.

Phase 3: Sexual Sins and Perversions. A third stage follows rapidly. It is a further stage in our subjection to dark powers. We are "given over" also to sexual impurity, to shameful lusts and to a depraved mind.

Therefore God *gave them over* in the sinful desires of their hearts to sexual impurity for the degrading of their bodies with one another. They exchanged the truth of God for a lie, and worshiped and served created things rather than the Creator—who is forever praised. Amen. Because of this, *God gave them over to shameful lusts.* Even their women exchanged natural relations for unnatural ones. In the same way the men also abandoned natural relations with women and were inflamed with lust for one another. Men committed indecent acts with other men, and received in themselves the due penalty for their perversion. (Rom 1:24-27)

Notice that vulnerability to various forms of lust and sexual perversion (and the attacks of dark powers in these forms) is here *part of the judgment.* God *gave us over,* as a community, to "sexual impurity for the degrading of (our) bodies"! If you struggle helplessly against sexual sin, you do so because that is part of God's judgment. To put it another way, God removed his protection against sexual perversion. He let you stumble blindly along an idolatrous road of sin until you lost yourself in a maze of sexual allurement.

Far from excusing our sexual lapses, we should open our eyes to our deeper sin, the sin of not honoring God as God in the way we conduct our lives.

Phase 4: Sexual Diseases. AIDS is not a judgment of God against homosexuals or drug addicts. After all, people get it who are neither homosexual nor drug addicts. Wives and children of affected men get it. God does not protect them. In Africa and Asia AIDS is primarily a heterosexual condition, and the innocent suffer with the guilty. AIDS is a judgment of God against society—a society which God has allowed to reap a whirlwind. AIDS has begun to invade the church, likewise representing his judgment. It is the result of the same sin, the sin of failing to honor God as he should be honored in our lives. Society and the church have been given over to the inevitable sequence—to unnatural sex, subsequently reaping "the due penalty for their perversion" (Rom 1:27).

Thus in the evolution of judgment, first comes blindness, then the sexual insanity into which our pride has led us. And it is the sexual insanity that is the real judgment. AIDS is merely a result, an eventual outworking of the judgment.

Phase 5: Satanic Defiance. The last five verses of Romans 1 describe the penultimate stage of earthly judgment. They present an appalling picture. Yet it is a picture of human behavior that we see all around us.

Furthermore, *since they did not think it worthwhile to retain the knowledge of God, he gave them over to a depraved mind,* to do what ought not to be done. They have become filled with every kind of wickedness, evil, greed and depravity. They are full of envy, murder, strife, deceit and malice. They are gossips, slanderers, God-haters, insolent, arrogant and boastful; they invent ways of doing evil; they disobey their parents; they are senseless, faithless, heartless, ruthless. *Although they know God's righteous decree that those who do such things deserve death,* they not only continue to do these very things but also approve of those who practice them. (Rom 1:28-32)

I have italicized two phrases in the passage. Both reemphasize the point Paul insists on. Blindness to the things of God is a blindness for which all human beings in every part of the globe are responsible. At that point God *gives us over* to the consequences of our choices. Then come the wars and catastrophes, which are today already quickening in their tempo.

God never loses his love for sinners, be their sin sexual promiscuity, perversion or whatever form. Jesus once said, " 'I desire mercy, not sacrifice.' For I have not come to call the righteous, but sinners" (Mt 9:13).

Real repentance is a profound work of God. I write about it in chapter sixteen. It begins with the illumination of the Holy Spirit as he removes the blindness, that strange spiritual insanity that is the first stage in judgment. It radically affects emotions, conscience, will. It is a new "seeing" that changes our attitudes about and our feelings toward God and sin.[5]

Is Doom Inevitable?

Is there no hope?

Away with the very idea! A Day of Deliverance has arrived. God is doing things today that fill me with joy and wonder. I write of redemption as well as doom—redemption from chains, from bondage. If I spend time dealing with the horror of our condition, I do so because the glory of our deliverance and of our Deliverer is thereby seen more clearly. Our God triumphs. He triumphs both in his judgments and in his deliverance.

Be certain, then, of one thing. Darkness will never overcome light. The smallest candle drives darkness from the largest auditorium. The only way to let darkness conquer you is by turning your back on light.

I invite you to walk with me, from the darkness and into the light.

CHAPTER 2

Nakedness: What Went Wrong?

"Isn't that like a man!" exclaimed Mrs. Dimble.
"There's not a mirror in the room."
"I don't believe we were meant to see ourselves," said Jane.
"He said something about being mirrors enough to one another."
C. S. LEWIS, *THAT HIDEOUS STRENGTH*

We no longer walk naked and unashamed in the Garden of Eden. Nor do our skin sensors respond to wind, rain and sun caressing our bodies. Our toes no longer grip the wet grass with pleasure. Oneness with creation has been broken. True, we take delight in nature. We swim, we walk, we sunbathe. Yet the quality of our delight has changed. We pursue sensation, making a god of it. We are less "in sync" with the created order, alienated in some degree from its silent rhythm. The rhythm itself has changed. God has cursed the ground we walk on.

Urbanization is not responsible for our being out of sync. Beautiful as the cursed earth still may be, it produces weeds and thorns. It also fights against decay and death. It is out of sync with itself. And we, also changed, are ashamed of our bodies, which once linked us to the earth. Once we were a part of it, destined to rule over it in ways we no longer can.

When Nakedness Was Not Naked

Were we truly *naked* in the garden? Or was it merely that we did not wear clothes? Was it, perhaps, that for the first time there came into existence *the awareness of nakedness* from a kind of mirror inside our souls?

I had a strange experience recently. I spend the first couple of hours or so in the early morning in silent prayer and meditation in the Scriptures. I try to listen to God more than talk to him. Slowly over the years I have been learning to distinguish his voice from the clutter of my thoughts and from evil suggestions. Not long ago I came to my study straight from shaving and showering, wearing only a warm bathrobe. I began to be silent before God, waiting on him. Almost at once I heard, "Take off your robe and stand before me naked!"

"You gotta be kidding!" I muttered—more to myself than to God. The command was repeated. Feeling foolish and glad no one else could see me, I did as I was told. I was not merely unclothed; I was naked—and embarrassed. I was neither in the shower nor having sex. It felt like the wrong setting for nakedness. I saw myself "in my soul-mirror," that is, in imagination, and was discountenanced by what I "saw," even though no human being was present.

I find it hard to put into words what happened next. I became conscious of his eyes, eyes that surveyed my body from head to toe. He did not look at me as a human being would. He was *clothing me, clothing me by the way he was looking at me,* as though the way *he* looked at me took away my nakedness. The sensation of being naked left me. God was clothing me with his eyes, clothing me in my experience with his righteousness, reminding me of who and what I was in Christ. I might still be technically naked, but now the shame—the embarrassment—was gone. I saw myself in "my mirror" no longer, but now in the mirror of his eyes. It would have been delightful if he had left me permanently with this freedom from embarrassment about being naked (though what I would do with such a gift in this sorry world I do not know). However, the experience passed.

Nevertheless, those moments of illumination taught me something profound. What was that righteous covering that covered me? Was it a radiance, a shining from within, the shining of Christ from inside me—was that what God saw? A radiance of righteousness that covered me but hid nothing? The true clothing for which leather and cloth are but sorry substitutes? I am sure it was. God's "seeing" reflects reality itself. And I suspect we shall all share the same experience that I enjoyed in a future yet to be. As Basil Atkinson puts it: "Covering acts towards nakedness as light does towards darkness. It does not conceal it. It removes it."[1]

Were we then truly naked in the Garden? I think not—not until we sinned. We were naked but clothed, clothed not with cloth or skins, but with something else—with an inner shining that some theologians have called innocence and others holiness. We need not worry about the distinction. What is important for now is that we grasp what went wrong. We sinned. We believed the serpent's lie. And at once our relationship with our own bodies, with one another, with creation and with God changed profoundly. We became self-conscious. The enslaving ability to see ourselves "from outside" was born. We began to be slaves of our own image.

The Mental Mirror Phenomenon

Before the Fall there were no mirrors . . . except the mirror of God's eyes. We saw ourselves in his gaze, in the manner with which he looked at us. Lewis reveals the implications of this in a moving passage in *Voyage to Venus*. A devil-possessed man is tempting a naked woman (the Green Lady) on the virgin planet. We are viewing an allegorical reenactment of Eden in which Eve is again being tempted to believe a lie and to disobey God. The evil man has slaughtered birds and made robes of their feathers. Intrigued, the woman tries on her robe; she is not sure whether she likes it. He produces a mirror so she can view herself.

The mirror is a new experience for her, and she is afraid. She perceives the extraordinary possibility of standing beside herself and looking upon herself from outside. Up to that point she has lived life from "inside herself." Now she sees that she could live life viewing herself from the outside, seeing herself as others see her. She doubts whether this is the way Maleldil, the Creator, meant her to live. She discards the robe of feathers but perceives what it means to view not only her body but her *person,* watching a drama of herself on the stage of life.

She did not look in the least like a woman thinking about a new dress. The expression on her face was noble. It was a great deal too noble. Greatness, tragedy, high sentiment—these were obviously what occupied her thoughts. Ransom (a philologist sent to the planet by Maleldil) perceived that the affair of the robes and the mirror had been only superficially concerned with what is commonly called female vanity. The image of her beautiful body had been offered to her only as a means to awake the far more perilous image of her great soul. The external and, as it were, dramatic conception of the self was the enemy's true aim. He was making her mind a theater in which that phantom self should hold the stage. He had already written the play.[2]

Our shame of nakedness reflects something far deeper than is first apparent. With the knowledge of good and evil came self-consciousness, a self-consciousness that was wider and deeper than the mere consciousness of our bodies. Have you ever sat down to analyze the stream of your thoughts? If you do, you may find yourself watching a soap opera in which your "phantom self" plays a leading role. Most people live out a fantasy role that they and the devil planned together. It governs their day-to-day interactions with others. We act our way through life on a stage we are secretly inventing. None of us lives entirely in reality—at least, not until the Holy Spirit has given us training in so doing. We live partly in fantasy, partly in what we can grasp of reality. We picked up this wretched package—shame of our bodies, confusion about our sexuality, longing for and fear of intimacy, a phantom role on an imaginary stage—all at the time of the Fall.

Genitalia: The New Essence of Nakedness

The redemption has not yet done away with our need to wear clothes. On most occasions where the Bible speaks of nakedness it refers to our sexual apparatus and commonly to sexual activity (see Lev 18). The restrictions the Bible imposes on nakedness are a result of the profound change that took place in us at the Fall. With its post-Fall connotation of the erotic, nakedness remains something about which we should exercise care.

God was concerned to protect his people from the sexual depravity of surrounding nations. Consider his instructions about sacrifices offered on an altar. In the days when men wore neither pants nor underwear, he took care to avoid male exposure during worship.[3] No one was to be given a chance to peek at male genitals from below.

> If you make an altar of stones for me, do not build it with dressed stones,
> for you will defile it if you use a tool on it. And do not go up to my altar
> on steps, lest your nakedness be exposed on it. (Ex 20:25-26)

Nakedness since the Fall is rightly associated with sex and with embarrassment about sex. This probably explains the curious incident about Noah's drunkenness (Gen 9:18-27). Noah was drunk and was discovered naked in his tent. So far as I am aware there was nothing shameful in that day about men seeing one another naked (under appropriate circumstances).

What was Noah doing in his drunkenness? Noah's curse of Ham implies more than an accidental breach of protocol. We do not know, but he was clearly caught doing something that produced bitter humiliation. Why else would he curse his own son? Frequently men try to masturbate when they are drunk and think they are alone. Was that what Ham saw? Did he snigger when he told his brothers? Were they more compassionate and respectful of their father's dignity than he was?

The Bible is outspoken. Even in our sex-crazed, sex-sodden age the Bible makes us blush with its language. For in this area it is not what you say that matters, but how and why you say it. God's harsh words through Ezekiel are not pornographic but cutting and frightening, yet at the same time strangely moving:

> On the day you were born your cord was not cut, nor were you washed with water to make you clean. . . . Then I passed by and saw you kicking about in your blood, and as you lay there in your blood I said to you, "Live!" . . . Your breasts were formed and your hair grew, you who were naked and bare. . . . and when I looked at you and saw that you were old enough for love, I spread the corner of my garment over you and covered your nakedness." (Ezek 16:4, 6-8)

But Jerusalem had played fast and loose with God's espousals. The graphic language of his jealous rage succeeds the graphic language of birth and growth. "I will bring upon you the blood vengeance of my wrath and jealous anger. Then I will hand you over to your lovers. . . . They will strip you of your clothes and take your fine jewelry and leave you naked and bare. They will bring a mob against you, who will stone you and hack you to pieces with their swords" (Ezek 16:38-40).

Of course, in Ezekiel 16 God is not really talking about sex. He is talking about our (or, if you like, his ancient people's) ingratitude to him and our (or their) betrayal of him. But he uses sexual language. He accuses us of adultery. He talks about stripping us "naked and bare," of shaming us. He refers to the blood associated with the birth process. Why? Once again it is because sex and nakedness and birth were familiar, everyday matters, yet still associated with feelings of shame since the Fall.

Sex is important. On earth it can be the highest and most beautiful expression of the intimacy that God plans between his people and himself. It
is the area at which Satan would therefore most want to strike, since it is
in many ways the key to all other relationships. Relationships lie at the core
of the Judeo-Christian faith. Christ came to reconcile all things to himself—
that is, to restore all relationships to what they were meant to be (Col 1:20-
22). Sex has to do with relationships. To the degree that we are messed up
there, we will be messed up in all relationships.

We are no longer comfortable with our own bodies, except when we are
concealed. At times our discomfort can make even marriage a torment. Satan
promised Eve a godlike status, but the reality proved shameful.

God's Holy Compassion in the Face of Evil

Does God know evil? Does he know it by experience? Let me put it this
way—God does not know evil in the sense that Satan implied in Genesis
("you will be as God, knowing good and evil"). You can know evil by experience, by doing evil and becoming evil. Such knowledge is darkness. It
is antiknowledge, bringing in its train the burdens of self-consciousness,
shame and guilt. Satan knew that such knowledge would overwhelm our
forefathers and all their descendants. God does not know evil in the sense
that we know it.

Or does he? He certainly knew it on the cross—not by doing it, but by
*un*doing it; he experienced guilt by bearing it, shame by taking our shame
upon himself. He *un*did evil by undergoing the death and darkness it brings.

Kindness has been his way from the start. It was shocking for us to discover
our vulnerability. His immediate action was to hide our shame by clothing
us. God clothed us, not because he is a puritanical prude, but because he had
compassion on our shame. It was a cheek-burning, terrifying shame.

If nakedness originally had symbolized anything, it was our openness, our
fearlessness, even joyfulness before a holy God and before one another. We
were his awed but delighted children, running to him naked when he visited
us in the evening. The association of sexuality and nakedness had to do with
the Fall. God's image in us and then our sexuality were two prime targets
of darkness.

The urge to be naked is still with us. It haunts our dreams, alternately
terrifying and delighting us. Years ago I used to dream I was in the center

of the city wearing nothing at all. Unable to find any concealment, I wondered how I could get back home. No one in the crowded streets seemed to be taking any notice of me, but I was acutely embarrassed. The dream symbolized my shame. The shame and fear of hearing God's voice in the Garden even tortured me in sleep.

The Barring of Eden

Nakedness still has to do with relationships—with ourselves, with one another, with the rest of creation and with God himself. Our longing for and fear of it reflect a simultaneous longing for and fear of God, one another, our own bodies and the whole creation. What sin banished us from, we long for and yet fear. We need intimate relationships; yet, whether we know it or not, nothing so scares us.

There was a time when I would have assured you with confidence that I had no fear of God—only a yearning to be closer to him. Since then, I have sometimes come closer. Indeed, there have been moments of sheer terror when I got closer than I was ready for. Yet still the longing possesses me, and my pursuit of him goes on. But now I know what his fear is.

Similarly, even though we may not be aware of it, there is a suppressed longing in us to be naked in the open air—in the woods, in lake and sea, to feel the sun and the breeze on our bodies, to sense our harmony with the creation. We associate that longing with eroticism, and certainly it can be erotic. Yet in its essence it is not so, and we must distinguish it from eroticism. Nudist colonies, reflecting the longing to be back in harmony with nature once again, pursue what is no longer possible. We cannot now return to what once was. Eden is over.

Even "naked" savages know the difference between being clothed and being naked. Long ago I spent brief periods among the Ayoreo people in the Bolivian jungle. Anyone looking at them would describe them as naked. The men wore only a thin fibre string, which hid nothing. Its apparent purpose was to hold the phallus as they jogged along jungle trails. A loose and flapping penis can be uncomfortable when jogging. Slowly the string of pineapple fibre had come to symbolize for them the difference between being clothed and being naked.

One day Jean Johnson, a pioneer missionary in the early settlement of Ayoreos, visited a crude shelter beneath which one of the men lay sick. She went to take medication to him. As she appeared in front of his lean-to, he gave signs of acute embarrassment and with agitation seemed to be requesting his wife to do something. She brought him his thin fibre string, and hastily he arranged it around his lower body. Only then did he appear relaxed and confident. He was no longer naked.

We smile—but we are no different. On the beach and around the swimming pool men and women can wear almost nothing. Some flaunt their bodily attributes and therefore their sexuality, but others are simply enjoying the pool. And both kinds of people are profoundly aware of the difference between wearing the little they wear and being naked. While nakedness is the same for all of us, the states we call clothed, in which we feel decently and adequately dressed, vary widely.

There are a few situations where to feel at ease with our nakedness is appropriate and legitimate—in the locker rooms of athletic clubs, for example. In contrast, there is only one situation where the fullness of intimacy is appropriate, and that is in the love relationship between a husband and wife. If there is ongoing discomfort with nakedness in such situations, it is commonly a sign that additional problems exist, not just those arising from the Fall.

Sex, Community and the Divine Image

"The LORD God said, 'It is not good for the man to be alone. I will make a helper suitable for him.' . . . The man and his wife were both naked, and they felt no shame" (Gen 2:18, 25). A helper. From Adam, the prototype human, comes someone else, someone who differs from him, who is something else. And so sexuality comes into being. Much more important, a helper comes into being, a person whose relationship is more than sexual, who is not designed merely to be a "sex object." For sex serves an end greater than procreation, greater even than communion between spouses. For with male and female, human society becomes a possibility.

Poet John Milton says, "Loneliness is the first thing which God's eye nam'd not good." Loneliness? Or isolation, *aloneness*? The two are not the same. In fact, Milton echoes the book of Genesis:

I ere thou spak'st
Knew it not good that for Man to be alone.[4]

The quotation comes from Milton's long poem *Paradise Lost*. In the poem, God is answering Adam's complaint. In Milton's Eden, Adam feels lonely and objects to his painful "solitude." Does Milton see the two (loneliness and aloneness) as synonymous? If so, I think even he is missing the real point. While loneliness may not be good, it is not God's intent here to label loneliness as such. Rather his attention is on aloneness, isolation. After all, there is no loneliness like that of a marriage full of misunderstanding.

We were created in God's image. God is community. *In God, in his very being, community has its origin.* He is a three-in-one God. Each of the three, the Father, the Son and the Spirit, is a Person. Each does not exist in solitary isolation, is not alone. Their oneness is something of a mystery to us, but a mystery we can have some understanding of. They are one in aim, one in their values and goals, one in a common consciousness.

As Persons, however, they each relate to the other two. Mutual love flows among them. The Father loves the Son, the Son honors and obeys the Father, and the Spirit comes to us sent from both of them.

Because we are communal beings, we reflect God's image. Physical love and sexual intimacy do so too. Sex, even at its worst and lowest, bears some distorted relationship to the divine image. (If you think about it carefully, you will realize that it is difficult to copulate without relating—whether lovingly or scornfully.) But it is in community most of all that humanity was intended to reflect the divine Being.

As we saw earlier, nakedness reflected the openness, the freedom, the absence of deception, the deep trust found in a society of two persons who reflected God's image. Like God, we were to live in a network of open and trusting relationships. We are neither fully alive nor Godlike when we are alienated in some degree from others. All the words in our language like *communion, community, father, mother, brother, sister, child, husband, wife* and *family* arise out of sexuality. Sex gives rise to community and relational beings. Distortion came with the Fall.

Pre-Fall Sex?

Older writers believed that the fruit Eve took represented sex and that the Fall introduced copulation into human experience. Lewis rightly disagrees. "Some people think that the fall of man had something to do with sex, but that is a mistake. (The story in the Book of Genesis rather suggests that some corruption of our sexual nature followed the fall and was its result, not its cause.)"[5]

Milton felt certain that sexual intercourse was part of the experience of our sires before the Fall.[6] While there is no mention of pre-Fall copulation in Scripture, we cannot thereby argue that it did not exist. But whether it did or not, it was neither the source of our shame nor the cause of the Fall.

Milton puts rapturous words in Adam's mouth. Adam is recounting his experience to Raphael, an angelic being, describing his first sight of Eve, his following and wooing her until

To the nuptial bower
I led her blushing like the morn: all Heaven
And happy constellations, on that hour
Shed their selectest influence.[7]

"I led her blushing." Did she blush? Blushing is the one sign that clearly indicates self-consciousness and shame. The parents of our race were clearly not self-conscious about their naked bodies; they were unashamed of their genital organs. But very quickly they discovered how their relationship with God had been impaired. They heard the sound of God walking in the garden and they hid. There was no longer the unself-conscious running to him like naked children. God called to Adam, not for his own sake, but for theirs, "Where are you?"

"I heard you in the garden, and I was afraid because I was naked; so I hid" (Gen 3:10).

Then came the critical question. "Who told you that you were naked?" *Until that point they had possessed no concept of what nakedness was.* How could they have? The experience that I recounted at the beginning of the chapter made me realize that an awareness of that sort can be gained only by living through it. Suddenly I was aware that as God looked at me I was no longer naked, merely unclothed and content to be so. Nakedness is a feeling about yourself when you are unclothed—an unprotected, vulnerable feeling of shame that we are never entirely free from. Even nude beach habitués would not think of strolling around the downtown area in the buff. You have to be sick, insane, demonized or drunk to do that.

Fear, Defensiveness and Community
"I was afraid," said Adam. Fear likewise began at the Fall, fear that impairs community life. It has profound interpersonal consequences. Fear disrupts the most intimate relationships, destroying communities.

Constantly I have men and women referred to me whose marriages are in crisis. The pattern is almost always the same. As each tells his or her story to me alone, the very words repeat themselves over and over, from couple to couple, so that I could almost write the script before we begin. "Yes, I admit I'm not perfect. I have faults too. *But . . .*" And then the speaker will continue for up to an hour if not interrupted. It is a standard formula.

If I should intervene to remind the speaker of the spouse's feelings, the script goes, "Yes, I know. I realize that. And I've already made it clear that I have faults too. But what you don't seem to understand is that . . ."

Why the pressure of speech? Why the desperate need to convince me of "the way it really is"? It is because the speakers (whether they know it or not) are driven by fear. Anger, too, and enormous frustration. But underneath both frustration and rage lies the same fear Adam confessed long ago. Fear of what? Fear of rejection—of rejection by the spouse, by the listener, but ultimately, and very deep down even in the case of atheists, fear of rejection by God. Each must therefore defend himself, herself. And in so doing we move toward aloneness and away from community.

The fear was just below the surface in Adam. Who else was there to reject him but his wife and his God? But in some of us it is very deep down, written into the coding of our body's cells. Hidden from us in inaccessible and darkened caves in our minds lies a dark terror of God's rage and rejection. And while we may deny its presence, even be totally unaware of it, it flickers from behind our eyelids too frequently to deceive anyone who has the discernment to see.

Hence the covering of our sex characteristics. It is symbolic of our deepest fear, that our hidden uglinesses will be uncovered and we will be dismissed with mockery and scorn. We may "know" in our heads that neither God nor our spouse would do so. We may protest the fact vehemently. Yet fear still lies hidden there.

It was precisely that fear which made Adam defensive. And in his defensiveness he played the "blame game." Question: "Who told you you were naked, Adam? Have you eaten what I told you not to?" Answer: "Well, not exactly. *The woman you gave me* offered me some, and . . ." *It was the woman. In fact, it was you, God. You should never have given her to me in the first place. Me? I would never have gone near the wretched tree!*

I am putting words in Adam's mouth, words Scripture gives no evidence of. What he did say was, "The woman you put here with me—she gave me some fruit from the tree, and I ate it" (Gen 3:12). On even the kindest reading of the words, defensiveness is present. Behind that defensiveness lies the fear he had previously confessed, the fear of a God he had never before feared, the fear that this God would now reject him—cast him away from his presence forever. Defensiveness and fear, both consequences of the Fall, destroy community.

Eve was no different. What in the world made you do it, Eve? "The serpent deceived me" (Gen 3:13). *It wasn't my fault.* Didn't you really *want* to be deceived, Eve? Didn't you prefer to believe the lie that dazzled you rather than the word of God?

Eve is of course doing what every human being has done ever since when feeling threatened. We defend ourselves (or "become defensive"). Eve is unable to see herself as she really is. She dares not. She is at least as afraid as Adam is. And her fear is the same sort of fear. In fact it is accompanied by the same "covering" behavior. She dares not see, so she has to cover, even from herself.

Even the world understands the principle at some level. Why else would they talk about the need to "cover one's tail"? Everyone understands the fear of exposure. When your tail or your rear end is exposed, people laugh at you for a fool. They can no longer take you seriously, and they dismiss you from their fellowship. Or they do worse. No wonder we cover our tails—both metaphorically and physically!

Dawn of the Age of Rape

God ordained that the belly-crawling, dust-eating serpent be at odds with the woman. This had less to do with the Wizard of Id cartoon strip and women's supposed fear of snakes than with the terrible bruising of the divine seed (Gen 3:14-15). Nevertheless, since human beings began to spin yarns round the fireside, serpent lore and dragon lore have flourished side by side, along with corruptions and elaborations of the original events.[8] A more sinister decree follows. Sexuality is to be marred by painful childbearing—and by something worse. "Your desire will be for your husband, and he will rule over you" (Gen 3:16).

One might think that men have more desire for women's bodies than women have for men's. But quickly we dismiss the notion. We need one another differently. Each may look to the other to supply needs that bother the other less. However, for sexual purposes men generally desire women's bodies more than women desire men's.

So to what does the predictive curse refer? "Your desire will be for your husband, and he will rule over you." Though I believe there is such a thing as male authority, I do not believe it is referred to here. I could be wrong, but I think something else is being discussed. One sinister twist that has arisen because of the Fall is that so far as sexual needs are concerned, a man can usually get what he wants. At least he can get it more easily than a woman can. But was that not so before the Fall? Rape would not have been contemplated before the Fall.

A woman is limited (if she is to have what she sometimes wants) to seduction. A man can commit rape. He usually is stronger and he has an erect penis with which to force an entrance into a woman's body. Neither seduction nor rape was part of God's original plan, and of the two rape is by far the more vicious and cruel. In fact many, if not most, men like to be seduced provided the seducer is a woman they feel okay about. We like it because we are less men than was Adam, our sire. Seduction sort of lets a man off the hook. If I am seduced I can argue that what happens is not my fault. She "asked for it."

A Misogynist God?

Yet if rape occurred because of God's curse, what are we to say of God? That he is a sadist? That he is heartless and cruel? That he is against women?

C. S. Lewis points out that every culture's idea of kindness and justice came to all the peoples of the earth from God. "What was I comparing this universe with when I called it unjust? Why did I, who was supposed to be part of the show, was bad and senseless from A to Z, so to speak, find myself in such violent reaction against it?"[9]

The Fall and its sexual and social consequences were our fault, not God's. We have been given the godlike dignity of real choices. We chose the course that led to the Fall and to the potential for rape. God respects that image we still bear which carries the stamp of his own dignity. He could no more make a spherical cube than give us that image and simultaneously not give it to us.[10] So male human beings wrongfully and rebelliously commit rape.

Experiencing the Meaning of the Cross

Some time ago in the early morning I lay on my face weeping. I had been meditating on the cross of our Lord Jesus. Having done a bit of research on Roman crucifixion, I knew that Christ was not decently covered, but naked on the cross. In my mind I was conscious of the cross as though it were looming above me on my left side. Suddenly words penetrated my thinking. *"Look on my nakedness."*

"No way!" I muttered, frightened, not knowing and not trusting what was happening.

But the voice was insistent. *"Look on my nakedness. Look at my shame. Look on my genital organs!"*

I was upset. Angrily I thumped the floor beneath me repeatedly with my fists, "No, no, no! No way! I *will not!"*

For a few moments there was silence. Then quietly, still from my left side, came, *"It's all right. You can look now. I'm clothed and I'm beside you."*

I did not look. I lay still, saying nothing, too frightened even to weep any more. The voice continued, *"And let me remind you that it was I who clothed mankind. Do you know why you could not look on me?"*

"No."

"It was because you would have looked with eyes of sin. There's a streak of the voyeur in you."

I cringed in shame. *"And do you know why my own sexual organs were exposed on the cross?"*

Still flat on my hidden face, I said nothing, humbled, ashamed, yet grateful, in spite of my fear, that he was speaking at all. I waited for him to go on.

"It was because of what you have done with yours."

"Oh, Lord!" I have never felt so small, so ashamed. And yet in a curious way I was being warmed with love and with gratitude.

Again there was silence. When next he spoke it was from my right side. *"You know, John, I know all about your sexual struggles."*

· I was suddenly angry. "Oh, no, you don't! I know what you're going to say. You're going to say that when you were tempted, Satan tempted you far more strongly than he ever tempted us, yet we always give way, and you never did. I know all that.

"What you don't know is what it's like for us. You never sinned. You don't know what guilt is all about. It's guilt that produces the tortured twistedness of our sexual temptations. You never had that to put up with!"

My anger slowly subsided into self-righteous self-pity.

Very quietly he said, *"And what do you suppose happened when the sun hid its face? Guilt came upon me, not my own guilt but yours, and the guilt of all the ages. I knew its torture. I knew what you talk about, and I can never forget. Why do you think I cried out 'Eloi, Eloi, lama sabachthani'?"*

And then I knew. I was overwhelmed. I struggled to my knees weeping and groped blindly for his hand, even though I knew there was no hand there. I wanted desperately to kiss it. I had never realized how close he was to us in our struggles, how truly he understood.

That is why I can write a book like this. I know God. I know why he created us and what went wrong. Most of all I know God the Son, who became a human being, and as a human being underwent all we suffer and more. He was holy. He never sinned. Yet he understands sin from the inside. He is in sync with us now, and he alone can restore our brokenness, the brokenness of every relationship in our lives. And he can do a major portion of that healing in this life.

No power on earth can resist him. The powers of hell tremble in his presence and cry out in fear.

But let us make no mistake about it, the powers of hell are emerging throughout the world in a resurgence of ancient religions and witchcraft. Christ alone, *Christus Victor,* has the answer. It is time to cry out to him for mercy.

CHAPTER 3
The Uniqueness of Sexual Sin

Flee from sexual immorality. All other sins a man commits are
outside his body, but he who sins sexually sins against his own body.
1 CORINTHIANS 6:18

We saw in chapter one that sexual sin is epidemic in the church. How did the epidemic arise? It arose because the powers of darkness have their own agenda for church life. Satan goes for sex first. His strategy has always stressed control over a people's sexual mores. Ever since our forefathers discovered the shame and embarrassment of their nakedness, the satanic strategy of making sexual sin a prime goal has steadily become more apparent in biblical and cultural history.

Sociologists and psychologists might offer us descriptive theories of sin's grip, but they would be just that—*descriptions*, not true explanations. For explanations we turn to Scripture. We must start to understand by grasping the biblical fact that sexual sin is unique.

Paul's statement in 1 Corinthians 6:18 is startling: "All other sins a man commits are outside his body, but he who sins sexually sins against his own body." He says that sexual sin differs from all other sin. The words "all other sins" clearly imply a distinction between sins that gratify sexual lust and every other sin in the book. Sexual sin is different. This is why Paul tells us to flee from it—to take flight, shun it, run from it. It is different, he says, different *because it does something to our own bodies*. The argument makes little sense at first. What does Paul mean?

The Bible nowhere says sexual sin is *morally worse* than other sins. Pride is the worst sin of all. In the words of C. S. Lewis, pride is the sin that made Satan Satan. Scripture deplores cruelty and violence more than wrongful sex. Yet the church throughout the centuries has recognized that in some distinctive way sexual sin is a sin to be shunned. Why?

If we are to understand why and in what way lewdness is a special case, we shall need to understand how Paul thinks. Being Jewish, he thinks like his Jewish contemporaries. He differs from most of us in two ways: in his *anthropology*, his view of what a human being is, and in his *historiography*, his understanding of the significance of Jewish history.

Pauline Anthropology

How does Paul view our humanity? In particular, how does he view the human body and sexuality? Western thinking in this area owes more to the Greeks than to the Hebrews. Today we either see our bodies as having only secondary importance—secondary to our souls or spirits, or else we are obsessed with them—their appearance, their well-being. Gnosticism is far from dead.

Gnostic heresies flourished during the early centuries of the church. They were based on the idea that our bodies either were the source of the evil in us or else did not matter. One variety of Gnosticism taught that what you did with your body was of no consequence. Only your higher faculties mattered. Carpocrates "urged his followers to sin." His son Epiphanes went further, teaching that promiscuity was God's law.[1]

Another form of Gnosticism was legalistic, especially about sex. Marriage was bad and women were evil. Procreation was also an evil. To have babies only led to multiplying souls under the sway of dark powers. A day was coming when women would be transformed into men—a sort of Eden without an Eve.

Greek views have continued to haunt theology for two thousand years, and I mention the fact because it contributes to our sexual difficulties. It is one factor in our struggle. Francis de Sales, for instance, while fully acknowledging the rightness of conjugal relations in marriage, was still influenced by neo-Platonism. Using the knowledge of the naturalists of his day, he cites the elephant as a model for human sexual behavior.

> I give you an example of (the elephant's) chastity. He never changes his mate, has a tender love for the one chosen, and couples with her only every three years. This is only during periods of five days and so privately that

he is never seen in the act. When he appears again on the sixth day the first thing he does is to go immediately to a river where he washes his entire body, as he does not want to return to the herd until completely cleaned.[2]

His view of sex arises out of a suspicion of bodily appetites. Notice what he has to say about eating:

> It is an infallible mark of a wayward, infamous, base, abject, and degraded mind to think about food and drink before mealtime, much more so to delight ourselves later with the pleasure we had in eating, keeping it alive in words and imagination and taking delight in recalling the sensual satisfaction had in swallowing those bits of food. . . . After dinner (spiritual people) wash their hands and mouth so as not to retain the taste or odor of what they have eaten.[3]

This is Greek thinking rather than Jewish. Paul will have none of it. Marriage is good and the body is good, not bad. The marriage bed is undefiled. The body is God-created, God-redeemed. It logically follows that the sexual parts of our bodies and the feelings they give rise to are a gift from God. He designed them, gave them to us. Therefore we must bless him for our sexual parts and sexual feelings. The hearty and grateful acceptance of our sexuality is an essential step in overcoming lust.

The passage in 1 Corinthians 6 presents a totally different perspective from Gnosticism and from Platonic thought. Examine it carefully. Notice what a high view Paul has of the human body. Eight times from verse 13 to verse 20 the term *body* occurs. Each mention is devoted to showing its glory.

More to the point, God the Son *currently exists in a human body*, uniting our human condition with divinity. He will remain so throughout eternity. In this way he exemplifies the great honor God bestows on what we, the Greeks and the Gnostics look down on—our bodies. At present, of course, our bodies are truly lowly bodies, lowly because of sin and the Fall, but not lowly in their creation.

At the resurrection my body will be raised from death. I shall wear it when I enter heaven. True, it will be changed, freed from corruption. But it will still be my body. I cannot altogether avoid a twinge of regret that I shall not have sex then, but I shall enjoy something even greater—the intimacy with God that sex points to. In that day we shall all be "as the angels in heaven," having gender but not sexuality.

Pauline Historiography

We have, however, only begun to answer the question, Why and how does sexual sin differ from all other sin? The most significant part of our inquiry remains. Far, far more important is the understanding that comes from Israel's ancient history.

Later in 1 Corinthians (10:1-10) Paul offers a quick review of the history of Israel following their exodus from Egypt under Moses' leadership. "For I do not want you to be ignorant of . . . our forefathers" he begins, for they committed many sins as they wandered in the wilderness and died there as a result. Then, he draws his conclusions. "Do not be idolaters, as some of them were; as it is written: 'The people sat down to eat and drink and got up to indulge in pagan revelry.' We should not commit sexual immorality, as some of them did—and in one day twenty-three thousand of them died" (1 Cor 10:1, 7-8).

Paul's mention of twenty-three thousand who died is a reference to a very significant incident in the history of Israel that occurred at Shittim. As we look more closely at this episode to understand the uniqueness of sexual sin, we shall consider several key concepts: (1) The incident at Shittim as a turning point in Israel's history; (2) the role and nature of pagan fertility religions and their impact on Israel; (3) genocide and divine judgment; and (4) Satan's territorial claims on earth.

Israel's Unfaithfulness at Shittim

After God brought Israel out of Egypt, Moses led the people in the wilderness for forty years. Shittim was the last encampment of the nation of Israel before they crossed the Jordan to the Promised Land.

The march of this formidable army had struck terror into many nearby tribes. As Israel approached King Balak of Moab, he was desperate. So he decided to hire Balaam the seer to place a curse on Israel (Num 22—24). Once Balaam's initial fear of God was overcome, and lured by a reward of Balak's gold, Balaam (amidst the well-known episodes with his talking donkey) made several futile attempts to curse Israel, only to find that, as he suspected, the Spirit of God was too strong for him. Frustrated, and seeing his chances for Balak's gold fading, he turned his prophetic gifts to divination. The book of Revelation fills in what Numbers leaves out. "Balaam . . . taught Balak to entice the Israelites to sin by eating food sacrificed to idols *and by committing sexual immorality*" (Rev 2:14).

Having failed to deter the army of Israel with curses, Balaam turned to other measures. He realized what the powers of darkness have known all along—that Israel's military might would be nothing if it could be induced to be unfaithful to God.[4] So as a result,

> While Israel was staying in Shittim, the men began to indulge in sexual immorality with Moabite women, who invited them to the sacrifices to their gods. The people ate and bowed down before these gods. So Israel joined in worshiping the Baal of Peor. And the LORD's anger burned against them. The LORD said to Moses, "Take all the leaders of these people, kill them and expose them in broad daylight before the LORD, so that the LORD's fierce anger may turn away from Israel." So Moses said to Israel's judges, "Each of you must put to death those of your men who have joined in worshiping the Baal of Peor." . . . Then the plague against the Israelites was stopped; but those who died in the plague numbered 24,000. (Num 25:1-5, 8-9)

I have not included the full story, which is brutal and bloody. Briefly, the leaders were to be put to death and their bodies hung from trees. It is not precisely certain what it means that they were to be exposed. The punishment for sexual sin sometimes called for the humiliation of naked exposure (see Ezek 16:35-37).[5] Nonetheless, the people as a whole were punished. A virulent plague began to decimate the Israelites. God's judgment had fallen. They had used their sexuality and their seed to worship gods who were no gods.

Fertility Cults
The pagan world into which Israel was moving worshiped fertility. Notice the origins both of the Moabite race and of the Ammonites. Moab and Ammon were Lot's descendants. Both races came into existence through incest between Lot and his daughters (Gen 19:36-38). The fact is significant. Both countries were hotbeds of the fertility cults. We do well to heed the doctrine of the seed in Scripture.

C. S. Lewis gives us a picture of the brutality, the sordidness and the strange allure of worship by sex in the novel *Till We Have Faces*. It is clear that Lewis is under no illusions about the awesome power behind fertility. G. K. Chesterton points out that before the revelation of God to his people, "there was nothing for the mass of men in the way of mysticism, except that concerned with the mystery of the nameless forces of nature, such as sex and growth and death."[6]

At the heart of fertility worship was the idea of an exchange. You gave seeds (whatever seeds were important to the economy) as an offering for the god's blessing on the seed of your crops and animals. In most cases, and this was the case in the Middle East, you gave the seed of your own body in the mystery of a ritualized sex act. It was a religious act, an act of false worship of a *quid pro quo* variety—your own seed in supposed exchange for fertility.

Basic to life in the Middle East were male and female "shrine" or "cult" prostitutes. The system seems to have been entrenched long before Moses. Judah, patriarch of the tribe of Judah, unwittingly engaged in sex with his own daughter-in-law, Tamar, who had disguised herself as a shrine prostitute in order to force Judah to give her a child (Gen 38:11-30). The Hebrew word used for *prostitute* in verses 21-22 refers to shrine prostitutes, those who engaged in acts of ritual sex.

Sacrifices made to idols had little meaning in themselves. Rather, the gift of your body and your body's seed mattered most. You gave your seed to the god to whom you would later offer a sacrifice. In return for your seed and your acknowledgment of the god's sovereignty, the god was supposed to guarantee a multiplication of your seed crops and to enhance your own personal fertility and that of your animals.

As I reflect on the important role of fertility religions in world history, I also wonder about the respective roles of male and female shrine prostitutes. Female shrine prostitutes symbolized mother earth and her fertility. What then of the male prostitutes? Was it that as they crouched on hands and knees (as some men do to receive the phallus of a lover) the symbolism became that of animal fertility? And was it by such a master stroke that Satan led the way to sodomy in its various expressions? Did male mounting another crouching male suggest the animal sex it symbolizes?

Friends are (as Lewis puts it) side by side, but lovers face to face. We are meant to adore God like that—face to face. If we bow or lie prostrate, we face downward. It is his pleasure and his grace that lift our heads to look with adoring longing into his face.

God had made it clear that he alone was the only source of life, fertility and prosperity (Deut 7:13-16). He alone made crops grow and animals reproduce. Only he gave rain. Locust armies were under his control. Fertility was a gift of his grace. In making sex a mysterious ritual (the seed of your body in exchange for the multiplication of your crops), the fertility religions revived Satan's rivalry with heaven. Therefore, God did not, could not, tolerate what happened at Shittim.

Sexual sin enslaves us to the "gods" to whom (in our case) we unwittingly yield ourselves. Every time we sin by misusing the sexual parts of our bodies, or by indulging in erotic fantasy, by pursuing pornography or paying for time on erotic telephone numbers, their power over our behavior increases. Sexual sin is sin because it is idolatry. And while idolatry can enter into many forms of sin, it does not do so in the way sexual sin seems to.

Paul knew about the idolatry of the ancient fertility religions. In 1 Corinthians 10 he picks up the theme he began in the sixth chapter. "For I do not want you to be ignorant of . . . our forefathers. . . . We should not commit sexual immorality, as some of them did—and in one day twenty-three thousand of them died" (1 Cor 10:1, 8). The twenty-three thousand refers to the judgment at Shittim. Other sins might involve other forms of idolatry and be "outside the body" (1 Cor 6:18). Sexual sin always involves the presentation of one's body (and therefore also of our whole selves) to the dark powers that wish to control it.

Like certain other sins, sexual sin grips. It tends to be repetitive, compulsive. I have heard experienced Christian leaders say, "Once a pastor has fallen into sexual sin, you will never be able to trust him again." I believe they are wrong, but I admit that healing and repentance must precede restoration to service.

The element that psychology and psychiatry miss in sinful compulsions is satanic power and control. Sexual sinners are under the control of darkness, not because it is more evil than other sins but because we are more easily controlled by sex. Hence its strategic significance in warfare. This may be more true of men than of women. Get your hands on a man's genitals, and you can do almost anything with him. You can reduce him to a shocked, groaning and vomiting weakling, or you can seduce him to give you what you want.

The fact that we lose control, finding ourselves hopelessly and helplessly in the grip of sexual urges now inflamed by satanic cohorts, is no excuse. We are responsible for the sexual sins we commit. We got ourselves into the mess by our own choice. Drunk drivers are responsible for the death of anyone they slaughter on the highway. Likewise, child molesters are account-able for the cruel wrong to their victims. We are to be held accountable for every sexual sin we commit. If we are the victims of dark powers, it is because we have chosen to be. (See Rom 1:20-25.)

And what does all this have to do with the church's victory over the powers of darkness now? Just this—that temptation to sexual sin is Satan's first stratagem in impairing our ability to fight. We preach the gospel to a lost world with our shield arms tied behind our backs and our ears deaf to divine orders.

The Judgment of Genocide

But let me return to Israel's military victories that terrorized all the surround-ing peoples. At God's command they defeated and completely wiped out whole towns and tribes. How had a slave rabble been transformed into an effective fighting force? Where did their military skill come from? Clearly, from divine leading, divine strategy and divine power. But why did God want the annihilation of nations worshiping Baal, Ashtoreth or Molech (see Deut 7:1-6)?

God certainly has every right to do what he wants with his own creation. Genocide means the wiping out of a species. In modern usage, it has come to mean wiping out a people descended from a common ancestor, even a whole nation. To modern liberal thinkers it is the ultimate crime, and cer-tainly it is an inconceivable horror. We can think of nothing more appalling, for we have never grasped the frightful nature of sin itself.

We ask, why would God order such a course of action? The answer, I believe, lies in the territorial claims by the rules of darkness over certain geographic areas of the earth. While some dispute this doctrine, let me summarize the scriptural evidence.

Satan's Territorial Claims

First, I must define what I mean. I believe Scripture tells us that earthly regions (principalities) can be ruled by specific evil beings, fallen angelic beings associated with Satan's rebellion. Since *principalities and powers can rule only through human beings who willingly collaborate by sinning* (in this case sexually), to rid the area of such control God called Israel to drastic mea-sures.

As for the human beings: In the nations Israel was to replace, ritualized sexual worship had continued for years, so that the economy, family life, the culture and political system were impregnated with it. When the sin of a nation was full and the rebellion had become fixed, the divine judgment of genocide followed.

As for the powers: That fallen angels exist, that they wrongly exercise control over earthly territories, that there are battles in heavenly places and that these battles are somehow related to earthly events—these things are certainly suggested by a number of biblical passages. (See Dan 10:4-21; Lk 4:5-7; Jn 12:31; 14:30; 16:11; Eph 6:12; Rev 12:12 and so on.)

Our forebears were given sovereignty under God. We forfeited our right to rule when we believed the word of the serpent, doing exactly what he suggested. In hearing and acting upon the word of the serpent, our forebears relinquished their right to govern the earth and gave their own rule to Satan. That is why God cursed the ground. Anything over which Satan rules is and *must be* cursed (Gen 3:17).

Jeremiah is crystal clear on the issue. He sees Molech ruling over Gad because members of the tribe serve Molech rather than the Lord. He urges Israel to rise up and overcome the Ammonites, whose influence over the inhabitants of Gad accounts for Molech's territorial rule there. "Concerning the Ammonites: This is what the LORD says: 'Has Israel no sons? Has she no heirs? Why then has Molech taken possession of Gad? Why do his people live in its towns? . . . for Molech will go into exile, together with his priests and officials' " (Jer 49:1, 3).

When the Germans invaded Norway in World War II, they did so with the aid of Vilkun Quisling, a Norwegian diplomat. Quisling's name became synonymous with "traitor." Thereafter, Norwegians were divided into those who supported the resistance movement and those who supported the collaborating civilian government. The latter were known as *quislings*. God sees Israel's persistent appeal to Molech for what God himself had given by grace as treachery and betrayal.

Jeremiah calls them to do with Ammon what he had originally made clear they should do, in order to free Dan's territory. Molech's people, priests and officials were to be exiled from Dan's earthly territory.

Satan's rule has always and only been exercised through a rebellious and fallen race, that is, through people. The nations worshiping the fertility gods had in the course of time become ripe for judgment. They were to be exterminated. *Israel was to exterminate them.*

> And when the LORD your God has delivered them over to you and you have defeated them, then you must destroy them totally. Make no treaty with them, and show them no mercy. (Deut 7:2)

> You must destroy all the peoples the LORD your God gives over to you. Do not look on them with pity and do not serve their gods, for that will be a snare to you. (Deut 7:16)

(See also Deut 2:32-34; 3:2-6 and elsewhere.) Since those nations refused to abandon their practices, only genocide, or annihilation, could liberate the territories Israel was to inherit from control by fallen angelic beings. Therefore, if Israel herself were to fall into idolatry, she would in effect be handing those same territories back to the very gods she was supposed to supplant.

It was essential for that not to happen. The lesson had to be made clear. Lewdness was out. Our bodies, carrying as they do the future generations of beings that bear the divine image, must not be handed over to demons in worship. The result was God's judgment.

Judgment and a God of Love

Let us face facts. The God of the Scriptures is both tender and fierce, just as the Jesus of the New Testament was by turns torn by compassion and filled with flaming ferocity. Judgment fell on Israel many times. God knows the deadly nature of sin. *We have no concept of the danger, the horrendous deadliness of sin, and therefore judgment bewilders us.*

The annihilation of a nation is not more awful than human defiance and rebellion against God. And when in the wisdom of God the time has become ripe for judgment to fall on a nation or people, judgment has always taken place, will always take place. The God of the Bible is a God of compassion, of patience, of mercy, but when he has to act, he does so. And his action is thorough. Moral cancer must go.

At times God uses the wickedness of one nation to bring judgment on another. Long before Nebuchadnezzar humbled himself before him, God spoke of "my servant Nebuchadnezzar" (Jer 25:9; 27:6). In the same way, "in order to fulfill the word of the Lord spoken by Jeremiah, the LORD moved the heart of Cyrus king of Persia" (2 Chron 36:22). In neither case is the godliness of these rulers implied.

Elsewhere I have told the story of when my first son, Scott, was just learning to walk and fell on a cement walkway, splitting the area below his chin so deeply that the floor of his mouth was exposed. We were appalled. Hospitals and doctors were 250 kilometers away over tortuous mountain roads. I had no surgical instruments with me. A quick catalog of our resources turned up a less-than-impressive array of one darning needle, coarse thread, one pair of rather blunt scissors and one pair of eyebrow tweezers. Infection in children develops rapidly, and infection in the floor of the mouth can have fatal complications. We also had a little sulfonamide powder. There was no local anesthetic. Rightly or wrongly, I decided to trim and stitch the wound with what we had.

We sterilized "the instruments." I could not help but look at the affair from Scott's point of view. I did my best to explain, but what can a one-year-old understand? Then he was placed on the dining room table—and judgment descended on him. Cruel adults seized his limbs and his head so that movement was impossible. Then the father he had trusted became a fearful monster inflicting unbelievable pain on him. How I wished that he could understand that I feared for his life. Mercifully, he still seemed to trust me when it was over. As for me, I had caught a glimpse of judgment from God's angle.

The Turning Point
The catastrophe at Shittim itself is appalling. What is important is that the terrible event, representing as it does the seriousness with which God viewed the incident, becomes a turning point in Israel's history.

You can tell that an event has unusual significance by the number of biblical allusions to it. Moses refers to Shittim once more in his speech in Deuteronomy. Joshua also refers to it. So also do Nehemiah, Hosea, Micah, Peter, Jude and John the apostle (Deut 23:4-5; Josh 13:22; 24:9-10; Neh 13:2; Hos 9:10-15; Mic 6:5-8; 2 Pet 2:15-16; Jude 11; Rev 2:14). Both Israel and the early church, both Old and New Testaments unite to see the significance of the tragedy. But it takes the prophet Micah to spot the whole story. He pours scorn on fertility idolatry and puts his finger on the lesson to be learned. "My people, remember what Balak king of Moab counseled and what Balaam son of Beor answered. *Remember [your journey] from Shittim to Gilgal,* that you may know the righteous acts of the LORD" (Mic 6:5).

Israel's history from this point until the time of their return from exile in Babylon (some 700 years later) centers around the struggle against worship by sex. Not until the time of Ezra and Nehemiah after the exile is this threat to Israel's whole destiny removed.

What were the measures God adopted to try to fortify the terrible lesson of Shittim as the Israelites entered the Promised Land? We shall look at the problem carefully in the next chapter.

CHAPTER 4
Overcoming Idolatry and Sexual Sin

Some tree, whose broad smooth leaves, together sewed,
And girded on our loins, may cover round
Those middle parts, that this new comer, Shame,
There sit not, and reproach us as unclean.
JOHN MILTON, *PARADISE LOST*

How could one man chase a thousand, or two put ten thousand to flight,
unless their Rock had sold them, unless the LORD had given
them up? . . . Their vine comes from the vine of Sodom and from the
fields of Gomorrah. Their grapes are filled with poison,
and their clusters with bitterness.
DEUTERONOMY 32:30, 32

Satan seized on our sexuality during human history's opening moments, covering us with shame at our own bodies. In doing so he polluted and distorted sex. He instantly achieved our alienation from the earth, from our own bodies, from one another and from God.

Then the eyes of both of them were opened, and they realized they were naked; so they sewed fig leaves together and made coverings for themselves. . . . (Adam) answered, "I heard you in the garden, and I was afraid because I was naked; so I hid." (Gen 3:7, 10)

Sex happens to be one means by which we learn to relate intimately.[1] I do not speak merely of brief moments of sexual ecstasy, for learning intimacy takes a lifetime—a lifetime of fidelity, of self-discovery and of the discovery of someone else.

Was Satan jealous that God should confer so high a privilege on time-bound, warm-blooded, naked bipeds? Was that why he went for our sexuality? It is easy to see how vulnerable we would be. Our sexual feelings and the organs that express them have explosive potential. Men more than women can virtually be controlled by sex.

Whatever the reason, Satan not only went for our sexuality when time began but has made it a prime means of control over humanity ever since. Sexual philandering by church members accounts in good measure for the impotence of the church's gospel presentation. When Satan has half the church in the grip of sexual sin we are fighting "principalities and powers" with our sword arms tied behind our backs.

God and Evil

God controls all things. He sets limits on evil beings—angels, demons, humans. I like the King James version of Psalm 76:10: "Surely the wrath of man shall praise thee, the remainder of wrath thou shalt restrain." God uses evil that flows from the Fall and from our own sin to bring judgment to pass. Thus disaster, disease, darkness and death come about by the choices of evil men and women, and by the powers of evil.

Satan is the immediate author of catastrophe. We sow the evil wind and we reap an evil whirlwind. Satan sends hurricanes, earthquakes, wars, plagues, famine. He does so within the hand of the God of judgment and holiness. The evil comes from Satan—but only within a God-created universe that allows real choices and real consequences to exist. So Paul the apostle receives "a messenger of Satan to buffet him." And because God has a good purpose in the buffeting, God ignores Paul's pleading to be delivered. God turns evil to good.

Satan has usurped earthly rule. God allowed this when he cursed the earth. We had to learn the nature of our choice by experience. Now the earth produces thorns and briars which were not part of the original creation. It also produces sickness and death. It is cursed. It is ruled by demons. It is a place of perpetual struggle against alienation.

I can only presume that evil powers do not comprehend the extent to which they fulfill the divine purposes! They do so insofar as God uses them in bringing about divine judgment. It is God's overall goal to eliminate them. In doing so he uses mankind—specifically his ancient people and the church.

Worship and Idolatry en Route to Gilgal

So we return to the journeys of Israel. Shittim was the last encampment of Israel before crossing the Jordan. Gilgal was their first after crossing the Jordan (Josh 3:1; 4:19). One represented tragedy and the other triumph.

The prophet Micah looked back to this journey when he urged, "My people, remember what Balak king of Moab counseled and what Balaam son of Beor answered. Remember [your journey] from Shittim to Gilgal, that you may know the righteous acts of the LORD" (Mic 6:5-8). To understand the significance of this trek, we are going to examine concepts the Israelites would automatically grasp better than we ourselves. Among these are:

☐ the nature of idolatry

☐ the lure of sexual imagery

☐ the significance of male circumcision in Israel

☐ the meaning of *devoted* things and people

Let me begin with idolatry.

The Nature of Idolatry

Prior to the incident at Shittim, God was preparing Israel to be the nation through whom the world's Deliverer would come. It is to become a nation free from any form of idolatry, occupying territory free from territorial claim by the fertility gods. The very ground has been polluted and must now be cleansed. Moses makes it clear that they are to be the instruments of judgment on those nations through whom territorial claim was exercised. They are to fight. On one level the battles are to be fought in time and space, with swords, spears, arrows and human determination to obey the God of Israel. On another level it will be a battle in the heavenlies, as human beings take part in celestial warfare by their faith and their obedience. Worship and idolatry are to be key issues.

The Israelites were in step with the Spirit. They were the recipients of divine instructions, given to Moses by God. They would form an instrument in God's hands to come against the powers of darkness, to aim at their destruction. Having used dark powers to bring judgment on mankind, God would now begin to use mankind to eliminate their influence in the countries they conquer. The Israelites were to eliminate idolatry.

What exactly *is* idolatry? It is false worship—worship of beings other than God, who alone merits worship. In the case of Israel and the surrounding nations it was worship by sex, by penis, by vagina. Worship is to give to something or someone else what belongs exclusively to God. In practice, it is also to "exchange the truth of God for a lie." Idolatry, then, must be understood by contrasting it with true worship.

To worship God, the God of Creation, is to know why we were born. At its lowest level worship is a deeply satisfying duty. It can be much more— it can be warfare or even ecstasy. Yet neither as duty, nor as warfare, nor yet as ecstasy does it have meaning if the basis of the worship is absent. Worship begins to arise when we hear the word of the Lord and respond to it. Our response is worship and reveals a trusting heart. Trust issues in obedience. *Unless we are those who hear God's word and obey it, our worship is meaningless.*

To hear the word of the Lord and do it is automatically to present our bodies not to dark powers but to the Lord as a living sacrifice. The moment you do God's will, you do it with your body. You let him use that body. The two things are one and the same. As Paul said, "Therefore, I urge you, brothers, in view of God's mercy, to offer your bodies as living sacrifices, holy and pleasing to God—this is your *spiritual act of worship*" (Rom 12:1).

Just as the basis of worship is to hear the word of the Lord and do it (thus presenting our bodies to God in worship), so idolatry is to hear the words of darkness and to act on them (thus presenting our bodies to the powers of darkness in worship). It is to trust the word and the wisdom of darkness. It is, I repeat, to present your body a living sacrifice to certain powers of darkness, which is exactly what Adam and Eve did. They listened to the serpent's word and acted upon it.

Worship begins with trust and obedience. We have been "rescued . . . from the dominion of darkness and brought us into the kingdom of the Son" (Col 1:13). Yet as we fall into idolatrous practices we cross the line again, choosing the dominion of darkness from which God rescued us. Where does the deepest essence of idolatry lie?

It does not lie in bowing to carved images or even in making meat offerings to the deity. Commenting on the folly of carving an image from wood, Isaiah writes:

> They know nothing, they understand nothing; their eyes are plastered over so they cannot see, and their minds closed so they cannot understand. No one stops to think, no one has the knowledge or understanding to say, "Half of it I used for fuel; I even baked bread over its coals, I roasted

meat and I ate. Shall I make a detestable thing from what is left? Shall I bow down to a block of wood?" (Is 44:18-19)

For the prophets an idol was less than nothing. Even the sacrifices made to the gods do not seem to be at the core of God's concern. To bow down to the idol was empty, meaningless folly. Paul shares the same view: "So then, about eating food sacrificed to idols: We know that an idol is nothing at all in the world and that there is no God but one" (1 Cor 8:4).

The only point in refraining from eating meat offered to idols is so that we might protect the consciences of weaker brethren, who do not see the issue clearly. But remember—idolatry is not a mere bowing to an idol. Idolatry is to hear the word of darkness, to trust it and to do it. Paul is under no misapprehension about the spiritual forces involved in idolatry. "Do I mean then that a sacrifice offered to an idol is anything, or that an idol is anything? No, but the sacrifices of pagans are offered to demons, not to God, and I do not want you to be participants with demons. You cannot drink the cup of the Lord and the cup of demons too; you cannot have a part in both the Lord's table and the table of demons" (1 Cor 10:19-21).

Worship begins when we hear the word of the Lord and do it. Idolatry begins when we listen to the word of darkness and do it. In Israel's case the word of darkness had to do with certain sexual practices. But before I leave the subject of images, let me emphasize that we must never forget the demon behind the image.

Sexual Images We Worship

Few, if any, of us have evil sexual images in our homes, but some of us are hooked on porn. Even mirrors that reflect our own images can have pornographic lure. Just as the images of ancient times were nothing, yet could have demonic power associated with them, so the images we see in our mirrors can have power over us. Calvin Klein commercials are noted for their erotic power. Have you ever seen a Calvin Klein image in your own mirror?

Years ago after an evening meeting in Malaysia, Lorrie and I counseled a Chinese girl. She seemed small, shriveled, shrouded in darkness. A student, she was obliged to live with her grandmother, whose house was filled with idols. Every room was crowded with these images, and the girl dreaded them. We prayed with her and told her she must face them, saying to them, "He that is in me is greater than he that is in you!"

When she came for follow-up the next night we did not recognize her, so great was the change. Radiant, she had been transformed. Fear and darkness had been abolished, light and joy replacing them.

We, too, are surrounded by images—in mirrors, in TV commercials, in magazines. I know a man in whose bedroom there are wall-length mirrors. He was a bit fat with a sizeable belly, but one night as he lay naked on his bed, a single light from the head of the bed played tricks with the image in the mirror, doing a Calvin Klein with it. A freak distortion, some trick of lighting, had made the image pleasing. He stared, gripped by an attraction and fascination he could not understand. Though the image had erotic power, yet it was not that he wanted sex with the image. What was happening? What was the lust he experienced?

He seemed unable to turn away. Then, uncertain, vaguely guilty and confused, he pulled the covers over him and turned off the light. Several days later as he was praying, God gave him understanding. The attraction was demonic. The image was not real and had no power in itself. Lust had arisen in him, the lust to *be* the image, to have erotic power to attract and control women, to exult in the feeling of his own sensual power over them. For several seconds he had played with the fascination. Unwittingly, he had been worshiping the demonic in the image.

Christ did not dwell in the image my friend was looking at, but in his own, real body. Nor was he sinning by lying on the bed naked. The sin lay in letting a distorted image lead him into lust. We are to live in reality, in real relationships. Just as the Chinese girl could tell the images surrounding her of the greatness of the one who indwelt her, so we can deal with images in mirrors, magazines and TV, turning from them to the great Victor who indwells our real bodies. As my friend understood, the truth set him free. As he confessed his sin, he knew a cleansing and joy, a restoration to fellowship with his Lord. He also had learned how to handle the images that surrounded him in his own environment.

In *The Last Battle*, C. S. Lewis grasps a point which eludes many of us as he tells how a heathen (Emeth, a Calormene warrior and a worshiper of the god Tash) went to heaven. Whether such things will ever happen I do not know. This may not be the point Lewis is making. In any case, the incident reflects more than one important truth.

The first has to do with justification. It is not knowledge that justifies but trust in a Person. If detailed knowledge of the atonement were essential for salvation, then Abraham, Moses, David and Elijah would all be in hell. It is faith that justifies and God who saves. If knowledge is important it is knowledge of a Person that matters, not the theological content that goes with that knowledge.

Emeth knows the character of God, even though he calls Aslan (Lewis's Christ figure) Tash. His actions and attitudes are those that can only spring from Spirit-induced repentance and real faith in the one living God. When he sees the demon behind the image of Tash, he is horrified. All along he has conceived something entirely different as his deity. And when he sees Aslan he describes his feelings: "He was more terrible than the flaming Mountain of Lagour, and in beauty he surpassed all that is in the world, even as the rose in bloom surpasses the dust of the desert. Then I fell at his feet and thought, Surely this is the hour of death. . . . Nevertheless, it is better to see the Lion and die than to be Tisroc of the world and live and not to have seen him."[2]

His heart had been Aslan's all along. Facts are important, but knowledge of a Person is essential. The story also illustrates the point I am making. The idol is not at the core of idolatry. Other actions link us more closely to certain false gods.

Should any doubt remain that the essence of idolatry lies in the action that God hates (the sexuality involved in certain forms of idolatry), let us look back at God's words through Moses: "And after they [the nations inhabiting the Promised Land] have been destroyed before you, be careful not to be ensnared by inquiring about their gods, saying, 'How do these nations serve their gods? We will do the same.' *You must not worship the LORD your God in their way, because in worshiping their gods, they do all kinds of detestable things the LORD hates*" (Deut 12:30-31).

"They do all kinds of detestable things." We may claim to worship the true God by asserting that we do not bow down before any images, or by claiming the most correct theology. But if we are heeding dark words and defending immoral practices, doing "all kinds of detestable things," then our worship is not acceptable. We must never worship our God in this way. Far more important than the bowing to an idol is the detestable practice associated with the worship.

Imagery and "the Word of Darkness"

I have spoken several times about listening to dark words. Dark words seduce us by the images they evoke. I mentioned that Eve, in the garden, was so lured. What is "the word of darkness"? In the case of sexual sin it may run something like this:

"God knows how your husband neglects you and makes you suffer. Why not give yourself to this other man who understands you so and shows you such tenderness?"

Or, "God made you the way you are. Celebrate your gayness and thank him. Do the thing that is in your heart!"

Or, "There's no harm in it. This magazine is an art form. Human bodies are beautiful. God gave us sex to enjoy. (But don't upset your wife by showing the stuff to her!)"

Or, "If you really love him (or her), keep doing it. It's okay. Why all the fuss about a marriage certificate? Your heart tells you the sex you had last night was holy."

When you accept and follow such words you do exactly what Eve did. You hear darkness and put its advice to work. You turn your face from God. You enter delusion and darkness. In so doing, you place yourself under the sovereignty of darkness. Your body is offered as a living sacrifice to the old fertility gods. And you may be sure that your offering will be accepted with delight. You will not thereby lose your salvation, but you will experience loss of self-control. You will lose the earthly experience of Christ's blood-bought deliverance from sexual sin.

Moses and the Price of Victory

With our discussion of idolatry and imagery as background, we return to the journey from Shittim to Gilgal. Moses, who does not cross the Jordan, is about to hand on the leadership of Israel to Joshua. Before Moses dies he reviews his life, including God's dealings with him and with Israel. Central to his thought is the issue of the worship of the one true God and the perils of idolatry.

God then gives Joshua extraordinary promises about victories that await him. No one will be able to stand against him.

I will give you every place where you set your foot, as I promised Moses.
Your territory will extend from the desert to Lebanon, and from the great

river, the Euphrates—all the Hittite country—to the Great Sea on the west. No one will be able to stand up against you all the days of your life. As I was with Moses, so I will be with you; I will never leave you nor forsake you. . . . Do not let this Book of the Law depart from your mouth; meditate on it day and night, so that you may be careful to do everything written in it. Then you will be prosperous and successful. (Josh 1:3-5,8)

The prosperity and success Joshua will enjoy are not financial. The victories that are to follow represent spiritual triumph in overcoming evil. The territory is controlled by deities that are no deities. Victory in this spiritual conflict depends on worshiping one God alone, on never being seduced into idolatry or even the trappings of idolatry.

The arrangement was a *covenanted relationship between God and his people*—victory as a reward for fidelity. The sign of that covenant was male circumcision. However, the Israelite male babies had not been circumcised in the desert. Moreover, all males over forty years old had died in the wilderness. Because of the covenant relationship, it was highly significant that circumcision should take place at that time. So after arriving at Gilgal, "The LORD said to Joshua, 'Make flint knives and circumcise the Israelites again' " (Josh 5:2).

This represented a new beginning. They were to renew the covenant, and circumcision of the male penis was the sign of the covenant in the same way a wedding ring is a sign of the marriage covenant. However, there are problems. Why was circumcision done on males? Why to a man's sexual organ? In either case, would it not have been better to devise a sign that would be visible, in the same way a wedding ring is?

I do not know the answer to such questions, but I can think of a number of possibilities. First, in some tribes the rite is practiced on girls. Presumably it teaches them, early in life, "what women are for"—to satisfy men's lusts. God views matters differently. The sign was to be in men. It might not be visible in public as my wedding ring, but that was irrelevant. All men are aware what their sexual organs look like. And other men become aware, too, when men bathe together. Perhaps, more significantly, it has to do with the fact that no man can go through a day without handling his penis, if only for purposes of urination. Thus, there would be a daily reminder of circumcision and of the covenant that could not be taken off as a ring but was marked on one's body for life.

There is also a deeper reason. Circumcision goes back to Abraham. God commanded him to be circumcised at a very significant turning point in his life (Gen 17:10-27). He had failed to have children by Sarah. Circumcision had a sacramental significance. As G. E. Farley puts it, it may have meant symbolically for Abraham that "I am yielding my powers of procreation, my stake in the future to Yahweh. I am becoming totally dependent on Him. If I have descendants enough to be a great nation it will be Yahweh's doing, not my own."[3]

The Circumcised Heart

A man's penis and his pride are linked together. I discovered this about myself in the health club at the "Y." We swam naked, and were naked together in the steam room, the shower room, the locker room. To sit on towels in the locker room, cooling down and chatting with other men, was one of the pleasures of life and a profoundly healthy pleasure. I recall how I would glance at other men's genitals from time to time. One man had an unusually large penis. "Hm! What a beauty! I wish mine were as big as his." There was no eroticism, but there certainly were pride and competitiveness in my absurd envy.

Male hubris, male pride. I thought of it again this morning as I found myself meditating on the circumcision of Jesus, trying to picture the ceremony in my mind. As I did, the word "indignity" popped unbidden into my head. It was as though they were offering the baby an indignity, an insult. The words were, of course, entirely out of place. Yet I saw their relevance at once. This is the way proud males think. The uncircumcised heart is a proud or "stiff-necked" heart in Scripture—the heart of a man not submitted to God (Acts 7:1; Deut 10:16). A circumcised phallus is meaningless if my heart is not circumcised.

The feeling is entirely illogical, nevertheless a man's penis symbolizes to him his manliness, his manhood. It should not, but it does. Big penis, more manly man. Nonsense, to be sure, yet not infrequently expressed when men have had a little too much to drink. I remember seeing an ancient bas relief, I think representing Hittite warriors going into battle. Helmets were on their heads. The upper parts of their bodies bore armor, while their lower legs were shielded with metal guards. They carried sword and shield. Yet their thighs, buttocks and genitals were proudly displayed. The bas relief was not an early example of pornography. Rather, the artist seemed to be saying, "See—they're men, doing what men do, engaging in war and fighting."

Circumcision? It means yielding this symbol of my manliness, my power to rule, my procreative abilities, to you, God. I cannot do what I like with them. I am to be ruled by you in this and in all things. I am to trust you and you alone for power, for my future.

This brings us to the next point. The Baalim were the principal deities in the countries they were to occupy. Baal worship was essentially the worship of the male penis, the symbol of potent fertility. We could say that Baal worship was the delusion that the male penis was a symbol of god. It could also be that the true God intended men and women alike to learn how concerned he was about what a man did with his phallus. That potent symbol of fertility, that sower of human seed, was of immense concern to God. The mark of his covenant was on it.

Closely related to what I have just said, penile potency can never be *omni*potent. That is, it must never operate, *can* never operate, in isolation from a higher authority. It must submit, if not to one god, then to another. It can do no other. Because it was designed to function under authority it can function in no other way—under either divine authority or diabolical pseudoauthority. Those are the only possibilities; that is the only choice.

Devoted Things

Israel was guaranteed victory against the nations they were to replace, because God had decreed that the time for their judgment had come. He had given those nations over to destruction, given them up. Otherwise Israel would not have experienced such an astonishing run of victories.

So important was it to break the territorial power of the fertility gods that God at times instructed the Israelites to eliminate not only all human inhabitants from an area, but animals as well. Even the artifacts of the civilization were to be destroyed. Usually metal was to be melted down and then devoted to God. Occasionally animals did not need to be destroyed.

Whatever faced destruction was referred to as *devoted*—devoted to destruction. Or, better, everything was to be devoted to God, some things for destruction, a little of it, once purged, for his service. Thus as Israel stood ready to take Jericho, Joshua cried, "Shout! For the LORD has given you the city! The city and all that is in it are to be *devoted to the LORD*" (Josh 6:16-

17). That which was not devoted to God for his use was to be devoted on his behalf to destruction. Hence at Jericho "the people shouted, and at the sound of the trumpet . . . the wall collapsed; so every man charged straight in, and they took the city. They *devoted the city to the LORD and destroyed with the sword every living thing in it—men and women, young and old, cattle, sheep and donkeys. . . . Then they burned the whole city and everything in it*, but they put the silver and gold and the articles of bronze and iron into the treasury of the LORD's house" (Josh 6:20-21, 24).

The idea of *devoted* things would be familiar to the people. It has at this stage been part of the law for some time (Lev 27:21). A field that has been devoted to the Lord is a holy field. Whatever a man devotes to the Lord becomes "most holy to the Lord."

A man can be "devoted to destruction," which means he must be put to death. He has ceased to be a human responsibility, and it now becomes God's responsibility to deal with him (Lev 27:28-29). Certain things that were devoted to the Lord (sacrificial offerings) were for the use of the priests and Levites (Num 18:14).

Wrongful possession of devoted things was perilous to God's people, both individually and corporately. Joshua's instructions are clear. "Keep away from the devoted things, so that you will not bring about your own destruction by taking any of them. *Otherwise you will make the camp of Israel liable to destruction and bring trouble on it*" (Josh 6:18).

Did Joshua later forget his own words? The military debacle at Ai follows the victory over Jericho, and Joshua and the elders are on their faces before God, their clothing torn and their heads covered with dust. God is not impressed. His words to Joshua seem curt. "Stand up! What are you doing down on your face? Israel has sinned; they have violated my covenant, which I commanded them to keep" (Josh 7:10-11).

Sinned? Violated the covenant? How? "They have taken some of the devoted things; they have stolen, they have lied, they have put them with their own possessions" (v. 11). And the result of cleaving to devoted things? "That is why the Israelites cannot stand against their enemies; they turn their backs and run because they have been made liable to destruction" (v. 12).

The lesson for us is plain. We cannot do warfare with the powers of darkness when we play around with devoted things. God will no longer fight with us. "I will not be with you anymore unless you destroy whatever among you is devoted to destruction." (v. 12).

What are devoted things in our case? Surely the lesson is plain! If articles of clothing, simple articles, were to be destroyed, how much more the sins that were associated with their use? Any form of sexual sin is a devoted thing. Why should it surprise us that the world shows no interest in the gospel? The church is filled with men, women and young people who cleave to devoted things.

The solution? "Go, consecrate the people. Tell them, 'Consecrate yourselves in preparation for tomorrow; for this is what the LORD, the God of Israel, says: That which is devoted is among you, O Israel. *You cannot stand against your enemies until you remove it* '" (v. 13).

We are to remove sin, and especially sexual sin. The task of eliminating it from the church may seem impossible. Nothing is impossible with God. The day of mercy is upon us. We are commanded to consecrate ourselves. Let us begin at once to do so.

The Problem

In this section of the book we are trying to understand the problem—the problem of the effect of the Fall on our experience. The sections that follow will deal with the interaction of Bible and theology and with our redemption, God's answer to the problem of sexual sin. Before we get into psychological and redemptive aspects, however, we need to look more carefully at a major social consequence of sexual promiscuity—violence in a society. We will do this in the next chapter.

CHAPTER 5
Sexual Sin and Violence

There are six things the LORD hates, seven that are detestable
to him: haughty eyes, a lying tongue, hands that shed innocent blood.
PROVERBS 6:17

*T*his will be a brief chapter, not about sexual sin, but about the
sequence of social changes that Paul tells us will inevitably follow
in any society—whether among God's people or not. I in-
clude this because I feel an urgency about the present situation. It cannot
go on. It must not. Judgment hangs over us, and I must cry out whether I
am heard or not.

You will recall that Paul describes the changes that follow sexual sin in
Romans 1:18-32. The sequence begins with our not allowing God to have
his place among us (vv. 18-20). Then follow darkness and idolatry (vv. 21-
23), then sexual sin and sexual perversion (vv. 24-27), and finally a totally
corrupt and disintegrating society of people who have been given over by
God "to a depraved mind, to do what ought not to be done" (vv. 28-32).

History records repeated occurrences of this grim sequence. It is my con-
tention that we are fast getting to the climax of another cycle in the world
as a whole, and we in the church are not too far behind. I point this out so
that we, the church, may begin to face the fact of sexual sin in our midst
now, lest we reap the full consequences—those divine judgments that began

with the flood and continued with catastrophic events in the life of Israel.

Prominent among the features of the abandoned society Paul describes is violence. The people affected by the process wind up full of murder and strife (v. 29). Such people are referred to as heartless and ruthless (v. 31). The society began to change once they had been given over to sexual impurity (v. 24). I, therefore, propose to look first at Scripture. Later we can look at a few statistics. I propose to look at Scripture first since I believe we need some sort of screen, a lens through which to gaze at and assess the world. Why is this necessary?

In *U.S. News and World Report,* John Leo comments on a question Marshall McLuhan used to ask: "If the temperature of the bath water rises one degree every ten minutes, how will the bather know when to scream? (Frogs don't! They allow themselves to be boiled.)"

Leo is quoting McLuhan to draw attention to an article by Senator Daniel Patrick Moynihan. The article, "Defining Deviancy Down," is about our tendency to pretend something catastrophic is not happening when in fact it is. Leo says, "Moynihan doesn't use the word *pretend.* He uses the psychological word *denial* and the sociological word *normalizing,* but they amount to the same thing. By normalizing he means that some excruciatingly hot bath water is now accepted as a normal, everyday feature of American life."[1]

And not only of American life, but of the life of the whole Western world, not to mention the Western church. But because terms are redefined constantly ("illegitimate birth" becomes "out-of-wedlock birth," then "single parenting") and because statistics are not "hard" but "soft" and easy to manipulate, we need a clarifying biblical lens to look through. So what about violence? What does Scripture say? Remember, I am looking at violence in one way only—as a sort of flag to indicate whether the many characteristics of the abandoned society now surround *us.*

The Biblical Perspective

The Bible shows repeatedly the sequence which Paul describes. The terrible shame of nakedness in Genesis 3 is followed in Genesis 4 by the first murder. Cain murders Abel. The scriptural sequence from that point on may be "explained" in a whole variety of different ways. That is not my point. We are not looking at explanations but at the sequence Paul describes in terms of divine judgment. Any explanation in terms of psychology, sociology or any of the human sciences is irrelevant. For in judgment God begins by progressively removing his hand of mercy and restraint from our behavior, allowing us to become subject to the sequence of Romans 1. The sequence has a spiritual, not a scientific, explanation. It obeys not human laws but divine ones.

Genesis 3—4 is followed by Genesis 6, where unnatural sex is mentioned. "The Nephilim were on the earth in those days—and also afterward—when the sons of God went to the daughters of men and had children by them" (Gen 6:4). And the result? "The Lord saw how great man's wickedness on the earth had become, and that every inclination of the thoughts of his heart was only evil all the time" (v. 5). What sort of evil? "Now the earth was corrupt in God's sight *and was full of violence*" (v. 11).

The sequence continues throughout the Old Testament: sexual sin, then violence. What effect of the sex-soaked idolatry figures most prominently in prophetic denunciations? Violence and abuse of the fatherless, the widow, the aged, the poor. "Do no wrong or violence to the alien, the fatherless or the widow, and do not shed innocent blood in this place" (Jer 22:3).

Once sex sin starts in a given society, violence follows. David the king has sex with Uriah's wife. (Phase 1: sexual sin.) Then, after doing his best to cover the sin, he arranges to have Uriah murdered. (Phase 2: violence.) David has forgotten (or else no longer cares) that Uriah bears God's image.

We protest: "This one doesn't count!" We say, "Don't you understand? The affair would have become public otherwise. That is the *real* explanation."

Our explanations are irrelevant. Judgment, not motivation, is the central issue here. A man who has "borrowed" another man's wife finds himself committing an even more appalling crime before he has time to think clearly. His mind had been darkened even before he committed adultery. He had become lazy, idle. So he sowed the wind and reaped a whirlwind before he came to his senses. One example of this same sequence is common today. Illicit sex followed by unwanted pregnancy and abortion. Phase 1: sex. Phase 2: abortion. They are links in the chain, part of an overall sequence.

All of these examples, whether inside or outside Scripture, can be explained in the deepest sense only in the light of Romans 1. God *gives us over* to sexual impurity (v. 24), then to the shameful lust of homosexuality (v. 26), and finally to a depraved mind to do whatever things we choose to (vv. 28-32). Prominent among these is violent behavior.

Do statistics bear this out? Might we be reaching yet another climax (or rather, low point) at the present time?

Is Violence Growing?

Statistics vary with the method of collection. Probably the most accurate index of violence is gathered from police crime statistics. House-to-house surveys are generally regarded as being more subject to inaccuracy. According to police statistics, violent crimes have increased steadily from 1960 to 1991 in the U.S.A. There were dips around 1976 as well as from 1981 to 1986, but in each case the subsequent increase more than canceled out the dip. In other words, the curve across the whole period continued to rise.

Whereas in 1960 the rate of violent crimes was less than 200 for every 100,000 of the U.S. population, the figure rose to almost 400 in 1970, then to just under 600 in 1980 and exactly 800 per 100,000 in 1990. There was even a 7 percent increase between 1990 and 1991. The general trend will continue even though there may be subsequent dips. "According to the UCR [the compilation and analysis by the FBI of all reported crimes] violence in the United States has increased in the past ten years. . . . the violence rate increased 25 percent . . . the rate of rapes more than 15 percent and assaults more than 47 percent. . . . In 1991 . . . the number of murders topped 24,000 for the first time in the nation's history."[2]

Curiously, the increase in violence does not correspond to the general crime rate. "Unlike violent crime, property crime has remained relatively stable during the past decade."[3] Is the United States more violent than other countries? "According to the Senate Judiciary Committee on violence, the United States is 'the most violent and self-destructive nation on earth.' The committee reports that . . . the U.S. murder rate is four times as great as Italy's, nine times England's and twice that of Northern Ireland."[4]

I am not competent to discuss these trends and will not make the attempt. Perhaps the hotly debated issue of the availability of weapons has some bearing on the question. The real question is: Does a sword of divine judgment hang over North America?

And what about other nations, especially Western nations?

Trends in Western Nations

It is trends that matter, not the amount of violence in a given country. The question everywhere is: Is violence on the increase? The United States may be a special case with an exaggerated proneness to violence. As a Canadian, I have never understood the gun control policy of the U.S.

Let me cut across a country-by-country analysis of violence trends and focus on war. One difficulty is to define war. The traditional approach centers around distinctions between civil wars within a country and wars affecting more than one nation. But the difficulties do not stop there. Students of war demand a comprehensive theoretical framework.

But in the minds of those who fight, rather than clearcut theories there is a wild range of emotions. And violence begins with the emotions that eventually drive you to it. Wars begin when political leaders experience a degree of rage or fear or a combination of both. They do not talk about their rage and fear, of course, but couch their emotions in rousing phrases. Among those who fight wars for the leaders, there are conflicting emotions: worry, fear, the need to put on a brave front. There is sometimes "rah-rah patriotism" along with naive enthusiasm. At other times there is anger, murderous rage, hatred, the tendency to depersonalize "the other side." Equally, there are resentments by the rank and file toward their superiors.

There may even be sudden total shifts of mood. For example, during World War I, one Christmas, there came a moment in the trenches when some soldiers on both sides were suddenly overwhelmed with wonder and a sense of their common humanity. On one side someone had begun to sing a Christmas carol, and soldiers on the other side joined in. An impromptu carol service began, involving enemies who had been engaged in mutual killing. Suddenly war seemed stupid and senseless. The common foe had all along been Satan, the pawn in God's hands as he executes judgment. The foe had been Satan, not one another. The singers probably did not grasp that fact, except in a vague and intuitive recognition of their common humanity.

Within all of us is a curious mixture of the divine image and satanic corruption. War is not simple. Only violence itself can be quantified. But how?

David Singer, who has contributed to several books on war, in an article in the book *The Long Postwar Peace* makes the obvious point that the peace between the great powers did not mean that there were no international wars. They have abounded. He cannot predict the future, and though he points out three possible ways of predicting what will happen, he reveals his own uncertainty about statistical methods by first excluding "tea leaves, chicken entrails, and the position of the stars."

Moreover, as Singer himself faces the future, he says, "My reading of the evidence leads, at best, to mild pessimism. First, those who live in the peripheral regions will not only remain peripheral in their access to the needs and wants of life, but will continue to experience more than their share of bloody violence. Second, and equally ominous, my sense is that the specter of World War III is by no means behind us."[5]

The violence in one country, however powerful, is no measure to go by. We must look at the "global village." And if an expert on war of David Singer's stature can summon up at best a mild pessimism on his own reading of the statistical and theoretical quagmire, I rest my case.

Except for this. On any reading of the evidence, armed conflict—both between nations and within national boundaries—has increased. From Uppsala University comes the statement that "the total number of armed conflicts in the world in 1990 were 82, and in 1991 71."[6] The fact that there were fewer in 1991 does not reflect a "downward trend" but merely a dip in this awful state of affairs.

A seething subsurface anger is what feeds modern wars. Inner rage, especially between ethnic groups, boils in the masses throughout the globe as I write. Deny it and you will be blind to the catastrophic judgment that is on the way. There is no question as to what is to follow, though I have no timetable to offer. Romans 1 remains the lens through which to view the international scene.

CHAPTER 6
The Question of Satanic Ritual Abuse

Our interpretation is a thing we bring to history and superimpose
upon it. . . . Therefore, the liberal, the Jesuit, the Fascist,
the Communist, and all the rest may sail away with their militant
versions of history, howling at one another across the
interstellar spaces, all claiming theirs is the absolute version.
HERBERT BUTTERFIELD

Allegations of child sexual abuse often disturb people in a way that elicits
the age-old human response of wanting to shoot the messenger
who brings the bad news. People find it more comfortable to
believe that children are natural liars.
KEVIN MARRON

I sense that Mephistopheles is still grinning.
WALTER SUNDBERG

D o Satanists and witches exist? Do they subject children to terrible
abuse? Does satanic sex exist? Is there any such thing? A debate
rages currently over these questions. We are faced by two sets
of people—some who claim to be victims of it and who give dramatic stories
of the way it has wrecked their lives, and others who are skeptics, who declare
they have investigated the stories and no solid evidence for their truth exists.
Christians and non-Christians are found in both groups. In the face of the
debate, how can we determine who is correct? How do we discover the facts?
Is there any smoke behind this fire?

The Controversy
Some believe that children are being ritually brutalized and sometimes killed

in satanic sacrificial offerings. An article by Greg and Gretchen Passantino, entitled "Hard Facts About Satanic Ritual Abuse,"[1] takes a skeptical view of satanic ritual abuse (SRA) after the authors had "conversations with dozens of its alleged adult survivors." While most of the survivors seem to the authors to believe their stories, the Passantinos point out that "sincerity cannot determine a story's veracity." And about this they are right. Their article also stressed the existence of a widespread belief in a "nearly omnipotent" satanic conspiracy.

In a 1989 feature of *The Cult Observer,* entitled "Satanism Watch," summaries of a number of newspaper articles appeared.[2] One from the *Los Angeles Times*[3] gave a report of a scholarly meeting in Salt Lake City, where someone stated there was "not a shred of evidence that the small number of satanic cults in this country is significant or spreading." Another quotes a Florida sheriff's office that cautions against playing down the threat of Satanism, stating that while "there is a risk of frightening the public and causing paranoia, we have to investigate every crime. Anytime it's minimized, it's a danger to society."[4] On the other hand, the *Washington Times* stated during that same period, "The reported rise of Satanism is unfounded, and the alarm surrounding it is largely the product of opportunists and evangelical publicists, according to a study released in November by the Committee for the Scientific Examination of Religion."[5]

The winter 1992/93 issue of the journal *Free Inquiry* devotes space to three articles on "The Satanic Cult Scare," two of them dismissing it and one urging its validity. Jeffrey Victor, a human sexuality expert, sets the tone for his article on civil liberties by quoting Ben Yehuda's 1920 remark that "sometimes societies create imaginary forms of deviance in order to have scapegoats for deep social and political tensions." Such is the case, he feels, with the current concern over Satanism. He states that the "satanic-cult scare is . . . a witch-hunt for moral 'subversives' and supposed criminals in a highly secretive conspiratorial network."[6]

On the other hand, Cynthia Kisser, executive director of the Cult Awareness Network, quotes many decisions by highly authoritative and responsible bodies who show concern about Satanism. Among them she cites a state supreme court ruling on the murder of a twelve-year-old girl. "Here the court ruled that evidence of Satanism and the satanic beliefs of murder defendant Scott Waterhouse were relevant and permissible."[7]

The final article in the same journal is written by Robert Hicks, a law enforcement specialist, who accuses Kisser of indulging in "wild, unsupported assertions" and who tries to tear her article to pieces.

A recent television program in Canada, called "The Fifth Estate," investigated the idea of SRA and concluded that there was absolutely no solid evidence for it.

Bob and Gretchen Passantino write, "Some true believers in satanic ritual abuse say that more than 100,000 'adult survivors' have undergone therapy and remembered . . . horrible abuses. Others more than double this number."[8] The Passantinos may themselves be true believers—believers in the nonexistence of SRA.

On the other hand, James G. Friesen, also writing about SRA, states, "When I first learned about satanic ritual abuse (SRA) from a tape on adult survivors, it went against my training about what to expect from people. I was in a state of disbelief for weeks. It was difficult to believe there are people who really do perform the terrible acts of SRA perpetrators. I still do not want to believe human beings are capable of slaughtering other human beings or of subjecting precious children to heinous crimes."[9] But Friesen is convinced that such is in fact the case.

The Core of the Matter
There you have it—two groups firing verbal missiles at one another. On both sides it is basically a matter of belief, even though writers talk in terms of "scientific evidence" or even "proof." We are faced with a situation where large numbers of people are convinced of diametrically opposed viewpoints about reality. Not only so, but professions are divided on the issues. There are social workers, psychologists, psychiatrists, police, lawyers, judges, journalists and politicians on both sides of the debate.

You will notice that both sides are discussing Satanism, and that Satanism is conceived of as a "vast conspiratorial network." That being so, the debate is unlikely ever to be resolved. The error is subtle but critical. We must turn our attention not to Satanism but to Satan; not to a human conspiracy but to a plot hatched by dark supernatural beings. Do they exist? Does Satan exist? If so, how active is he on earth? If dark powers are active, it should not surprise us that some people might worship them, or even that the number of worshipers might be on the increase. After all, witches have been historically very much a part of the human scene.

The issue of conspiracy is a sort of red herring. We need have no fear of a vast conspiracy, whether by New Agers, Satanists or neopagans. People of common interests form groups and organize conferences, and they are doing so more and more—and quite openly. But the only conspiracy I am aware of is the conspiracy in heavenly realms among wicked fallen angels. Yet the false and futile debate rages on.

Politics and Debates

Where two sets of "true believers" fiercely oppose one another, at least one side and perhaps both have political reasons for their beliefs. Political parties always do, but they will consistently deny it, sometimes with blind sincerity. This could be the case here. I am currently reading Farley Mowat's book *Never Cry Wolf.* The Canadian government years ago sent Mowat to study the habits of arctic wolves. All the information they supplied him with portrayed the wolves as fierce and extremely dangerous brutes who were decimating caribou herds. The government wished him to get firm evidence for this view of the wolves and to devise a plan for their extermination.

His book is at once amusing and informative. Mowat's first encounter with the male leader of a small wolf pack terrified him. Evidently it also terrified the arctic wolf. Each fled from the other! Gradually he came to live among them and observe them, only to discover that the staple of their diet was arctic mice. They hunted caribou only during the season when the caribou herds migrated through their territory, confining their predatory behavior, even then, to the diseased among the herd and thus securing healthier stocks of caribou, better able to survive predatory attacks.

His research was not welcomed, however, by the Canadian government. The depletion of the herds was actually due more to hunters and trappers. The hunters mounted a powerful lobby, with a vested interest in the extermination of "deadly arctic wolves," "deadly" both to mankind and to caribou. I cannot say that the same politicized problem characterizes the psychology of people who do not want to believe in the growth of witchcraft, or of others who want too much to believe in it, but I have my suspicions. Pride and politics walk arm in arm.

How can we know the truth?

Balance

Debates often shift the center of interest away from a larger problem. The evil of SRA pales before a greater evil, the evil of the sexual abuse of children by people far removed from witchcraft. This of course is where our main concern should lie. We must see the debate in the context of brutality against these children, of child sexual abuse in the home, the church and the community. While in the current climate of panic false accusations are being made, real child abuse is very common. Incest and domestic violence are growing. The number of prosecutions is rising.

The abuse I experienced as an eleven-year-old from a Christian worker makes me sensitive about this. My abuser may have been satanically inspired, but he was not a Satanist. (Yet is the stride from satanically inspired sexual abuse to witchcraft and Satanism such a long one?)

Incest is undoubtedly numerically commoner than the more bizarre and dramatic SRA. It is also more serious, in that it is often perpetrated by professing Christian parents, grandparents and other relatives and predators, some of whom struggle vainly against their proclivity, hiding it. Most churches are helpless to deal with the problem. It is this that reminds us that the powers of darkness are behind the church's apparent irrelevance. Satan and his rabble are alive and increasing in power, while many churches seem unaware of their danger.

Therefore, when we think of SRA we must see it as part of a larger pattern. Satan is behind the emerging pattern, damaging the lives of children in their own homes, commonly homes of the "respectable" variety, but also homes of parents who practice witchcraft.

Earlier I stressed that it was not Satanism but Satan and demons that must interest us. Another reason for the skepticism of some Christians may be that they have never experienced a live demon. To believe demons exist is one thing. To meet one is quite another. And when I talk of meeting a demon, I am not talking about a subjective experience that no one else can verify, but about a dramatic manifestation of a demonic presence in someone to whom such a thing had never previously taken place, and that was totally unexpected—by me, by the victims and by other observers who were present.

To have such experiences is suddenly to be aware that one is surrounded by other worlds, other beings, other powers. In my case the awareness fades quickly, for the influence of the material world of Newtonian science is so much a part of my background and training—and, as Lewis puts it, a good dose of "real life" quickly dispels the feeling of surrounding angels and demons. I am not a "natural" believer. But the repeated demonic manifestations that occur when I approach demonized persons, or when I pray for someone, not knowing they are demonized, restores my belief.

Christianity and Academic Disciplines

Another factor has to do with the spectacles through which one examines reality. Has your life ever been changed by a book? A book entitled *Christianity and History* influenced me profoundly when I was still an undergraduate. In it Herbert Butterfield, a Cambridge professor of history and a Christian, discussed his own academic discipline both as a don and a Christian. He was one of the comparatively rare breed of academics who saw the limitations of his particular field. Butterfield refused to allow that field to blind him to how he, as a Christian, should view the world around him and its history. His is the quote at the head of this chapter.

He saw that even theology was often tied to contemporary science. In the opening chapter of his book, Butterfield comments on the fact that "much unnecessary anguish has been produced for Christians throughout the ages because the Church has so often imagined the Gospel to be tied to the science of a particular epoch (Aristotelian physics and Ptolemaic astronomy, for example), with the result that men have felt that the one must stand or fall with the other."[10]

The gospel still is tied to Newtonian science, to an idea of physical reality that flies in the face of quantum mechanics. Not that twentieth-century science may be any better, though at least it gets us out of the trap of a too rigidly fixed form of the created universe.

Butterfield was concerned about reality, about what is. He saw the folly of supposing that any academic discipline, however valuable, could arrive at ultimate meanings. At the same time he saw the rightness of bringing a point of view to history—and he felt that the Christian point of view was the real key to understanding it. But he was fully aware he was doing so, conscious that his thinking was based on certain presuppositions, and that he built on a foundation of solid rock. "Interpretation is a thing we bring to history and superimpose upon it. . . . Therefore, the liberal, the Jesuit, the Fascist, the Communist, and all the rest may sail away with their militant versions of history, howling at one another across the interstellar spaces, all claiming theirs is the absolute version."[11]

The art of seeing what is there is simple but costly. You must wear the right spectacles. You may need to discard your present glasses and opt for a pair that are better constructed for biblical vision.

Sex, Sacrifice and Sorcery in Scripture

In Scripture the idolatry of the fertility cults, witchcraft and sorcery all were part and parcel of one another. We may not make sacrifices to idols today, but as I have already made clear, we are into the same thing without the superstition. Let me then begin with Scripture and with the reminder that witchcraft used to accompany the fertility cults, with their associated child sacrifice and ritual sex. It existed in the Old Testament and the New. I must establish this clearly. I know this does not prove that it still exists. Nor does it, in itself, prove that witchcraft had (and has) access to satanic power. But it does establish a more-than-occasional social relationship between these things. Satan may shuffle his cards a little, using sleight of hand to shove in an ace of agnosticism (in respect to idolatry), but he retains the same essential hand.

Judah's most evil king was Manasseh. He reinstated fertility worship following the reforms of his father, Hezekiah. Under Manasseh the association of sexual depravity and witchcraft reached new heights. Witchcraft was widespread in the land. "He sacrificed his sons in the fire in the Valley of Ben Hinnom, practiced sorcery, divination and witchcraft, and consulted mediums and spiritists. He did much evil in the eyes of the LORD, provoking him to anger" (2 Chron 33:6).

Child sacrifice? Rare today? I am not so sure. Human nature does not change. Wherever in Scripture the worship of sex affected human society, child sacrifice arose. Sorcery, fertility religions, divination, witchcraft, mediums and spiritists have throughout history been part of paganism's package. We now live in a paganized society and a post-Christian era.

In chapter four I commented that Micah had the discernment to see the significance of the journey from Shittim to Gilgal (Mic 6:5-8). Micah also shows God's judgment against the associated witchcraft and fertility idolatry. "I will destroy your witchcraft and you will no longer cast spells. I will destroy your carved images and your sacred stones from among you; you will no longer bow down to the work of your hands. I will uproot from among you your Asherah poles and demolish your cities" (Mic 5:12-14).

Asherah poles, prominent among pagans of the Old Testament, were associated with ritual sex. Sexual sin, without fertility cults, is associated with witchcraft in the New Testament. Paul talks about the two things one after another. The association was a clear one in his mind, even if it may not be in ours. The two are found in the same society because they are products of increasing carnality in the members of that society. "The acts of the sinful nature are obvious: sexual immorality, impurity and debauchery; idolatry and witchcraft" (Gal 5:19-20).

Science, Philosophy and Christianity
I am a theist, and my theism is biblical theism, arising out of my limited understanding of the Judeo-Christian sacred writings. Limited as my understanding may be, it is all I have. Therefore, I gladly wear my conclusions as spectacles on my nose. For the only way to sort out the mass of confusion we are faced with is to look at it through the right lenses. Through my lenses I see the world around me. Without them I would grope bewildered and befogged.

When I think about Satan and Satanism in the world of today, I come to my world with a set of expectations. What I *believe* colors what I shall *see*. My basic philosophy must penetrate the deceptive fog of apparent reality. I do not remove my spectacles in an attempt to be more "scientific." In the much-quoted words of Sir James Jean, modern science tells me that the universe "begins to look more like a great thought than a machine." As for science's supposed laws, John Wheeler declares, "There is no law except the law that there is no law."[12] Therefore, I want to be biblical much more than I want to be scientific.

In this way I hope I shall see what is really there. I shall be thus in touch with reality—not with just an imaginary reality of my own creation, or with the deceptive chimera surrounding me. For I am not being obscurantist so much as recognizing the narrowness of all individual disciplines and particularly of the scientific method.

So truth about the occult lies where? It lies where our knowledge of Scripture would lead us to expect. The Bible, among other things, tells the story of an age-long conflict between good and evil, between darkness and light, between the forces of heaven and those of hell. The theme is one in which hymn writers and poets delight. Whether in Dante's *The Divine Comedy* or Milton's *Paradise Lost* and *Paradise Regained,* or in the host of lesser tales, pagan and Christian alike, all are plays and poems about the conflict between good and evil, expressing that which is deepest to our humanity.

Twice in the book of Job, Satan describes his activity as "roaming through the earth and going back and forth in it" (Job 1:7; 2:2). "But woe to the earth," cried the loud voice from heaven, "because the devil has gone down to you! He is filled with fury because he knows his time is short" (Rev 12:12).

He still roams the earth. Peter warns, "Your enemy the devil prowls around like a roaring lion looking for someone to devour" (1 Pet 5:8). Even Paul Tillich rejected the scholarly notion that the devil is merely the externalization of dark aspects of human experience. Walter Sundberg, summarizing Tillich on Satan, reminds us that "to take up the ancient myth of warfare between the divine and the demonic is to repossess the deep structures of reality before they were fragmented in the destruction of matter and spirit."[13]

Sorcery Then and Now

Today's world grows more and more like the world of the New Testament. Civilization flourishes. Communication and travel tie the world together. English, the latest lingua franca, is spoken everywhere. United Nations and United States forces have replaced the Roman legions. North American musical culture, European banking, and a worldwide system of stock exchanges in instant communication present us with an updated version of the Mediterranean world in Roman times.

Nowhere is the power of sorcery in that world more evident than in the account of Paul's ministry in Ephesus. There the two warring forces, light and darkness, meet as demonic beings themselves, demonstrating that they know the reality of divine power and its superiority over satanic power. Extraordinary divine power had been manifested (Acts 19:11)—power unlike any that had previously been seen in a pagan environment.

It was assumed that the magical incantation "In the name of Jesus" was a new secret of power, but the sons of the Jewish chief priest, trying to cash in on the formula, came to grief, running from the demonic encounter naked and bleeding. The result? "When this became known to the Jews and Greeks living in Ephesus, they were all seized with fear, and the name of the Lord Jesus was held in high honor. Many of those who believed now came and openly confessed their evil deeds. A number who had practiced sorcery brought their scrolls together and burned them publicly. When they calculated the value of the scrolls, the total came to fifty thousand drachmas. In this way the word of the Lord spread widely and grew in power" (Acts 19:17-20).

Witchcraft was clearly widespread in Ephesus, and also, we presume, in the Mediterranean world generally. The plight of the sons of Sceva itself reminds us that satanic power is nothing to fool around with. It is real. But it quails before the power of Jesus and before those who walk in his power. The burning of the scrolls tells us that people who knew power had seen a superior power, and had known that it was a holy power and that they must therefore repent. Supernatural power was an integral part of the New Testament world and is of ours also. Dark power is as ancient as Eden and as contemporary as next year's elections. It has ebbed and flowed throughout history, going under cover when it is persecuted, emerging cautiously when belief in its existence dies down, flourishing when the worship of our bodies and violence are commonplace.

The apostle John, on receiving revelation about the church in Thyatira, writes, "Nevertheless, I have this against you: You tolerate that woman Jezebel, who calls herself a prophetess. By her teaching she misleads my servants into sexual immorality and the eating of food sacrificed to idols. I have given her time to repent of her immorality, but she is unwilling. So I will cast her on a bed of suffering, and I will make those who commit adultery with her suffer intensely, unless they repent of her ways" (Rev 2:20-22).

Jezebel, the Ultimate Witch

Jezebel, whose person and powers even Elijah feared, seems to be a biblical symbol of witchcraft's power of seduction and manipulation. Elijah feared her; this becomes evident by his flight from her. Unafraid of her wimpy husband, Ahab, unafraid of the prophets of Baal, Elijah was yet afraid of Jezebel's threats. "So Jezebel sent a messenger to Elijah to say, 'May the gods deal with me, be it ever so severely, if by this time tomorrow I do not make your life like that of one of them.' Elijah was afraid and ran for his life" (1 Kings 19:2-3).

Not only was Jezebel's end terrible, but also it reflects God's abhorrence of witchcraft. Burial and grave sites were of great importance in Israel's culture, so that Jehu felt Jezebel should be properly buried. Having previously ordered that Jezebel be thrown out of a tower window, he later ordered her burial. However, no burial was possible.

When they went out to bury her, they found nothing except her skull, her feet and her hands. They went back and told Jehu, who said, "This is the word of the LORD that he spoke through his servant Elijah the Tishbite: On the plot of ground at Jezreel dogs will devour Jezebel's flesh. Jezebel's body will be like refuse on the ground in the plot at Jezreel, so that no one will be able to say, 'This is Jezebel.' " (2 Kings 9:35-37)

Two things are clear. The first is that, associated with pagan worship, *witch-craft existed in Bible times.* The second is that *God abhors witchcraft and is determined to stamp it out among his people at any cost.*

Witchcraft and Power

Did witchcraft in those days exercise true power—not just political—but "spiritual"/magical power? People who call themselves witches certainly exist. But do they have power? Did they in Bible times?

Indeed they did. If the Bible is true, then Pharaoh's priests displayed magical power. Their rods turned into serpents (Ex 7:10-12). They turned Nile water into blood (Ex 7:20-22). They even produced frogs from the Nile by their secret arts. The witch at Endor produced the spirit of Samuel and somehow instantly knew that she was in the presence of King Saul. Calling up spirits of the dead was a practice forbidden not only by the king but by God himself. Yet, though she dreaded discovery, the witch of Endor certainly had the power to do it. Clearly magical power existed then. I believe it still does.

Magical power exists because Satan exists. And Satan, defeated or not, still exercises a great deal of power. But there are other things Scripture makes clear about Satan. He is proud, an arch-liar and manipulator, and with our unaided wisdom we are no match for him.

The Satan Seller, Mike Warnke's bestselling book of his experiences as a witch leading a satanic movement, convinced many people of the sinister reality of modern witchcraft. His exposure suggests that he may have been guilty of exaggeration.[14] The exposure could be also be the arch-liar's attempt to confuse issues and deepen our cynicism. It will be tragic if we allow this to happen. The assumption some will make is, "I always knew there was nothing to the business of witchcraft." What matters is not whether or not Mike Warnke was spinning a yarn, but whether Satan, "the prince of this world," is active and powerful among us still.

At the risk of saying it too many times, I repeat: *The issue before us is not Satanism, but Satan—not the extent of witchcraft, but the present activity of demons.*

The Importance of Knowing What to Expect

What then am I saying? Am I saying that those who believe in a conspiracy are correct? Not really. I am saying that the belief in a conspiracy interests me little. Perhaps many of the supposed victims are victims of their own imagination. On the other hand, the fact that I wear biblical spectacles means I shall not be surprised if hideously damaged victims of witchcraft should cross my path more than occasionally. Wearing the spectacles I do, I shall expect to find witchcraft and sorcery increasing wherever sex is worshiped and violence rises.

When you walk through the woods looking for a rare bird, you are more likely to find it if you carry field glasses and walk with woodsmanlike cunning. There are far more birds in the woods than you will ever see. Even if you are looking for more common birds, you may not see any, especially if you walk through the woods at the wrong time, or carelessly. Remember, the birds are really there, even though you may neither see nor hear them. And so is Satan. You may even conclude, because of your careless approach, that birds do not exist. You may conclude also that witchcraft ended long ago. But in both cases you will be mistaken. Both kinds of believer—the believer in witchcraft's universal horror and the believer in the negligible extent of witchcraft—need to carry biblical field glasses and to walk through witchcraft's woods with circumspection.

Smoke and Fire

It is true that if you are suddenly presented with someone's story, and the story depends on the subjective evidence of the person who tells the story, there is not much to go on. But there are things you cannot fake, hard evidence that frequently accompanies real victims. It consists of anal and vaginal scarring. And there are doctors who testify about examinations that bear out these facts. When the findings are combined with memories and nightmares, one then knows one has a genuine example of satanic ritual abuse.

Our local newspaper[15] recently reported such a case. The author gave the name Pat to the woman who gave him the story. He notes, "When she (Pat) was 27 years old she had to have her uterus removed due to abnormally thick scar tissue. She had never had an abortion." That is, she had no awareness of having had one. I am uncertain what Pat understood by "abnormally thick scarring," but in reported cases of SRA, characteristic findings include vaginal and rectal scarring.

Pat is not a Christian. She wound up in Wicca as a white witch. Satan does not really mind which of his many avenues we choose. But as a witch who believes in the goodness and benign nature of the mother goddess, she is determined to fight the other kind of witchcraft. She will do so even if "it has to be like in the old way—sacrifice me as a lamb, put me on the altar—if that's what it takes to wake up this world . . . because this stuff is really, really happening."

Sorcery was a natural companion of pagan idolatry. Following the Reformation, the naturalist philosophical movements on the European continent, and the empiricism of philosophers like Hume, Berkeley and Locke, together with the growth of empiricist science, all tended to diminish the importance of witchcraft in the public mind. It was at that time diminished just in the same way as it had previously been exaggerated. Lewis reminds us that Satan welcomes atheists and witches equally.

Now the pendulum is swinging rapidly to the other extreme. When this happens it always swings too far. At the moment we are near the apex of the swing. But there is never smoke without a fire. So far as I am concerned, the bizarre nature of the practices of witchcraft allow me neither to raise my eyebrows nor to shrug my shoulders. We must ask God to give us enough experience and discernment not to relish the latest wild story as proof of our beliefs. We need to cry to him for wisdom about where the truth lies in a given case, for there are many exploiters of attention and pity who are only too willing to lead us down some garden path of their own creating.

CHAPTER 7
Satanic Sex

Let no one be found among you who sacrifices his son or daughter
in the fire, who practices divination or sorcery, interprets
omens, engages in witchcraft, or casts spells, or who
is a medium or spiritist or who consults the dead.
DEUTERONOMY 18:10-11

*T*here are believers and unbelievers in witchcraft, in satanic ritual abuse, and in the growing significance of witchcraft. On both sides it is a matter of belief, for in this world absolute proof is nonexistent. Evidence, yes; proof, no. I am myself a believer, a believer on the basis of what Scripture teaches about the association of sexual sin, violence and witchcraft, and on the basis of what I observe of the growth of sexual promiscuity and violence since World War II.

Satanic Ritual Abuse (SRA)
I have no doubt that SRA exists. The debate should center around how common it is. Satanic ritual abuse is cruel abuse, mostly of infants and young children, who grow accustomed to it and assume there is nothing wrong with it. It commonly goes unnoticed by professionals dealing with childhood sexual abuse simply because they are unaware of its existence, or, if aware, they have little idea of its extent. What you don't expect, you do not look for. Police and the courts were initially cynical, especially since some early reports of it could not be substantiated.[1]

I hesitate to write about the effects of Satanism and witchcraft on children for the same reasons Kevin Marron states in *Ritual Abuse* (quoted at the opening of chapter six): People often want to shoot the messenger who brings the bad news. In the book he gives an account of the first Canadian public inquiry on the topic, which began in October 1985 and lasted eighteen months in a Family Court.

The hearing concerned the wardship of the children. There were descriptions of ritual murders, mainly of children. Because of police failure to follow up the children's stories and the subsequent difficulty of identifying grave sites, the law was hampered. Over the course of the trial the mother, much to the chagrin of her lawyer, admitted her own criminal involvement with the satanic rituals.

Satanic ritual abuse exists. No woman freely opens herself up to criminal charges in an open inquiry, against the advice of her lawyer, unless she is admitting the truth.

The story included horrific episodes of orgies, cannibalism, ritual murder of many children. I read the book on a plane trip from Ottawa to Vancouver. I am not squeamish, having worked in city hospital emergency rooms and taken part in postmortem examinations. Nevertheless, at one point, as I read how one of the little girls was placed for punishment in a recently reopened grave at night, I lost control of my stomach. The child had screamed in terror on feeling the hair and the decomposing, liquefying body of a woman's corpse beneath her. I tore my seat belt off and hurried to the washroom.

Are Children's Reports Reliable?
Do children tell the truth? There is a good deal of evidence that while they can be embarrassingly truthful at times, our assessment of their statements is hampered by their need to tell us what we want to hear in order to please us. This is especially true when they are frightened or when they have a great need to please the adult they are with. However, they lack the skills to keep what they know to be the truth from us, if we know how *not* to question them. They automatically talk among themselves, and sometimes talk to themselves when they think they are alone.

Key to assessing the validity both of Marron's book and of the eventual decision by the presiding judge were the skills and the integrity of a woman who acted as foster mother to the two little girls who were the main focus of the inquiry.

Catherine McInnes projected a wholesome, grandmotherly image. She sat up straight in the witness stand, dressed in a dark serge suit with a white blouse that was fastened at the top by a cameo brooch. She looked like someone who would give moral principles, recipes, folk remedies and household hints, rather than some of the most graphic descriptions of sexual abuse and sadistic violence ever heard in a Canadian courtroom.[2]

In addition, psychological testing had indicated that the children's accounts were truthful. We can be sure of the truthfulness also from the way in which the stories came out.

Catherine McInnes never questioned the children. She was an experienced foster mother who kept a careful diary. In that diary she recorded conversations between the girls, who seemed at times unaware of her presence. Both children were still under eight at the time of the hearing (and younger still—five years and three years, I believe—when the Children's Aid Society had placed them with Catherine, at their mother's request). At times the older girl would, in angry fear, say things like, "You mustn't talk about it. You know what they told us. We must *never say anything!*"

Because Catherine showed no curiosity and did not display any emotion at what the children would say from time to time, they began to feel safer. Gradually they even began to confide in her. They were reluctant to spend time with the man who acted as their father. After one visit the younger girl told Catherine, "Gary puts his finger where the pee comes out." The child dropped on the floor and spread her legs. "I lay down like this and he puts his finger in and wiggles it and I scream. . . . You don't tell people you know. He thumps the wall when he has finished. . . . Gary squeezes the thing he pees with, then he pees into a towel."

Later that same day she said, "Elizabeth got dead. A killer got her. He had a knife. He was a killer. . . . Me and Gary, and Mum and Janice and Elizabeth went for a drive . . ." Catherine noted down the remarks on the only thing she had to write on at that moment—a drug store bag. She also wrote, "Should I tell and be a fool, or be quiet and be a bigger one?"[3]

It was only the beginning. Piece by piece a series of inconceivable horrors poured spontaneously from the lips of the two young children, in their own language, and with their obviously limited grasp of the implications of their words. They accepted the normality of the adult behavior. It was the only world they knew.

At the end of the trial the judge rebuked the police for their failure to follow up a great deal of the evidence, and he declared himself to be satisfied about the essential truth of the girls' stories.

What we need to grasp is that men and particularly women who are victims of such abuse earlier in their lives will be turning in increasing numbers to Christians for help during the next few years. Among them there may be manipulative attention seekers, so we will need discernment and spiritual power to help effectively. The damage done to small children in their early years can have appalling effects in later life, psychologically, spiritually and socially.

Cases are coming to light with increasing frequency. Police are taking note of what is happening, gradually assuming a more responsible attitude. Their effectiveness is limited for many reasons. After all, how able are they to contain even the drug problem? The rising crime rate? Hampered by lack of personnel, they will never stamp out Satanism. More significantly, they will never do so because they are fighting spiritual powers with human weapons.

Ken Blue[4] warned a police officer in our area, whose assignment was to investigate witchcraft and Satanism, that without Christ he was in great danger. Shortly afterward that police officer took his own life.

The Emergence of the Occult

Suddenly a number of churches are finding themselves facing what the church down the ages has faced—the powerful reality of witchcraft. It should not surprise us if our sex-sated and violence-crazed society should turn out to be seething with sorcery. Both are manifestations of Satan's rule on earth. I would like to devote the rest of this chapter to a quick look at where we are in the West and what we face as a church.

Dark powers are at work appointing human priests and priestesses to carry out their orders, many of them declared witches, warlocks, Satanists, or priests and priestesses in the resurgent pagan religions. They are not an invincible conspiratorial network; they are tragically deceived people, many of whom have turned from Christianity because they saw it as powerless. Rituals sometimes parody Christian services. I believe the number of witches and Satanists exceeds official estimates. All over the world, including the Western world, the old religions are rapidly returning. It is important to realize that not all who profess pagan power possess it. Others do—and I have met both kinds.

Witchcraft in a Primitive Setting

My first experience with a witch doctor took place in a primitive Bolivian tribe, the Ayoreos, and it convinced me that witch doctors must be frauds. Many of us gathered around him as he tried to heal a woman of abdominal pain. The healing session took place beneath the open sky at night—when there were clouds and no moon. We couldn't see a thing. In the dark he bit her naked abdomen—and then allowed us to light lanterns. He held up a tiny bag for us to look at, claiming it was a growth which he had removed. It was made of brand new pineapple fibers. Inside the tiny bag was fresh red earth. The little bag smelled—of pineapple fiber and fresh earth. He expected the tribespeople to believe that this was what he had actually bitten from and removed from the woman's belly. He was a manifest fraud, and his Ayore followers were at that point playing the sucker.

But since that time I have met real workers of magic, both in primitive settings and in the civilized world.

In *The Masks of Melancholy* I mention the North American Indian shaman who asked me to help him recover his sexual potency, having explained to me the technique for having sex with demons. At one point a change came over his countenance as he faced me. He said, "I've never met anyone like you before! You have *the power.*" He had seen on me a power I didn't even know I possessed. He had also perceived that it was of a different order from those powers he himself fooled around with. He was the second occultist to tell me that. Since then I have used that power with increasing frequency as I have listened to the voice of the Spirit.

Engaged to Satan

Not long ago a young woman approached me after a meeting, requesting my help. She felt she was possessed by demons. She trembled, speaking in a low voice, and had difficulty retaining control of herself. Overwhelmed by very many people who sought my help at that moment, I suggested she come to see me following the Sunday morning service in a local Vineyard fellowship.

She came there with her husband, and as I went to greet her, a demonic manifestation began.[5] I sat next to her, while her husband sat on her other side. She half turned from me, avoiding both her husband's eyes and my own. Once again, her body trembled. She made no sound, but sat, with her hands on her lap gripping a bunch of tissues, repeatedly tearing tiny pieces of paper and dropping them on the floor. I addressed her quietly and repeatedly, but always her body would jerk in a characteristic gesture that reminded me of a terrified animal. It was a "go away" gesture. Her dignity was gone and only terror remained.

In no time we were surrounded by other church members, who had perceived what was happening. Full of demon-hunting enthusiasm, they called on the name of Jesus, issued various commands, prayed in tongues. But the more they did, the more the young woman began to show signs of violence, growled, ground her teeth. The longer the process continued and the louder it got, the less I was able to intervene effectively. Demons can hear well. There is no need for noise.

Let me digress for a moment. I have never enjoyed dealing with demons. It is the spiritual equivalent of cleaning a filthy toilet bowl. When I help someone controlled by demons, I have as little to do with the demon(s) as possible, limiting my dealings with them to commanding them to leave their victims and, when necessary, commanding them to give me their names. I never engage in arguments with them. If they speak (as they sometimes do), I command them to be silent, telling them I will speak only with their victim. In most cases control and dismissal have been easy. But occasionally it has been anything but easy.

On this occasion I requested the demon chasers (whose chorus was reaching a crescendo) to leave us in peace. When they had gone I asked the woman's husband for information. The manifestation gradually subsided as I talked with her husband. He told me his wife, all her life heavily involved in the occult, had been chosen as a bride of Satan. Two weeks before the "marriage" and its consummation were to take place, Christ found her. However, she was not immediately delivered from her many demons. She sought the help of Christians experienced in deliverance, and more recently she had spent time with a team who finally had told her that all demons had left her and that she must resist any deceptive feelings that might suggest to her that her demons were still present.

Clearly she had either been misinformed or else, because she was not at that moment filled by the Spirit of holiness, the demons had returned. I recognized from long experience that a very prolonged and time-consuming battle lay ahead. I also recognized that it would have been irresponsible and unethical of me to tackle the matter then and there, and so made arrangements for her to see two men with outstanding gifts and international reputations.

Training Future Witches
A bride of Satan may be chosen by satanic cult leaders even before she is born. Certain women, cult members or daughters of cult members, may have the "privilege" of producing a child for use by the cult, once they have been ritually impregnated.

Members of satanic cults train themselves to gain spiritual power by violating every human instinct, eating and drinking human waste products, torturing small animals as long as possible before slaughtering them, teaching their own children from a young age to do as they do themselves, and ultimately practicing human sacrifice, using as victims newborn infants born to a "breeder."[6] Young children are commonly victims. Occasionally an adult cult member may be deceived, then sacrificed in a ceremony about which he or she had not been "clued in."

The greater the "self-control" of would-be witches (their capacity to violate every divinely implanted revulsion of evil), the greater their power. Cult members are believed to include judges, doctors, psychiatrists, psychologists, police chiefs and other prominent members of society. Their sexual practices are perverse, since the violation of divinely ordained sex is a central aspect of their pursuit of spiritual power.

Again, these men and women may have a local association, but they are not part of a massive, secret conspiracy. The overall picture of witchcraft/ Satanism is one of many small movements coordinated by the dark spiritual powers themselves. The movements reflect a wide variety of understanding and culture. Some are highly sophisticated. Others are crude, cheap and vulgar.

Organization
We have an annual psychic fair in our local mall. Several months ago we received advertising about the region's sixth annual "witch camp," to be held

not far from where we live. Courses were offered in several tracks, from beginners to advanced. At the public training level, Satanism is becoming more highly organized. Curiously, the dates of the witch camp coincided with those of a large Christian worship conference. Both conferences attracted international applicants. Both conferences were advertised. They were an integral part of the Canadian free enterprise system.

Slowly the extent of witchcraft activities is coming to light. The number of cases dealt with in courts of law is increasing. It is generally suspected that a proportion of the younger children who disappear are sacrificed in satanic rituals. There is growing evidence from court trials in the U.S. and Canada that this is so. But murder can take many forms, forms that would have seemed inconceivable only a few years ago.

A teacher in a denominational boys' school here recently invited three witches to address his class. One of them posed the rhetorical question, "Why worship one God if you can worship two?" She then invited questions. One boy asked about child sacrifice. The witch responded, "We used to sacrifice babies, but we no longer do so. We also used to dance together naked, but now we wear gowns." A male witch intervened at that point, suggesting that the discussion was getting into unprofitable areas.

I learned about the matter from a concerned parent who realized that while an appeal to the principal was certainly called for, in the long run prayer for the young people in our city was the major weapon. She came to me for advice about starting a group for prayer.

The Tempo Increases

Why am I including this information? I do so because, though Christians profess to believe in the existence of a devil, few of us have any real grasp of the extent of his power and activity in the church and the world around us. (And this is particularly true in relation to sex.) Every month it becomes more open, so that now occasional television programs invite professed witches and warlocks to appear, while more serious programs discuss the social problems caused by what seems to be the widespread but hitherto well-concealed practice of witchcraft. Witches used to avoid publicity.

In recent weeks three pastors in different areas have phoned me seeking counsel about how to help and shelter women seeking to escape from satanic cults. In each case the woman had been in the cult as long as she could remember. They had been child victims before their adult involvement. Each reported threats of violence from other cult members and from members of their own families. In two instances the threats were carried out. You may ask me why they do not call other churches and pastors for help. I can only suppose that such people learn by word of mouth (if they learn at all) where they can get help.

Satanists Invade the Church

Twice in the past three years Satanists have invaded Sunday morning worship in the church I attend, even though we had not up to that point had any involvement with cult members. On the first occasion we were merely puzzled as a female witch carried out rituals in the front of the church. We assumed she was just a woman who was "a bit strange" and decided it would be kind to ignore her. Only in retrospect did we realize what had happened. A few weeks later four male witches (appropriately dressed) stood up at the back of the church. They raised their arms, seeming to perform some sort of ritual. Few of us saw them. (Our backs were turned to them. We were intent on the preacher.) The Holy Spirit's presence in power could be felt by all of us, and there seemed to be an unusual anointing on the preacher. The four faltered in their performance, then left. Then, in a recent service in the Anaheim Vineyard when I was present, staff members of the church quietly kept two male Satanists under surveillance while they searched, both in the service and elsewhere in the building, for a woman who had fled from them.

I have noticed that confrontations between Satanists and certain Christian groups are increasing in frequency, invariably in churches where God's power is being manifest. I am friendly with the Anglican minister of a chapel on Vancouver Island. Recently he told me his church received a request from a group of men. They wished to rent the building for an all-night time of "prayer and fellowship." Puzzled, the church secretary requested the names of some of the men involved. All were members of the "group of thirty," a band of professional men—some of them psychologists, lawyers, psychiatrists—all of whom were professed satanists determinedly opposing those Christian groups that seemed to be making significant advances. The group had no interest in robbing the church of ornaments on the altar; they were engaged in the more serious business of seeking to undermine the church's spiritual power. The group's own power is drawn from satanic prayer and worship and diabolical rituals.

Multiple Personality Disorder (MPD)

Multiple personality disorder is a condition in which people have the core of their person split into a number of personalities, sometimes called *alters* or *personas*. Some victims (often referred to as *multiples*) experience, as we all do, sudden changes of mood and behavior that puzzle them. In their case the shifts are more pronounced and dramatic than in the rest of us. But they do not recognize the condition that plagues them.

In a more extreme form, a woman, let's call her Jane, may wake up one morning no longer calling herself Jane and no longer behaving anything like Jane. She is now Mary and may or may not have any awareness of Jane. Like Jane, she thinks of herself as a complete person with her own memory and her own history. In other cases the identity of some alters is kept secret.

Mary (in the example above) may know exactly who she is. If she is aware of Jane, she probably thinks of her as a member of a group of people whom she can describe and with whose relationships she may be familiar. Less extreme forms are less easy to detect, unless the unusual range of personality manifestations arouses suspicion. Therapists dealing with such a person seek to integrate the various alters into one, having first tried to identify all the alters (often a formidable and time-consuming task) and to familiarize themselves with the pattern of the alters' relationships.

Lay Christians reading popular accounts of multiple personality tend to equate the various alters with demons. The explanation never fits all the facts. There is a better explanation of how alters are related to demons. Faced with terrible trauma, children with a certain psychological makeup have the capacity to escape into the fantasy (which can rapidly become more than a fantasy) of being another child and living under other conditions. They avoid pain and fear in this way. Such children begin to spend major portions of their time in an unreal world. They do so to protect themselves from unthinkable horrors.

A number of recent researchers now relate many, possibly most, victims of MPD to SRA. Faced with the horrors of SRA, the victims escape into alters as a protective device. Demonization can be involved, but it is the demonization of individual alters. One step preliminary to integration, used by some helpers, has been to lead individual alters to Jesus and to cast out any demonic beings attached to a particular alter.

One woman who sometimes telephones me for advice (as she helps a victim of MPD) described her discovery of an alter whose existence she had never suspected. At that stage the young woman she was helping was almost well. One night she overheard her crying, but crying as a small child cries. She went to the young woman's bedroom, where the following conversation took place. I will call the helper Pat and the young woman Janis.

Janis (in the scared voice of a three-year-old): Who are you?

Pat: A friend. Don't be afraid.

Janis: Where am I?

Pat: Where did you think you were?

Janis: In the box.

Pat: The box? What box do you mean?

Janis: The box where they put you when you're bad.[7] *(Janis begins to cry.)* They were squirting water into it.

Pat: Water?

Janis: Daddy was squirting water in. But I'm not bad. I'm going to do what Daddy says. Elizabeth didn't an' she drownded. But I'm not going to be drownded. I'm going to be a good girl.

It was evident that the new alter had made itself known as a result of a memory, perhaps in the form of a dream. Pat was a Christian worker, working under supervision. She had by this time a fair amount of experience and saw that she must try to help the new alter. After attempting to reassure the child alter of her safety, as the dialogue continued, Pat began talking about Jesus as though she were talking to a child.

Janis: Jesus is bad. He kills little kids.

Pat: No, Jesus is not bad. He loves little children.

Janis: No he doesn't. He does bad things to them.[8]

Pat: I'm going to ask Jesus to let you see him. *(She prays.)* Let me know if you see him.

Janis: He's with some kids. *(Pause.)* He's telling them a story.

Pat: Why don't you go nearer so you can listen?

We have no means of knowing how Janis drew nearer. But somehow she did, and evidently the Holy Spirit began to reveal to her the winsomeness of the Son of God. Janis the three-year-old child found peace, and Janis the young woman was one step nearer to full integration.

Not all victims of SRA develop MPD. One woman we have been trying to help simply has no memories of the first twelve years of her life. Horrifying pictures (some in the form of "flashbacks") come to her at odd times, but she cannot relate to them as memories. Once in a prayer session with her and several others, I had a vision I never again want to see. As a result, I know one or two of the things that have happened to her. But she is not ready to integrate them into her memories at the time I write this.

Dr. James G. Friesen, a Canadian psychologist working in California, may know as much as anyone in North America about the relationship between SRA and MPD.[9] Along with other Christian psychiatrists and psychologists, he runs a clinic for sufferers. Recently, having encouraged the publishers to publish his book, and having written a foreword to it, I was glad to see *Uncovering the Mystery of MPD* published by Here's Life Publishers.

My Reservations About the Treatment of MPD
The psychological treatment of MPD can be lengthy and therefore very expensive if carried out by a professional. For an MPD victim with twenty alters, it will take many sessions to discover them all and longer to bring them all together in a process of integration. The process is lengthy and time-consuming. Although laborers are worthy of their hire, one wonders how justifiable the expense will be. A further question arises. Already the number of persons alleged to be suffering from the condition seems to exceed the number of available therapists. If this increase should be real, and if it should continue to grow, where will the needed resources come from?

I am convinced that the church's mission to the poor is her most important mission. Messianic gospel preaching is characteristically to the poor (Lk 7:22), but poor people do not have money to pay for professional skills. I can envisage the possibility of a time, probably a time of general economic hardship, when the principal responsibility for helping witchcraft victims will fall on the church. At this date the church is not ready for that.

But there are a few people, not professionally qualified, who seem gifted with the ability to get through hindrances to treatment that professionals struggle with. They work on a different principle from professionals. Instead of beginning with an attempt to discover the many alters, they begin with the principle of the unity of the personality.

It seems to me that the very process of "discovering" the alters is a sort of reinforcement in the client's mind of their reality as separate beings. Biblically the personality is unitary. Some people claim more success by stressing this to the client. In addition they simply pray that God will bring about the integrating process.

Former Victims as Counselors

People escaping from a background of SRA, or who have been chosen as breeders, are fragile, vulnerable people. At present I lack the knowledge and the wisdom to say at what point they themselves might be ready to be used as counselors to help others. I know of two cases where doing so proved ill-advised, and I will mention one of these.

The essence of witchcraft is manipulation, particularly with power. A true servant of God uses God's power only to do God's will. A sorcerer wants to have power *for the sake of having it.* The sorcerer's victims, manipulated constantly, themselves become manipulative. Manipulation, always diabolical, is a habit hard to shake, very difficult to unlearn. Victims of witchcraft have usually learned it well. It is very important that those who help witchcraft's victims do so without a trace of manipulation.

In addition, the experience of a victim of witchcraft can become the sole point of reference to reality. It can be mixed with the teachings of witchcraft as to the nature of a human being and with the true experiences of power which advanced witches undergo. The teachings are erroneous—true satanic deceptions. *Nevertheless, they work!* Persons who have for a significant portion of their lives been involved in witchcraft therefore may still have a fragile hold on the nature of reality, in addition to showing manipulative tendencies.

We need great humility in making discoveries of this sort. Knowledge in anything so esoteric tends to excite us—and therefore to blind us. Jane (a pseudonym) was an experienced counselor who made the mistake of prematurely setting up a victim, Beatrice (also a pseudonym), as a counselor. Jane writes:

Beatrice came into the church as a very traumatized woman, but as she began to read and practice the Word and develop relations of trust, she grew as a Christian. Some of her clients came to church and became Christians. We were excited about what God was doing and while we were puzzled over what she said about the cult, we accepted that such things were possible and that those coming out of the occult needed acceptance more than they needed to fit our world view.

An older and more experienced person, in a letter to Jane, commented:

I sensed, early on, that you would eventually have problems of trust, belief, reliability with Beatrice. She seemed (to me, skeptical as always) too bound up in her memories, too enamored of them, too certain that her memories, aside from marking and crippling her, gave her a kind of *panache,* even to the point of working professionally with others similarly stricken.

Jane concludes:

Our excitement and, more subtly, our pride in what God was doing, in combination with our own needs, dulled our discernment. We started to believe things that, in looking back, had no basis in objective reality. . . . Could we have challenged some of (Beatrice's) therapeutic practices and assumptions?

What we must never forget is that few people have any experience of dealing with victims of witchcraft, behind which lies all the malice of Satan toward God. We are fools to believe we are qualified to enter into such a conflict in our own wisdom; we must recognize our need for and continued dependence on the Holy Spirit for discernment.

The Nature of Christian Warfare

This is the day of God's mercy to sinners in society—and in the church. Our main weapon in the battle with the powers of darkness is the gospel. We are not called on to rule society as a Christian elite, nor even to reform society. We are called to obey Christ, and in so doing to allow the Holy Spirit to awaken society to its peril, causing large segments of it to turn in repentance and faith to God. When that happens society will be reformed. Our aim, however, is not societal reformation, but the declaration of the kingdom of God which divides society with the sword of truth.

Our main task is not even to tackle or take on the powers of darkness. We will inevitably be at war with them if we are effective in obeying Christ. To be sure, we need to know something about their methods of warfare. But they themselves are not our main assignment. Our main assignment is the rescue and redemption of perishing human beings. Our goal is to reach a lost world, to carry out the Great Commission.

The church, though an army, is at this point a badly battered army with many wounded. Many church members are compromised, unable to fight. We have secretly kept *devoted things* for ourselves, and therefore we are constantly defeated in battles with dark powers. I believe many churches have an unwritten understanding with the powers of darkness: "We'll leave you alone if you'll leave us alone."

The Day of Deliverance

Belial and Moloch were henchmen of Satan in Milton's *Paradise Lost.* They are still on the earth, the one (in Milton's view) the champion of phallus, the other of violence and murder. And both claim the unwitting loyalty of members of Christian churches. Along with them, whatever satanic henchmen govern witchcraft also bring ruinous evil on human society. Christian households are being destroyed by one or other of the motley crew from within. However, in the mercy of God, this is the day in which God is dealing with sexual sin and violence among his own people. This is the day in which we renounce our idols and the pseudodeities behind them. This is the day in which we forsake idolatry and return to God.

How do I know that the day of God's deliverance has arrived? The first time I fully expounded the material I deal with in chapters two and three in a European country, the effects were startling. I rarely make an appeal and never a long one. All I ever say—*and I say it only once*—is, "If you wish to acknowledge your sin and need prayer for help, come forward!" Then I wait. If no one comes—fine.

On that occasion in Europe, young men began to *run* forward. Soon an avalanche of people, men, women, young, old, broke loose, making hurry impossible by the density with which they crowded together. Of four thousand Christian leaders present, an estimated two thousand five hundred pushed forward, seeking prayer for unavailing struggles against their sex drives. The stairways from the balconies were jammed, as were the corridors, the aisles and the area around the platform. Only small islands of people remained in the seating area. Every available space was congested with standing men and women. It was an impossible situation. The majority were members of conservative churches. Before long, we began to hear the agonized cries of desperate men and women and the shrieks of demons.

These reactions owe nothing to any ability I personally may have. They are the result of both the working of the Spirit and the victory of the Son of God. God is making men and women desperate and opening wide the door to repentance and hope. The effects have not always been quite so dramatic, though the material on violence (which is, I believe, the inevitable social consequence of sexual promiscuity) shows some astonishing effects. In the meantime we have become better equipped to deal with large numbers of people needing prayer and counsel for sexual sin.

We have also taken care to discourage people from coming forward unless they know that God has spoken to them. Recently in a meeting of over three thousand Christian people (including a high proportion of pastors and Christian leaders), almost one-third came forward to acknowledge and seek help for their inability to control rage and, in the case of some, violence in the home. Those confessing their need of help were conducted to two large rooms where they could receive extensive prayer and help. Again, large numbers of demons spontaneously manifested themselves.

Unless and until the church faces up to her need for deliverance from sexual sin and violence in the home *and deals with that need,* the power of God will not be on the church's evangelism in the way it could be. But the power of God *is* on the church at this moment to deal with sex and violence. We live in the day of Christ's deliverance. Powerful as the dark powers may be, they are no match for their Creator and our Redeemer, who is in our midst to save us all from the tyrannies that have held sway for too long.

The moment we start to "clean up our act," the warfare will begin. Yet unless and until churches clean up immorality and violence among their members, they will remain in darkness, ignorant of their blindness. Their successes in battle will be minor and their defeats major. Fine buildings, excellent programs, highly trained pastors are all relatively unimportant in comparison with dealing with the hidden skeletons in our closets.

It is with this task in mind that I write.

PART II
Men, Women
& Sex

In part two I want to look at men's and women's sexuality both as a psychiatrist and as a Christian. Psychiatrists try to heal damaged emotions. As a psychiatrist I think in terms of pathology, of disease. As a Christian I think in moral terms about sin, salvation and sanctification. I cannot think both psychiatrically and "Christianly" without at the same time asking what a manly man or a womanly woman is. Is there validity to such concepts? What makes a man a man, or a woman a woman? What is the relation between *being* and *role*?

Clearly, too, I must look at gender, a word the Bible never actually uses but implies by the models of manhood and womanhood it gives us. For it is to Scripture, not to the human sciences, that I appeal. Where science agrees with Scripture, I say, "Science is beginning to learn wisdom." Where science disagrees, I try to point out its error from the biblical principles I am learning to prove by experience. For me, scientific truth must conform to Scripture.

It is not that I ignore science. God is good in permitting, indeed in encouraging, us to explore his designs. But we have gone overboard. We have thrown away our real heritage and worshiped the gods of human knowledge. I try to correct this serious imbalance by emphasizing where our hope must lie.

Part two has six chapters. Chapter eight affects both singles and married people but deals more particularly with marriage. It addresses two related subjects, our attitude to (feelings about) our bodies, and the relation of that attitude to the divorce between affection and eros in marriage. Chapter nine deals with masturbation, where my own thinking has undergone a significant shift since I wrote *Eros Defiled*. The Bible is silent on masturbation, so I look at general principles in relation to Scripture. In a similar fashion I look at sexual identity confusion in chapter ten.

Chapter eleven discusses the most extreme form of sexual identity confusion, that which is associated with homosexuality. I discuss the roots of homosexuality, both in its possible genetic and its environmental aspects. Finally, chapters twelve and thirteen look at the issues of manliness and womanliness—and my personal view that the war between the sexes is primarily the fault of men, and that it dates back to what happened at the Fall.

CHAPTER 8
The Marriage of Sex and Love

There dwell an accursed people, full of pride and lust. There when a man takes a maiden in marriage they do not lie together, but each lies with a cunningly fashioned image of the other.
C. S. LEWIS, *THAT HIDEOUS STRENGTH*

*S*ex and love are supposed to go together, integrated as one whole, one entity. Sex concerns the physical, erotic side of love. Sex is also about love that is tender and giving, that makes me long to give all I have and am to someone. Each is good, even when considered alone. Together they have the strength of steel and the sparkle of diamonds.

As a result of the Fall, however, men and women experience love and sex separately. Nevertheless, love and sex are meant to be married to each other. Many of us who are married hang on to one of them, not caring so much about the other. Others of us hope that someday the two—the physical and emotional sides—will be reconciled.

Referring to men, Sam Keen asserts, "Most of us have a difficult time forging a marriage between the heart and the penis. We can't get our sex and our potency together."[1] A common pattern in marriage is for a man to be preoccupied with his sex drive while his wife feels starved of affection. But the two, affection and sex, are meant to be one, to be so much a part of one another as to be indistinguishable.

Marriage: Doorway to Freedom

Let me talk about marriage. I still believe marriage—the conventional notion of it—is one (not the only) high road to true freedom, whether we are talking about personal freedom or sexual freedom. In saying that, I certainly do not imply there is freedom only for the married. I am trying to avoid worldly cynicism about both marriage and singleness. Chastity is difficult—some would say impossible. Marriage can look like a trap. Lured by sex and/or affection, we crawl into the trap like lobsters after bait. How then can I speak of the freeing nature of marriage?

Mike Mason describes his own struggle with honeymoon panic in the prologue of *The Mystery of Marriage*. Vividly he shares the feelings of fear and gloom that came over him as, along with his new wife, he visited former friends in a Trappist monastery. Yet as Mike and his wife drove on, a glimpse of a couple of hawks dancing an aerial *pas de deux* compelled them to stop the car to watch:

> There was something in this soaring dance of the pair of them, with a whole sky all to themselves, which spoke directly to me, not just of play and freedom on a summer's day, but of the shining beauty of love, the pure ease and joy of companionship.[2]

That "shining beauty" and that freedom of an aerial dance "with a whole sky all to themselves" are integral parts of God's gift of marriage between man and woman. It is a freedom and beauty which married people uniquely may experience. I shall deal with marriage only incidentally and then only with the uniting of sex and love. Yet I must dismiss at once the notion that marriage is limiting. Or if it is, it is so only in the way prison gates are limiting when you are leaving the prison. You might have to squeeze through the prison doors to get out, but once out you are free. And the prison I am talking about, please remember, is not the prison of singleness, but the prison of wrong thinking about both marriage and singleness.

Freedom (at least the Greek idea of it) is doing what you were designed to do. Human beings have bodies and hearts designed for marriage and adaptable to singleness. There is freedom to be found, true freedom, in either. My father, expressing the cynicism I speak of, used to sing,

Oh, when I was single my pockets did jingle;

Oh, I wish I were single again!

Both marriage and singleness should be what the ocean is to a fish, what the sky is to a bird, what powdery snow is to an expert skier. They are rarely so conceived. The freedom of the slopes awaits the skier—but only the expert and experienced skier. First must come discipline, the discipline of learning how to stand, how to move and how to stop moving, how to cooperate with slope and surface, how to overcome fear, how to recognize and handle danger. Only then does true freedom yield its wonders. Until that point the skier's freedom is limited.

Inexperience and incompetence may themselves cause serious injury. If you recover from the injury, one of several things may happen. You may give up and never find out what real skiing freedom is, or you may continue but never gain confidence. However, if your commitment to skiing is whole-hearted and deep, having learned a valuable lesson you may continue pursuing a high road to freedom.

The same is certainly true both of marriage and singleness. Their skills must be learned, and the learning may bring painful injuries. But let me, for a moment, focus on marriage. Mason puts it this way:

> Love aims at revelation, at a clarifying and defining of our true natures. It is a sort of sharpening process, a paring away of dull and lifeless exteriors so that the keen new edge of a person's true self can begin to flash and gleam in the light of day.
>
> A diamond cannot be cut with a tin saw, and neither can a hawk fly with a butterfly. A person, to grow keen and shining and real, needs love, which is to say, needs another person: "As iron sharpens iron, so one person sharpens another" (Proverbs 27:17). And sharpening is a painful process: extract the pain from love and there is nothing left.[3]

We come to marriage not only untrained but damaged and largely unsanctified. "Lifeless exteriors" need to be stripped off and painful injuries healed. Some of us are damaged emotionally, especially sexually, and it is this sort of damage I address in this book.

Learning Freedom on Your Own

In some of her conferences Leanne Payne talks about "bent" men and women: those who, particularly within marriage, are bent toward their partners rather than reaching upward toward God. They are men and women who depend upon their partners for their fulfillment. We bring fulfillment in Christ *to* marriage. We do not look to marriage for a fulfillment that can only come from him. Single men and women who feel incomplete outside marriage because of their affectional and sexual needs are certain to be frustrated within marriage as well.

If we define *healing* (emotional) as a degree of restoration to what God intended us to be at creation, then healing and sanctification become synonymous, and healing becomes a part of wholeness. We should not look to marriage for sanctification except in the painful sense Mason talks about. We are continuously to be bringing sanctification *to* marriage. When each leans on Christ rather than on the other, each brings strength to the partnership. Structures with mutually leaning parts are unstable, liable to collapse.

Marriage should reflect the oneness of the Trinity. Such is God's intention for it. As Father, Son and Spirit are one, so are we to be. In our case the oneness is the oneness each of us should enjoy with God.

My focus is not on marriage itself. Rather, I am to be concerned about my own maturity within the marriage, about *my* sin and immaturity, not that of my spouse. The focus in many books about marriage is on how to have a good marriage. Our marriages improve greatly when we get past being "bent" (mutually leaning) men and women and become God-leaning instead. To be so has greater importance than anything else in life, for both singles and marrieds.

God does not call married men and women to perfect marriages. He calls them to godliness within marriage. He calls singles to godliness as singles. It is every bit as tough to be godly in either state, each having its peculiarly sanctifying aspects. Godliness is about being set free, free as a single person or as a married person. In married people, godliness may not advance at the same rate in both spouses. Even so, my prime business is to obey God, whatever effect this may have on my marriage. To put the marriage before personal obedience is idolatry. Marital counseling can be helpful, but once the marriage is made central, Christ ceases to be central. As each partner makes Christ central, the marriage advances.

The Nature of Sexual Love
For each spouse individually, when affection and *eros* come together, lessons are learned as to what true love is all about. Sexual love is bodily love, love we learn through our bodies. We are bodily creatures, and God teaches us through our bodies.

Agape is the word the New Testament uses when it talks about the love of God. It is the love we Christians are supposed to have for God and our fellows. There is a feeling among Christians that *agape* must not be mentioned in the same breath as *eros*—bodily, physical love. Sexual love, we feel, is infinitely lower than *agape*. It is seen as inferior—as somewhat gross, unspiritual. But as C. S. Lewis points out, in the matter of the varieties of love, "The highest does not stand without the lowest."[4]

A major component in our problem is that we do not feel at home in our bodies. It is almost as though we don't live in them, as though we are off somewhere in a world of thought, or that we would be if we were not constantly reminded of our bodies by their hungers, their smells, the never-ceasing growth of hair on them. So we bathe them, shave them, powder them, perfume and clothe them, all with the object of making them fit for the exalted world we inhabit. To such hygienic practices I have no objection. It is the motive behind it all that I suspect.

I suppose there is a sense in which bodily, sexual love, while not being an inferior form of love, is a lower love. It is lower in the sense of being more elementary, more basic, just as learning the alphabet is basic to learning to read, or learning to recognize and reproduce sounds is a prelude to learning to talk. To learn bodily love is to learn the basics of a more difficult lesson, the lesson of *agape* love. We must never despise or look down on our bodies. They are divine instruments.

Do I imply that only married people have a shot at learning *agape* love? I don't intend to. Marriage is one way to learn it, but some of the greatest God-lovers of all time have been single people, so marriage cannot be the only way. What I do say is that *agape* love for a spouse cannot be truly learned unless we learn to "love and to cherish" our own bodies.

Ephesians 5:28-29 tell us, "In this same way, husbands ought to love their wives as their own bodies. He who loves his wife loves himself. After all, no one ever hated his own body, but he feeds and cares for it, just as Christ does the church."

To enter a true experience of sexual love is to be on a high road to learning *agape* love.

Curiously, celibate mystics speak of divine love in sexual terms. Groping for language in which to describe what they experience of God's love, they are forced to use the language of the Song of Solomon. Contrary to the belief of some psychoanalytic writers, this is not because they are sexually frustrated. Far from frustrated, most of them are profoundly fulfilled. They experience love, ultimate love, that higher love of which sexual love is a symbol and a picture. Human language lacks the words to describe what they experience, the nearest being the language of the love that can exist between a man and a woman.

The Breadth of Sexual Love

Of course we must not limit our understanding of sexual love to the erotic sensations that accompany *making* love. Sexual love is deeper and broader than brief ecstasy. For a woman it includes gestation—the nine-month saga of the growth of a new life inside her body, that amazing poem of leisurely but profound changes. Her body both sings and groans—a singing and a groaning that are sexual in nature.

Nor is a man's sexual love mere orgasmic ecstasy. When a man feels tiny baby fingers curling around his own little finger, the sensations of wonder and affection as well as the urge to care for and protect arise out of sexual love. It is no longer erotic arousal, and it is certainly not the lust of a child molester. Rather, it is that which erotic arousal has led to: the joy of what is happening to him in that moment, the experience of a tiny replica of his own hand grasping his finger. Flesh that came from him now clings to him. The ecstasy at the beginning was a part of the greater whole.

In the same way, when a grandmother examines the photographs of her grandchildren and glows with pride and wonder at the second-generation fruit of her own body, it is sexual love she is experiencing. *Sexual love includes all that arises out of sex*—and grandchildren certainly do! We must not narrow sexual love down to what happens in bed or in a hayloft. It is a deep and broad God-given thing which covers a wide range of in-the-body experiences.

Sexual love is family love. It is the dependent and utterly selfish need-love of the child for its mother. In marriage it embraces friendship, a love necessary to every married couple. Friendship is first learned not outside the home, but among siblings in a family. It is also developed between parents and children as the children mature. Our habit of limiting the term *sexual* to erotogenic sensations is a master stroke of Satan, played out through idiocies of advertising. For it is Satan's design to split eroticism off from the totality of bodily love. And when he has achieved that, he weaves sexual chains around us.

C. S. Lewis writes about those particular chains both in his children's and in one of his adult fantasies, when he describes those pleasures which never satisfy but serve only to create a craving for more. Pleasures that come in the line of obedience to God do not leave us with craving, even though they may be repeated many times. We experience cravings, cravings for food that exceed our need for it and that ruin our health, cravings for sex that drive us insane with their endless demands and their failure truly to satisfy.

The Nature of Sexual Lust

Legitimate, God-given desire becomes lust the moment we make a god of it. To worship food is food lust. To be neurotic about getting our full quota of sleep becomes sleep lust. To be enslaved to erotic sensations represents sexual lust.

Lust never satisfies. One craves more and more while getting less and less out of it. In C. S. Lewis's *The Lion, the Witch and the Wardrobe*, Edmund (one of the four children in the story) enters a wardrobe in an old house, only to discover that the wardrobe is a gateway to another world. He meets a witch queen who asks him what he would like. Edmund chooses Turkish delight and the queen conjures up a box of it by magic—a box containing several pounds of pleasure. He has never tasted such delicious Turkish delight.

The queen knows that Edmund's brother and two sisters are aware of the wardrobe, and she wishes to lure them also into her power. The Turkish delight is her weapon, her means of control over Edmund. It is enchanted Turkish delight which cannot satisfy, and "anyone who had once tasted it would want more and more of it, and would even, if they were allowed, go on eating it till they killed themselves."[5] Edmund looks at the empty box, longing for more, but the queen will give him more only if he brings his brother and sisters to her.

Sex can be a craving when love and sexual desire are split. It matters little what form the sexual activity takes—heterosexual sex within the marriage bond, or any other erotic delight. When love and sexual desire are split (an exceedingly common state of affairs), erotic sex becomes like Edmund's enchanted Turkish delight. Ultimately, the craving leads to illicit or pathological forms of sex. The devil has achieved his aim. We fall into cravings that drive us into addiction to pornography, to masturbation, to excessive needs for sexual intercourse, heterosexual or homosexual, to child molestation and every form of perversion. Common to all of them is a hunger that can never be satisfied, that leaves us emptier than we were before.

Sexual love was never meant to be like that. When affection and fidelity blend with *eros*, true love flowers, for (as Lewis has explained) the higher will not stand without the lower. Sexual activity then becomes an expression of love, not of need. Indeed the two (love and sex) seem one. Love expressed sexually under those conditions is always deeply satisfying. It does not leave an aching hunger, for it was designed to satisfy, not to torture. Nor does it enslave.

There is something more. Edmund's craving for the enchanted Turkish delight has destroyed his normal taste for food. Later in the story he shares a meal of freshly caught fried fish. "He had eaten his share of the dinner, but he hadn't really enjoyed it because he was thinking all the time about Turkish delight—and there's nothing that spoils the taste of good ordinary food half so much as the memory of bad magic food."[6] Our enjoyment of the real thing is enhanced once the "bad-magic" sex is abandoned.

Perverted sex is always diabolical. It is every bit as much enchanted as Edmund's Turkish delight. As long as we crave it we are unable to relish the real thing. It needs the power of Christ to break the enchantment and restore what is lost.

Two Case Histories

In everyday experience, the divorce between eroticism and affection takes one of two forms: sometimes a yearning for erotic sensation is paramount, sometimes a craving for tenderness and love.

I have been consulted by many women who dislike their bodies and are embarrassed by and ashamed of them, whatever their actual shape and size may be. From many case histories I will now construct an imaginary case history. Since the case history will include details which are common to many such women (it is surprising how the same details crop up repeatedly and how many expressions are repeated), it will seem like the story of any female reader who shares the same problem. So I would say, "If the shoe fits—wear it!"

I'll call my imaginary woman Irene. Irene is a single mom of thirty-three whose husband was killed in a car accident five years ago. She has two children, a boy of ten and a girl of eight. She is attractive—blue-eyed, with almost black hair. In spite of having to struggle financially, she still takes care of herself, dresses neatly, uses makeup and is not overweight. She is about to marry a widower ten years older than herself but is apprehensive about the sexual aspects of the marriage.

Irene is a Roman Catholic, part of the Catholic charismatic movement. "I read in *Eros Defiled* that sex is supposed to be good and beautiful. My priest (he's young) says the same thing, and I start to cry when he does so. As a matter of fact, I cry whenever I read a particular sentence in your book, because that's what I want—to know its beauty." She pauses. "I'm not pursuing sex. I just want to stop hating it, to know it as God means it to be. I know it's not wrong, but I can't stop *feeling* it is."

Irene was born when her mother was sick and her father old. She can only remember the one as an invalid and the other as overwhelmed with the care of providing for his large family. She read romantic novels of the "pure" variety, which fed her with the notion that marriage was about love. "They kissed—but I always associated kisses with affection—even 'passionate' kisses—and never with sex. I thought *passion* meant adoration."

Church and its activities were important to her, and a church-based youth group eventually became the center of her social life. One day when she was seventeen a twenty-four-year-old man (who sounded like a smooth operator) so manipulated things that he accompanied her home after dark. On the way home a struggle took place which could have become a rape but didn't. She ran home trembling, too ashamed to tell anyone what had happened.

Eventually she fell in love and got engaged. The engagement lasted two years. During the engagement "he seemed to have a much greater sexual need than I had, and it was a perpetual struggle to hold him off. But I did. I told him it was wrong. We must wait until we married. It was the one thing that made for difficulties in our engagement."

I asked her how the honeymoon had gone. "We just went away for a weekend. We couldn't afford more. Even that was awful. Then we had to live at my in-laws' home at first."

"That must have made your first sexual encounters difficult."

She dropped her head. "It did."

After a moment or two of silence I asked her, "How do you feel about your own body?"

"I hate it. I'm ashamed of it. I don't like looking at it."

I made some comment about the kind of difficulties some women face who are molested as children by some older family member or friend. Again she looked at the floor. "I was hoping you wouldn't raise that," she said, "but now that you have done so . . ."

Irene had been molested repeatedly by an older brother when she was small. Her parents were the "no-touch variety" and in any case were too absorbed with their own problems to display physical affection. Irene knew nothing about hugs and kisses in the family. Her prime physical contact had been with a brother who forced his attentions on her in secret.

Already we have talked about the sexual molestation of children and the damage it causes. Here we will note only two things. First, there was Irene's hatred of sex, her feeling about its wrongness and her fear of her own and her husband's bodies. Second, there was her longing for affection and even physical touches indicating affection, something she had never known in her childhood.

Fearing One's Body

Irene's story represents one way in which sex and love get separated in our experience. In men it commonly occurs in a different manner.

I myself was delighted to get married. I knew God had brought Lorrie and me together. Our early sexual experiences I would rate as good for my wife, excellent for me. I knew all the textbook rules, all about consideration for one's partner, about the differences in sexual responses in men and women. After all, I was a doctor. Lorrie was a virgin when we married. I was what I would call a *technical* virgin. You'll see what I mean as I continue. However, the early days of our marriage were supremely joyful ones. For my part, I had never known such happiness. And though I now recognize how uninformed and shallow we really were, I can only be grateful for that beginning. It could have been so different. *God took us as we were and where we were, drawing us gently and gradually into the deeper lessons of marriage.*

I came to marriage unhealed from my past. For one thing, I had been molested as a young boy by a Christian worker. He could arouse me, he did so whenever he had the chance, and I hated him with a deep hatred. There were other things in my past, my habit of masturbating, the sex play of British schoolboys, the almost total absence of touching in my family. All of these left me vulnerable.

The masturbation was under control a lot of the time. But I would begin again, sometimes after a year or more of abstinence. Then came a dream which changed everything. I have had such dreams all my life from time to time. I remember after a long "silence" begging the Lord to speak to me in a dream. Dreams that come from the Lord are so different from other dreams in my own experience. Usually I wake up startled and moved after having one.

I will not bore you with the details of the dream that came. Suffice it to say that for once I was a little puzzled about its meaning. Usually I was stunned by the power of the message dreams from God carried. Though they were all highly symbolic, I would know the meaning of them even before I woke up. In fact it was the sudden awareness of the dream's meaning that would waken me.

This dream was different. Sex had been the last thing I had been thinking of when I made my request for a dream. Yet I knew at once it was about sex, but I had to interpret the dream this time, and I interpreted it to mean that I had problems with masturbation from time to time simply because I was naked too often. I slept naked, swam naked at the "Y," and enjoyed being naked under other appropriate circumstances. There seemed to be no erotic arousal about it. At that time I just felt good about my body. Even so, I still masturbated occasionally, usually naked. I got more of a kick that way. But I despised myself for "needing" the habit and struggled constantly against it.

My interpretation of the dream was badly mistaken, but I am glad about the mistake now. It served to reinforce the lesson about the importance of a right attitude to our bodies and our sexuality. I was obedient to what I *thought* God was saying, and that is always good. My God brings good even from my mistakes. What happened was that in my efforts to avoid any naked-ness outside bathing and sex, I became more and more aware of the erotic potential of that nakedness. Gradually even showering became a problem. I had to struggle against lustful thoughts, far more than when I was free to be naked.

One day God spoke—simply, powerfully, clearly. "I want you to start being naked again. You are to be naked in your bathroom whenever you are there in the morning and at night. You are to be free to be naked in the bedroom. You are to sleep naked—and to be naked whenever you choose when it is appropriate."

I was very afraid. I knew it was God, but I could not face him. I was already having trouble. It made no sense.

"What if I masturbate?"

"Yes, that *is* a risk. But whenever you are naked you must constantly call to mind that I, by my Spirit, inhabit your body, and that I am also all around you, so that in a double sense you are in my presence."

I was bewildered. Scared. If I remember correctly, I prayed over the matter two or three days. For by this time there were erotic sensations along with nakedness. I was painfully aware of the sexual aspects of nakedness, and was sometimes sexually aroused merely by being naked. I was terrified of being naked, yet at the same time I *wanted* to be naked. Wasn't that temptation? Didn't the Scripture say we were to flee temptation?

Before God's word to me I had still masturbated from time to time. *From that day on I never masturbated again.* What is more, during all the years since, I have never even wanted to.

My Reasons for Sharing

Yet I do not present this account as a model of how to quit masturbating. In later chapters I will talk about masturbation and about sexual identity confusion, both of which were problems to me. God's leading to each of us in terms of our sanctification is to be unique. His programs are tailor-made to fit our individual difficulties.

There are several important reasons behind my sharing the account. One is to show that you will never know what God's tailor-made plan for your own sexual difficulties is unless you learn the sound of his voice and how to distinguish it from your own thoughts and imaginations. Jesus taught us that his sheep listen, or pay heed to, his voice (Jn 10:27). You cannot pay heed to a voice you don't even hear. In part three I shall go into this in more detail.

I have another reason. One of the biggest differences for me, once I obeyed God's word to me, was the change in my sexual relations with Lorrie. My attitude to her and to her body changed in the degree that my attitude to my own body changed. And it continued to change for years after that. I had long recognized that there was little difference morally between my masturbation and many of the times we made love. Sometimes I was merely using her body to get the orgasm I lusted for. I didn't want to be like that, and I tried to "be considerate," to ask her how she was doing. I was "following the book," but it did not come from my heart. My real interest was in me, in what *I* got out of it.

Slowly that changed. For one thing, I began to find I was no longer the victim of my body's drives. In the approach to lovemaking, it did not matter if on one occasion I was thoroughly sexually stirred up but Lorrie wasn't. I no longer felt that I would burst or go crazy if I didn't get "that wonderful feeling of relief." So I stopped trying to lay guilt trips on Lorrie. By the grace and gift of God, *I* was in control, not my body. And my body responded appropriately. Raging desire subsided soon enough. It turned out to be merely a scarecrow.

Using someone else's body to relieve oneself represents love in the partner who gives, not in the partner who takes. It is good as far as it goes. It can be a stage in learning to love. But it can also be a stage in deepening the divorce between love and sex. Eventually things will go one way or the other.

The quotation at the head of this chapter is from C. S. Lewis's novel *That Hideous Strength*. Ransom, a Christ figure, is establishing his identity before Merlin, who has entered the twentieth century. In doing so Ransom reveals his knowledge of the vile sexual practices of the moon folk, who engage in sexual relations not with their true partners but with images of them. Lewis is asserting that many people do in practice what I had often done, merely gratifying their lusts, scarcely thinking of their partners. They might just as well be copulating with "cunningly fashioned images" of them.

> There [on the moon] dwell an accursed people, full of pride and lust. There when a man takes a maiden in marriage they do not lie together, but each lies with a cunningly fashioned image of the other, made to move and to be warm by devilish arts, for real flesh will not please them, they are so dainty in their dreams of lust. Their real children they fabricate by vile arts in a secret place.[7]

Lust had never satisfied me. An orgasm would leave me wanting more, whether I could have it or not. I have said elsewhere that the devil's sadistic joke is to cause us to need more and more stimulation for less satisfaction in return. For sex and love, *eros* and *agape*, were meant to be welded and wedded. And to the degree that they are, *making* love becomes infinitely more satisfying. If there is a universal lesson in what I have shared it is this: *A wrong attitude to our bodies renders impossible that welding and wedding of* eros *and* agape.

There were endless spinoffs to my trembling obedience to the word of God that came to me. One was the (at first) frantic need to remember I was in God's presence. It led to deeper awareness of the valueless, self-centered flotsam and jetsam that flowed endlessly over the surface of my mind, as well as of my *real* self (in Christ) which waited there, deeper than the floating garbage. It proved also to be the beginning of a long and endlessly ongoing series of sanctifying lessons, some of the sexual parts being included in various parts of this book.

The progressive acceptance of my body and its parts was thoroughly wholesome. I remember in the early days standing naked before God, my head thrown back and my arms reaching skyward, crying in deep pain, "Look on me, God! Look at this body you gave me! It's full of moral twistedness and lust. Take the twistedness away, Lord! See what is in me and deal with it!"

Since then, on a number of occasions I have stood again naked in his presence (usually just after getting out of bed), blessing, praising and worshiping him for his great goodness in creating my body and giving it to me. Most particularly I bless him for the sexual parts of it, and for the feelings associated with them, deeply conscious that my sexuality must be used to his glory and according to his instructions.

Respect for the Body
Hatred of our bodies? God desires to inculcate *respect*—not fear—respect and honor for him, and respect and honor (even joy) for what he created. He wishes us to be thankful for our bodies, which are a gift from him. I had feared my own penis, feared the rapidity with which it became aroused when I saw it or touched it. The fear was understandable, but it was not the same as respect. It also excluded any sense of thankfulness. The sexual parts of us demand "greater honor" and also to be treated with modesty because they are less presentable publicly (1 Cor 12:23). We should all be profoundly grateful for our sexual parts, and *should express that gratitude in worship and praise.*

Fear of the body? Everything created by God, including our bodies, is good, and according to Paul it is to be received with thanksgiving, being sanctified by the word of God and prayer (1 Tim 4:1-5). And while exhibitionism and immodesty are inappropriate and sinful, a natural awareness of and enjoyment of one's body and all its parts, and a wholehearted rejoicing in God's creation of, sanctification of and indwelling of it is important. "After all," writes Paul, "no one ever hated his own body, but he feeds and cares for it, just as Christ does the church" (Eph 5:29).

The Conquest of Sex-Related Fear

Irene and I, then, both experienced a degree of divorce between the experience of sex and that of love. Irene loved and enjoyed receiving and giving affection—even by touch and caress. But once an invisible line was crossed, hatred and fear set in. I, on the other hand, mostly enjoyed erotic arousal. For me, nearly every caress, every touch became erotic eventually, even when the touch was an expression of affection. But following my dream and my "obedience," because the thing became so uncontrollable, I hated and feared my own body, just as Irene was humiliated by and ashamed of hers.

Underlying both fears lay essentially the same reason. Irene felt (though she did not *believe*) that sex was unclean and sinful. I had less of a problem at that point, but the association of masturbation and nakedness for me had created a terror of sexual arousal, especially when I was away from home. But knowing this—at least knowing it intellectually—helped little in overcoming temptation.

Many people are afraid of their bodies without realizing it. Only when God's Spirit put his finger on this in my own life did I become aware of it. What I thought was godly care in avoiding certain temptations—temptations related to my own nakedness—turned out to be a fear of my body and to have pathological roots. I had not called it fear, but *common sense* about nakedness. Had God's Spirit not drawn my attention to the fact that it was fear and, more significant, that certain incidents in my childhood lay beneath the fear and were its cause, I would never have known.

Payne comments on this question.

Our humanity . . . we fail to accept. This is a lingering result of earlier gnostic incursions into Christian thought, thought which has always tempted us to replace a dying to the old man with a misguided hatred of our . . . bodies, thought which has always tempted us to deny that God would find His dwelling in a temple of flesh.[8]

Why should some of us fear our bodies? On the surface it is because we associate many of their sensations with erotic sex, and that our sex urges are almost uncontrollable. If this is the case, it becomes easy to feel that erotic feelings are in themselves evil (except when in marriage we are actually engaged in sexual intercourse—and sometimes even then).

There is indeed hope. The person who fears, John tells us, "is not made perfect in love." Indeed, "perfect love drives out fear" (1 Jn 4:18). Fears of the kind Irene and I suffered never came from God.

Many other men and women I know have overcome their fears in relation to sex after what has been called prayer healing or inner healing. Because inner healing is controversial and widely misunderstood I want to deal with it more fully later. It is, as a matter of fact, the way Irene came into healing.

Not Respecting One's Body
Other people have no such fears. They are much less inhibited about display-ing their nakedness, especially in sexual settings. In Spanish there is an expression of contempt: *sin verguenza*. Literally meaning "without shame," it does not refer to the experience our forefathers had before the Fall when they were "naked but unashamed." Rather it refers to the shamelessness of persons who laugh because they can make others blush by flaunting their sins. It is to glory in one's shame, to be proud of one's sin. Such people cheapen sexuality and do not respect the bodies God gave them.

They are symbolized in my mind by an adolescent boy I saw from a train window in Peru. Watched by an admiring crony or two who egged him on, he stood totally naked on the hillside a few yards from the train as it rushed by, his legs widely spaced, a grin on his face as he waved one arm in greeting, while with his other hand he masturbated. It was as though he was taunting us, laughing at us.

A more sinister example of the same thing comes from the life of Charles Manson. A magazine account of an interview with him described him en-gaging nonchalantly in sex with one of his women in the open air while the reporter conducted the interview. It was the quintessence of evil, the per-formance of a *sin verguenza,* who had lost all respect for his own or anyone else's body, seeing in them *only* bodies.

Only when people call down the dark powers, either consciously or un-consciously, do they go to such extremes of shamelessness. It is the very opposite of that for which God made us in his own image. For the present all I wish to point out is the way in which love and sex can become divorced.

They are meant to be together. The giving and receiving of love can and should be fully expressed and deeply felt in "lovemaking."

Should they be divorced in your own case, take heart. It is the will of God that they come together again. I cannot say that my solution will be yours, and in any case we will get to solutions in due course. But be assured of two things. First, there is a depth to the love that expresses itself in sexual coupling which a focus on orgasms misses entirely. And second, God plans that depth for you. It is your heritage in Christ, and he waits to give it to you.

CHAPTER 9
Sex for
the Castaway

**The LORD God said, "It is not good for the man to be alone.
I will make a helper suitable for him."**
GENESIS 2:18

I once read a haunting story about an Indian woman who became a castaway on an island off the California coast. She survived there by her courage and ingenuity, and she was rescued in 1853 after being isolated for eighteen years. No one was ever able to learn her language, so nobody could grasp all the details of her story, which she tried to communicate by signs and gestures. The rest of her tribe perished in the wreck of a ship taking them to the coast.

The woman herself had actually boarded the ship that was to take her small tribe away from their home island. But, realizing that her younger brother had not gotten on board, she had leaped from the ship as it had set out from the island and had swum ashore to find him. Within a year or so her little brother had been killed by wild dogs and she remained stranded and alone.

Her attempts to leave the island by canoe proved too dangerous, one attempt nearly costing her life. After doing research into what information exists about her, Scott O'Dell attempted to supply details of what may have happened during those eighteen years, constructing a beautiful and moving novel.

In O'Dell's story the woman hides herself fearfully from her eventual rescuers, but the sound of human voices awakes in her the longing to be among her own species again. Certainly the real-life woman had been eager enough to leave the island in 1853. There was something about the sound of human speech, even in a language she did not understand, that drew her away from her much-loved animal companions. She craved companionship with her kind. She later describes her experience when the captain of the rescue vessel addressed her in words she did not understand.

I shook my head and smiled at him. He spoke again, slowly this time, and though his words sounded the same as before and meant nothing to me, they now seemed sweet. They were the sound of a human voice. There is no sound like this in all the world.[1]

Sex and the Castaway

Sex is not intended only for procreation but also, and more importantly, for communication. In the previous chapter I described how hard I had found it to quit masturbating. In *Eros Defiled* I first made my feelings clear, and I shall refer to what I wrote there in this chapter from time to time. My ideas have become clearer since I wrote that book, but the chapter in it is still well worth reading and will not be replaced by this chapter.

I define masturbation as *bodily manipulation in pursuit of an orgasm.*[2] In *Eros Defiled* I compared masturbation with the experience of a castaway on a desert island.[3] Isolation of that kind breeds a yearning, a craving for the sound of a human voice, for the companionship of other human beings. I have always maintained that masturbation is an undesirable anomaly since sex is meant, among other things, to be interpersonal communion. Sexual union has also been seen down the centuries as an anticipation of the loving intimacy that will one day exist between God and his people.

The Significance of Shame

What started me thinking again about masturbation was the amount of shame it still causes today. We are not ashamed about sex in marriage; we can even talk about it in social gatherings. Healthy people are not ashamed of being naked under appropriate circumstances. I have known enough of the pain and the shame of my own masturbating to have compassion for someone who struggles in the Valley of Humiliation. But the modern tendency is different. Opinions have changed. Many young people nowadays masturbate freely—but discreetly. And millions of older and married people do the same. It is something most married people prefer not to think about.

I have already rejected the view that masturbation is a normal release of sexual tension. Yet is it true that masturbators experience no shame? I question it, though certainly people nowadays have a much easier time suppressing shame than people of my age did. But is not shame one key to understanding sexual issues? Paul seems to think so (1 Cor 11:6).

I believe the shame is still there, suppressed or not, hidden under pseudosophistication. And if I am right, surely the fact is significant. If you have shame *about something you have been taught is normal,* then "nature itself" is trying to teach you something. And when I say that "nature itself" tries to teach you, I am talking about primary shame, as opposed to cultural shame.

For instance, I have known a training hospital chaplain to address a small circle of trainee chaplains at the beginning of their morning instruction session as follows: "Good morning! I would like those who had sex with their partners last night to smile for me." Several trainees smiled, not to comply with the trainer's request, but because they couldn't help themselves. Their smiles reflected embarrassment, amusement and pleasure. They would not have had the same reaction had he made the same request about masturbation. We may be "not ashamed" of masturbating, but no one is secretly proud of doing so, except perhaps boys who have just learned how.

High school boys, a little older, may boast about masturbation, but they are really boasting about their early steps in prostitution. Today, as I was out for a walk, I passed a group of four of them outside the local high school. As I approached I heard one of them, presumably talking about a person who paid money to watch him masturbate, say, "I masturbate for fifteen bucks." He laughed. Then after I had passed he cried exultantly, "I jerk off for money!"

Adults are different. Married adults, especially, experience difficulty in using the word "masturbation" in a social group. Even in a therapy group I know about, which meets under skilled leadership to receive help for sexual perversions, it was a long time before anyone forced their mouths and vocal cords to pronounce what they had begun to call "the 'M' word"! How many pastors could get their tongues around it in the pulpit? This should tell us something.

The shame of masturbation is primary shame, and primary shame can teach us when we are misusing our sexuality. I speak about it publicly, but I never enjoy doing so (any more than I enjoyed sharing my own experiences about it), for I too dislike getting my tongue around the word. It is a little easier to write than to pronounce. We all recognize that we experience shame even about discussing masturbation. Yet in spite of this we insist that masturbation is "perfectly normal." Could it be that there is some guilt, as well as shame, here?

I suspect the real reason we hesitate to call it sin is precisely because of its universality. What we call our reasons are more probably rationalizations. Let us bear in mind that many women and most of us who are men either once masturbated or still do. Counselors, psychologists, psychiatrists, pastors are no exception to the rule. They, too, masturbate. They must; after all, it is unlikely that as a class they form the great exception to the rule. Could this be a factor in their stance? After all, if you do it yourself you have to either quit or create a rationale for it.

In *Eros Defiled* I wrote about masturbation with compassion. I still have compassion for the victims of masturbation, but the time has now come for me to challenge the views that prevail and to call on Christians to face reality. Masturbation is sin. It is not *grave* sin, not nearly as serious as pride, or cruelty, or even unkindness. But still it is sin.

A Wrong Attitude to Masturbation

Let me state my reasons for calling it sin at all. It is sin because sexuality was not given us for that purpose. In masturbating we use our bodily parts for a purpose God never intended for them. To say that the release of sexual tension justifies it is what my grandmother would have called "all my eye and Peggy Martin"—or what logicians might call specious reasoning.

My first argument, then, for calling masturbation sin is what could be called the *argument of design*. My body is mine only in the sense that I am responsible for its proper use. I am its steward. For what was my body designed? The Westminster Confession asks a similar if not identical question. "What is the chief end of man?" The answer the authors give is, "Man's chief end is to glorify God and to enjoy him forever."

Paul expresses the same end for our bodies. He concludes, "So glorify God in your body" (1 Cor 6:20 RSV). The argument I have been using from chapter three onward concerns the offering of our bodies to God as an act of worship. In the NIV version of Romans 6, Paul even mentions the *parts* of our bodies, saying, "Do not offer the parts of your body to sin, as instruments of wickedness . . . offer the parts of your body to him [God] as instruments of righteousness. For sin shall not be your master" (Rom 6:13-14).

My body was not designed to masturbate. My body was designed to be used exclusively to glorify God. To use it in any other way is to rob God of something that is his by right, for there are no morally neutral actions.

You say: So everything becomes black and white. Are there no shades of gray? Yes, plenty of them. But even the whitest shade of gray has some black in it. So if you should go on to say, "Well, it really doesn't matter that much, does it?" then I must insist that sin always matters. Our sin brought about the death of Christ.

Just as speech was given to us in order that we might communicate truths rather than lies or gossip, so the sexual parts of our bodies were designed to copulate. Remember, copulation is far more than orgasmic experiences. It was to be a sharing, a sort of gateway to deeper sharing, a never-ending mutual revelation of the depths of our souls. Yet copulation can be entirely selfish, a mere using of somebody's body to gratify myself, which is little different from masturbation.

My second argument for calling masturbation sin—closely related to the first argument—is that masturbation is *a form of idolatry*. Our bodies are to be offered to God. Masturbation is to make a god of my bodily sensations, of relief from the tension that I feel. Again, I know that married lovemaking can itself be a selfish pursuit of bodily sensation. But I repeat: it was not designed to be. At that point it becomes lust.

Yet I know how some men and women struggle. How bitter some people feel in their vain struggle against it! Younger people, young marrieds away from their spouses, have a particularly difficult time. I know a man whose problem *began* with marriage. Like all sin, masturbation must be dealt with compassionately and in love. I may be in my sixties, but I remember very clearly what it used to be like. Those were dark days when I hated myself. (I do not excuse my past actions, even though, looking back, I can explain them. Nor did my release from the habit occur gradually, dying out as the need for it diminished. It came by the Spirit's revelation.) Let us be compassionate with those who struggle.

Pastoral Counsel

I remember a pastor telling me of an experience in his teens. He had accepted Christ though he was raised in a non-Christian home. His church and all its activities became life and family to him. However, he was deeply concerned about his inability to quit masturbating.

One day he told his pastor about it, standing shame-faced and contrite before the pastor's desk. I could hardly believe him when he described the minister's reaction. It was to order him out of his office. His actual words were, "You filthy little pig! Get out of my sight!" The following Sunday the minister referred from the pulpit to what had happened. Since my friend's reason for seeking help was that he already *felt* like a "filthy little pig," the response only served to increase his pain and loneliness. It was a reprehensible outburst on the part of a man who had forgotten (or perhaps had never understood) the nature of his true calling. Someone struggling in this way needs both understanding and helpful counsel.

I have nothing but compassion for the victims of masturbation (and I see them as victims), especially for those who struggle against shame and self-loathing. I have less for those counselors who encourage it. Masturbation is to make a god of my bodily sensations, and there is but one God. To make a god of my sensations is to become an idolater.

The Psychological Damage

I shall spend most of the rest of this chapter discussing the harm masturbation causes, harm in the form of increasing our susceptibility to a wide variety of sexual behaviors and of fostering any natural tendency to live in an unreal world.

Classical behavioral psychology tells us that pleasure, even more than pain, shapes behavior in all life forms. We learn without realizing we are learning. When you do something and it gives you pleasure, you are more likely to do it again. Even worms learn (in time) to avoid certain surfaces. More intelligent life forms learn faster. Especially children. Buy a child ice cream, and the child will want it every time you pass the store. The pleasure of the ice cream has "stamped in" ice cream-eating behavior.

If a young, unmarried woman masturbates with pleasurable fantasies of another woman's body, the immediate effect of the masturbation will be a sort of relief, an easing of any sexual tension. The long-term effect will be that the pleasure of the experience will increase her proclivity to homosexuality in real life.

Or when a married man masturbates contemplating in his mind the body of a woman with whom he once had an affair, he "stamps in" three things: first, the tendency to repeat the performance—to the detriment of his relationship with his wife; second, and at first perhaps only slightly, the possibility of seeking the woman out in real life and having an affair with her, or of seducing someone else; and third, the increasing tendency to be self-absorbed in any sexual relationship.

Sex is communication, communication with real persons. No communication takes place with a fantasy, and none takes place when you are merely focusing on your own body. In masturbating, you are really communicating with yourself—or with something you have conjured into being from your own inner resources. What you are teaching yourself also undermines your capacity for communion with others. A behaviorist would say that by means of erotic pleasure you are "stamping in" *an attraction to isolation.* You are pushing a pattern of self-manipulation toward becoming an addiction, increasing your chances of acting out what you have fantasied, yet simultaneously fostering a choice of your own company. Therefore, sexual experiences cease to be experiences of giving, or of sharing, ever becoming more self-centered.

Communication skills and habits do not stand still. Either they grow or else they regress. And when I talk about a communication skill, I do not refer merely to keeping up your end of a conversation. You can do that without communicating at all. I am talking about a deeper sort of freedom, the freedom to be yourself in any company, joyful freedom from artificiality, freedom for Christians to talk, when it is appropriate, about the things that matter most to them. Coupled with this should be the capacity to hear. It involves sensitivity to what people are *not* saying. It involves empathy, the empathy of having no fear of other people.

I remember a pastor years ago who told me, "When I am away from my wife I masturbate, but I think about my wife when I do so. What I am really doing is having sex with her." Was he right about this? Of course not! You can do anything you want with a fantasy. Fantasies are remarkably cooperative. The pastor's real wife would not necessarily be. Indeed, one value of sexual intercourse with a real person lies in the fact that the wishes of two people may not coincide. Something will then have to be negotiated, unless the parties are into force and manipulation.

But at least you open up to the possibility of real communication. There is no such possibility with a fantasy. In other words, sexual intercourse with a real person (as I keep insisting) is a gateway to deeper sharing.

A More Fearful Possibility

Charles Williams, a member of the group of writers with whom Chesterton, Lewis, Sayers and Tolkien are associated, wrote a number of mystical and allegorical novels. In *Descent into Hell,* his antihero is Lawrence Wentworth, a historian of note. Wentworth was a greedy, self-centered and jealous man spurned by the woman he loved. Williams never uses the word masturbation, but it seems obvious that this is what Wentworth begins to practice—masturbation with fantasies of his former lover. The diabolical voice of his fantasy lover tells him, contradicting the divine musing in Genesis 2, "It's good for man to be alone." That is exactly what masturbation is—sex with myself, communication with me. His fantasy lover tells him he is getting back to the roots of sex, but that she is even "better than Eve, closer than Eve. . . . Come along, come along: farther in, farther in: down under, down under."[4]

In the context, *farther in* seems to refer not to penile penetration but to self-deception, and *down under* to joining the mentally and spiritually dead. Lawrence Wentworth is at that point making "hellward" choices. He is also having erotic experiences in the moonlight:

> He felt hands moving over him, the moonlight changing to hands as it reached him, moonlight hands, cool and thrilling. The hands were delighting in him.[5]

Whenever we abuse our sexual gifts, we not only become victims of the ancient gods, we play god ourselves, especially so in masturbating, making ourselves the center of our own universe. Earlier I talked of the differences between masturbation with a fantasy and sex with a real person. With a fantasy, of course, there is no risk of an undesirable pregnancy. The fact troubled Wentworth.

> He had no need of the devices against fertility which, wisely or unwisely, the terrible dilemmas of men compel them to use, for he consummated a marriage whose infertility was secured. This . . . troubled him, for it reminded him.[6]

It reminded him that his lover *was* a fantasy. But the pleasure was too easily accessible to trouble him greatly. Not only was she readily accessible, but he could perform any manner of sex he chose with her.

> He could not conceive a manner of coming that, sooner or later, she did not take, not a manner of love that, sooner or later, she did not fulfil.[7]

Moreover, what he was doing was a huge consolation.

> In the early summer dawns it wakened him to whisper farewells, and his heavy, drugged sleep only understood that here also it was fulfilling his need . . . for it promised him, leaning naked over him, that it would always return.[8]

Unreality

The real danger is always what I discussed in chapters three and four, the danger of coming under the control of dark powers, just as in any form of misuse of our sexuality. Masturbation certainly tends to be compulsive. Victims may claim (like many alcoholics) that they "could stop any time." One of Satan's goals is to lead us into an unreal world. And one of the signs that I am in unreality, under Satan's control, is that God's power in my life can be deflected by sin.

In my case the habit was certainly compulsive. I was *not* in control, could not quit entirely. I had lost that freedom wherewith Christ had made me free—until he rescued me. In my case, and many years ago, a personal word from the Lord changed matters. One night as I lay reflecting, he drew near and told me the practice grieved him, and that he wished me to quit. With the word of the Lord came the power of the Lord, and I was set free from a bondage I alone could never have broken. But such is not everyone's experience. Later, I deliberately sinned again, and though I still had some control, for a number of years I continued to struggle. My freedom now is too valuable ever to lose again.

The Seduction of the Unreal

Williams represents life as proceeding in one of two directions, toward unreality or reality, toward the vividness of life or the world of shadows. The poet-playwright in *Descent into Hell* refers to the choice of unreality as *Gomorrah,* as opposed to Sodom, reflecting extrabiblical accounts of the difference in the two cities.

We know all about Sodom nowadays, but we know the other even better. Men can be in love with men, and women with women, and still be in love and make sounds and speeches, but don't you know how quiet the streets of Gomorrah are? Haven't you seen the pools that everlastingly reflect the faces of those who walk with their own phantasms, but the phantasms aren't reflected, and can't be?[9]

Unreality is the master stroke of the Deceiver. It produced our blindness to our sins and our tendency to hide from God and one another. It produces psychological denial, defensiveness in the face of criticism and suppression of our shame. To live in it is a habit, the habit of choosing unreality. Instead, remembering in whose presence we live, we should think every thought, speak every word, perform every action before God. (And I believe few of us would be so abandoned as to masturbate in his presence.)

I still remember the Indian shaman in our alcohol detoxification unit who called me over to his bedside to ask my help for his impotence. His eyes, alight with wonder and passionate enthusiasm over his sexual experiences with spirits, stood in stark contrast with his despairing lament both over his being forsaken by the spirits and—even worse!—over his subsequent loss of potency.

Victims are not free. We were redeemed that we might no longer be under the dominion of darkness but might be really free. And only God's Son can restore our freedom. Freedom is something positive. It is not merely freedom *from* but freedom *to* something. We are freed from slavery in order that we might live to and for Christ. Freedom is being what we were designed to be, doing what we were designed to do. We were not designed to be a race of masturbators. Which we are.

"It's Impossible Not To"

Now for the brighter side. Nothing is impossible with God. For married and for single folk, for pubescent youngsters and for dirty old men and women, the norm is, actually, *not* to masturbate. Freedom under God is what he created us for, and freedom in Christ is what the Son died to restore to us.

We must realize, of course, that God has his own priorities, his own order for sorting us out and making us holy. The thing that may humiliate us the most is not necessarily what God wants to deal with in us first. God desires to free you from your ambivalence—the many contradictory desires which pull you this way and that. It is possible for you to be freed, but ambivalence will have to go first.

If you masturbate regularly and then you stop, nothing dreadful will happen. The fear that something will burst is simply not true. No boiler will rupture and no kettle inside you explode. Rather, your experience will be like that of a mechanical toy when it is fully wound. You will be fully ready to perform sexually, but the tension in your "spring" will not affect your inner rest, because the spring is locked in that state. In the same way, a married person does not have to have sex even when gloriously aroused. The arousal can be allowed to subside. Interpersonal relationships are impossible, in fact, if both partners insist on getting all they think they need right away.

Can God deliver you? Of course he can. If he isn't doing so at the moment, he may, incredible though it may seem to you, have a prior concern with something else in your life. While I remain firm in my conviction that masturbation has to go, I recognize that God has his own order in dealing with sin. Sin is always serious. But when an injured man comes into the hospital, his injuries must be dealt with one at a time. By all means ask God to help you, but do not focus too much on this one thing. Focus on positive virtues like loving your neighbor as yourself. Or if you focus on sin, think of someone you may have hurt this week—by your sarcasm, your coldness, your forgetfulness, your laziness, your lack of tact and courtesy. Then confess these and set them right.

Again, thank God for all your sexual feelings. Don't hate them. They may be as difficult to manage as a canoe in the rapids, but they represent one of God's richest gifts to you. He made you to feel sexual desire. Be glad and rejoice in it. Thank him, too, for the day when you will be master of your sexual drives. Though it tarry, it will come, if you let God be master in other areas in your life.

Do you despise yourself? You can quit doing that right now. Refuse to listen to the torturous accusations of the accuser of the brethren, who accuses you day and night (Rev 12:10). If you are cast down, God waits for you with arms wide open. By all means groan, but take your shame to the throne of grace where the blood will wash it away. Your will is being freed. And it will be freed from the grip of masturbation too, one day. So learn to laugh at your chains, in faith. Thomas R. Kelly says, "Humility does not rest . . . upon bafflement and discouragement and self-disgust at our shabby lives, a brow-beaten, dog-slinking attitude. It rests upon the disclosure of the consummate wonder of God."[10] He also says, "When you catch yourself again, lose no time in self-recriminations, but breathe a silent prayer for forgiveness and begin again, just where you are. Offer this broken worship up to Him and say: 'This is what I am except Thou aid me.' Admit no discouragement, but ever return quietly to Him and wait in His Presence."[11]

We are nothing apart from his help. He knows it. We know it. To admit what we are (for instance, to say, "Among other things, I masturbate—and it's wrong") is to begin to walk with God. Honesty with ourselves, with God and at times with one another will be a step toward health and spiritual growth.

CHAPTER 10
Sex and Gender Confusion

The earthquake that is shaking men and women, their roles
and interrelationships, is part and parcel of the world culture's tectonic
plates. The changes in our gender roles are only one aspect
of the upheaval that accompanies the death of one
epoch and the birth of another.
SAM KEEN, *FIRE IN THE BELLY*

*S*ex and gender are not the same. Our *sexual* identity has to do with
our being *male* or *female*, man or woman, boy or girl. Our sex is
determined by the shape of our bodies and their organs, by our hormones and the brain centers that control them. It is physical in nature, rooted
in our biology.

Our *gender* identity has to do with something slightly different—our sense
of being man*ly* or woman*ly*. *Masculine* and *feminine* have to do with character,
and disposition, and above all with our feelings about ourselves as men or
women. Obviously sex and gender are to some extent dependent on the
other. But the wide variety of characteristics in both men and women would
suggest that the correlation is not exact.

For years I suffered agonies of self-doubt about gender identity, not doubt
about sexual identity. I doubted being a real boy, a real man. I am not sure
how aware of it I was most of the time. Only in retrospect can I see it. My
deepest problem was not knowing my real feelings. I think of a Very Large
Lady I once knew. My mother proudly asked me (I was six or seven at the

time) to play a piece of music for her. I played it well—at least, I played it exactly the way for which my music teacher had praised me.

"Does he always play so slow?" the Very Large Lady said. "Can't he play any faster?"

I was humiliated, crushed. I was sure it was the "sissy" thing again. Real boys, I suddenly knew, would play at top speed. Ever after that, I infuriated music teachers and parents by unconsciously increasing the tempo as I played, soon galloping through any piece of music and ruining it in the process, long after I had forgotten why I had a need to do so.

For years I was haunted at an unconscious level by a Very Large and Utterly Terrifying Lady who pursued me shrieking, "You are not a real boy!" and later, "You are not a real man!" However, until I was ready to face the shrieker in my unconscious, the shrieks were muffled, and I remained in bondage to my need to behave in certain ways, ways I falsely thought of as manly.

The shape of our bodies, the nature of our internal organs, the sort of hormones the hypothalamus produces determine our sex. They have some, but less, bearing on gender—on our sense of being manly or womanly, on masculinity and femininity. Gender has to do with the masculine and the feminine in us. Psychoanalyst Karl Stern tells us in *The Flight from Woman* that "Man in his fullness is bisexual."[1] By this he means that every man (and every woman also) contains both masculinity and femininity.

Manliness and Womanliness

So what is—not the female—but the feminine? The traditional view is that God, the source of both masculinity and femininity, is more masculine than the most masculine male. What does this mean? How can God, who clearly is the source of the feminine as well as the masculine, be *more* masculine than male human beings?

A key difference, noted by C. S. Lewis, is that the male is the initiator and the female the responder. In this sense God acts in a male way toward his world and his people. It is in this sense that God, who is neither male nor female, is more masculine than the most masculine male. God speaks, and *ex nihilo* the universe is initiated into being. He takes initiative with every human being—in creating us, speaking to us, sending his Son for us. His masculinity is expressed in this way. He is basically not one who reacts, but who *acts*.

Thus when any of us (male or female) responds to God's initiative, our response is essentially feminine in nature. In any divine-human encounter, *God always takes the initiative, and we humans respond*—either with faith and trust or else with rebellion.

Appearances can be misleading. It may appear at times that we take matters into our own hands, taking the initiative ourselves. But it is never so. When David cries out in distress to God (in Ps 38, for example), he does so for two reasons. First, God has taken the initiative to implant a hunger for himself in David. Second, God has already given David a lot of training in hopeless situations, precisely so that David might learn to cry out. Once again, God initiates. *David's psalms are responses to circumstances into which God has brought him.*

Prayer is prayer only when it is a response to what God is doing in us. God is always and supremely the initiator. We are all responders, women usually having a greater gift for responsiveness and sensitivity than men. These qualities, rather than lace, frills and perfume, lie at the root of what we call femininity.

In addition, both men and women bear some of God's nurturing qualities—women usually more than men. Women bear children from their own bodies, feeding them with milk manufactured in their own breasts. So it is understandable that most women show more patience with children, greater tolerance of their ceaseless activity and noise, more compassion. When men show these qualities, they respond to the feminine in themselves. When women fail to show it, their femininity is not yet fully developed.

Men and women alike are thus gifted. Yet just as women are more gifted with gifts of femininity than men, so men are more given to initiating. We live in a day of profound confusion about such issues, as both men and women search for answers, men especially searching for their true identity.[2]

We sometimes say, "Jim's a real man," or "Bettina's all woman." We imply degrees of proximity to manliness and womanliness. Some people never think about such questions because they have buried their fears in their unconscious minds, but there are men who secretly wish they were more like other men, while some women wish that they had the same interests and instincts they see in other women.

When I was a boy, I dreaded visits to the barber's shop. All the men there read sports papers and discussed bets on horses and greyhounds. They smoked; they sometimes went to the door to hawk and spit. I felt like an intruder in a foreign world. I was sensitive, imaginative. I was sure they must despise me. Was I a real boy? If only I had known it, I was nearer to real boyhood than I suspected.

Thoughts and fears of this nature often give rise to the question, *Is there something wrong with me?* And beneath that fear lies a question we do not always like to face—*am I gay?* Such questions have to do with the sense of manliness or womanliness that I am talking about, our gender identities. Fortunately, my own doubts arose before I was aware of homosexuality.

Model of Womanhood

The implication that arises from the statement "Bettina's all woman" must be examined. Is there an ideal for womanliness and manliness, and if so, what is it in each case? *To whom do we look for a model?* Stereotypes of both men and women break down when we examine them.

For Jews and Protestant Christians the ideal woman might be found in Proverbs 31. Catholics would think of Mary as the model for womanhood. My own feeling is that it might be better if Protestants, while not abandoning the Proverbs 31 woman, did the same.

To look on Mary as a model does not necessarily imply worship. Her submission to the angelic tidings is remarkable not only as an example of womanly submission, but of astounding faith and courage. Her response displays both masculine and feminine qualities. She knew she would face mockery and possibly lose a husband. The vision itself must have been a terrifying ordeal. In fear she asked the angel how she would become pregnant. The answer would have made matters infinitely worse for most women—but Mary rose superbly to the astounding challenge:

> The angel answered, "The Holy Spirit will come upon you, and the power of the Most High will overshadow you. So the holy one to be born will be called the Son of God. Even Elizabeth your relative is going to have a child in her old age, and she who was said to be barren is in her sixth month. For nothing is impossible with God."
>
> "I am the Lord's servant," Mary answered. "May it be to me as you have said." Then the angel left her. (Lk 1:35-38)

At the same time, the woman of Proverbs 31 is nothing to despise as a model for womanhood. Feminists might argue that she is depicted as her husband's slave. He enjoys the privilege of power—"sits in the gate" (is one of the city's leaders) while she by her slavish devotion to him and his household keeps him there. On the other hand, women who have an excessive need to be submissive and to devote themselves to their husband's pleasure and success will feel uncomfortable with her independent ways. This paragon of a woman teaches, organizes her household, handles money independently and makes successful forays into the "male" world of business and finance. We need to revise our notions of the biblical picture of ideal womanhood.

Model of Manhood

In every culture there is an ideal form of manliness and womanliness. "Be strong, Philistines! Be men, or you will be subject to the Hebrews, as they have been to you. Be men, and fight!" the Philistines were told, as they faced Israel on one occasion (1 Sam 4:9). The Philistines clearly had their own point of view about manliness.

But so has the apostle Paul. In 1 Corinthians 16:13 we find him echoing the words of the Philistines. "Be on your guard; stand firm in the faith; be men of courage; be strong." For Paul, masculinity and therefore the greatest element in manliness means strength in the face of opposition and persecution.

For men, Jesus is the model of manliness. We are presented by Western society with such models as the jock, the wimp, the womanizer and Rambo. Jesus was none of these, yet if there is to be found an ideal of true manliness anywhere, then we must look to the portrait of him as it is found in the Gospels. I shall do that later. For now, it is enough to make one comment about Jesus—that we rarely think of him in terms of his maleness and his masculinity. If the question is raised, we feel that we must say, "Yes, of course. Jesus is most certainly a manly man." Yet Jesus—at least the distorted image of him that comes through preaching and storytelling—does not conform to our confused idea of what a manly man should look like.

We must, therefore, use words like *manly* and *womanly* more carefully. After all, there are clear biblical models of manliness and womanliness.

Gender Identity

Which is the basic, which the more fundamental? Gender or sex? C. S. Lewis puts it this way:

Our ancestors did not make mountains male because they projected male characteristics into them. The real process is the reverse. Gender is a reality, and a more fundamental reality than sex. Sex is, in fact, merely the adaptation to organic life of a fundamental polarity which divides all created beings. Female sex is simply one of the things that have feminine gender; there are many others, and Masculine and Feminine meet us on planes of reality where male and female would be simply meaningless.[3]

Lewis makes this statement in his novel *Voyage to Venus*.[4] Earlier, his hero, Ransom, has encountered two powerful guardian spirits of the planets Venus and Mars. He describes them in this way:

They were taller than Sorns, the giants whom we met in Mars. They were perhaps thirty feet high. They were white like white-hot iron. . . . Both the bodies were naked, and both were free from any sexual characteristics, both primary and secondary. That, one would have expected. But whence came this curious difference between them? . . . Malacandra was like rhythm and Perelandra like melody. . . . what Ransom saw at that moment was the real meaning of gender.[5]

Gender, then, is not the same as sex. If Lewis is right, it is more basic to the whole of the created order than sex. God and the angelic hosts have gender. They do not have sex.

But, so what? Are not men to be masculine and women feminine? Well, not exactly. I do not know all that happened when God drew a rib out of the first man and from it formed woman. The account is so brief that innumerable fanciful but contradictory theories exist about it, all supposedly based on the words of the text. It may be that what I am about to say is equally fanciful, but at least it may help us to understand the distinction between sex and gender.

The Prototype Human

I like to think of Adam before the mysterious operation not as the prototype *male* human, but simply as the prototype *human being*. I am told that there is support in the Hebrew text for the idea. I also like to think that when the operation took place, most of the feminine qualities but also some of the masculine qualities were used to form the woman, and that some of the feminine qualities but most of the masculine qualities remained. After all, how could men and women relate to one another, unless each were to contain within their inner selves something of the other's nature? How else would mutual understanding be possible? Men and women both experience "mixed gender" characteristics, even though men are male and women are female.

When as a man I look at a woman neither through chauvinistic eyes nor with shallow romanticism, but with true manliness, I can understand her. That is because, different though we may be, there is something within me that sympathizes with her nature—a string that vibrates responsively. I am not talking about sexual attraction, but about understanding and friendship. And the same can be true when a woman looks at a man. Women who say, "I can't understand men," are denying the masculinity in their own beings. Men who say, "Women make no sense at all to me," deny that which is feminine in themselves, and in so doing deny their God-given capacity to understand women. Both men and women of that sort are really less than complete men and women.

After all the (prototype) man was made in the image and likeness of God. And in God's person, and from his being, come all the properties we call masculine and feminine. We think of masculinity in terms of initiative and strength, qualities God supremely displays. We have already seen that he takes the initiative sovereignly and always. His strength is infinite.

On the other hand we think of sensitivity, nurturing and responsiveness as feminine qualities. God has feminine qualities too. He tells the inhabitants of Jerusalem, "As a mother comforts her child, so will I comfort you" (Is 66:13). Moses describes God's reactions to Israel as follows: "like an eagle that stirs up its nest and hovers over its young, that spreads its wings to catch them and carries them on its pinions. The Lord alone led him [Israel]" (Deut 32:11-12). The perfect God displayed the feminine qualities of a mother eagle.

In deep distress Jesus once cried out, "O Jerusalem, Jerusalem, you who kill the prophets and stone those sent to you, how often I have longed to gather your children together, as a hen gathers her chicks under her wings" (Lk 13:34). The perfect man expresses the "feminine" feelings of a mother hen.

We may take it then that God's ideal for manhood includes qualities we call feminine. If, for example, sensitivity is not a male quality, where do male artists, poets and musicians get their sensitivity from? Are they less men than professional football players or men who drive trucks, drink beer and wear cowboy boots? Some might say yes. Or is it simply that male artists have made more use of the feminine side of their natures? Are some men perhaps afraid—afraid because of cultural stereotypes of manliness we have created, of their feminine traits?

Similarly, is there something wrong with drive and initiative in a woman? Remember, the Proverbs 31 woman displays both of these "masculine" qualities. "She considers a field and buys it; out of her earnings she plants a vineyard. She sets about her work vigorously; her arms are strong for her tasks. She sees that her trading is profitable. . . . She makes linen garments and sells them, and supplies the merchants with sashes. She is clothed with strength and dignity; she can laugh at the days to come" (Prov 31:16-18, 24-25).

Let it be established then that males major in qualities we call masculine, and minor in qualities we call feminine, and that females major in the feminine and minor in the masculine. Men should not be afraid of the feminine side of their natures, nor women of their masculine traits. Our natures will be unbalanced and incomplete if we are, for men without feminine traits *are not yet fully men,* and women with no masculine side to them are *lacking in the full development of their womanhood.*

Gender Identity Confusion

Gender identity confusion, the final result of the Fall that I shall discuss, is the failure of my manhood or my womanhood to reach its full maturity. It is a *forme fruste* of my true being, the failure of my real self to flower. Sometimes (but not always) it may result in the consciousness that my body has one sex, but that my experience is not the same as secure members of my sex. But there are grades and degrees of the confusion. Only when it is very severe does it make heterosexual life intolerable. Moderate grades of it may raise the doubt in my mind from time to time as to whether *there is something wrong with me—perhaps I'm gay.* But often there is not even that.

What then is gender identity confusion? We all know to what *sex* we belong. The very form of our bodies, the shape of our sexual apparatus makes the matter clear. Men are men and women are women. How could there be any confusion?

But gender confusion can foul up our sexuality and the bodily mechanisms of sexual response. It can mess up the way our bodies function. Confusion about our gender identity will affect our bodily responses to members of our own and the opposite sex and thus our relationships with both. Normally we will be attracted to members of our own sex for companionship and common interests, and to the opposite sex for companionship and also for romance and marriage. But where there is confusion about our gender identity we may be attracted physically to members of our own sex instead of, or as well as, to members of the opposite sex.

Men in Western cultures, middle-class men particularly, are lonely. We're afraid that to want or to seek close companionship with a man might mean we are gay. So we congregate as men, but rarely do we deeply share the concerns of our hearts. Women are better at it than men. With a dawning men's movement, men are getting in touch with other men once again.

Sexual identity confusion can be associated with homosexual temptations, homosexual dreams and preoccupation with the bodies and the genitals of members of one's own sex, as well as with a flight from the gender characteristics of one's own sex. But it can be concerned with much more. Even the excessive "jockness" of jocks, the "supermacho" qualities of some men can arise in this way. Payne tells us gender confusion lies behind the story of "the husband who from time to time jumps in bed with other women in order to assure himself he is still a man . . . [or of] the young man who is guilt ridden over occasional sexual affairs, unable to commit himself to a woman, and now in clinical depression, contemplating suicide."[6]

Payne is right. Last week I had two long-distance calls from Christian men. One was striving to live a holy life but could not stop himself from turning around to look at every half-attractive woman he passed on the street. "I know I could get involved so easily. I was a male nymphomaniac before I became a Christian. And I can't stop myself from fantasizing about it. It haunts me." The other man, a pastor, preaches victory in Christ and secretly visits brothels. *Both suffer the effects of identity confusion.*

Inevitably sexual identity confusion and gender identity confusion go together. A few moments ago I asserted that masculinity and femininity existed before creation itself and are more basic to the whole of existence. That fact may make it easier to understand Lewis's idea that God is infinitely more masculine than the most masculine man. Remember we are not talking about maleness, but about masculinity, a quality shared in different degrees by both men and women.

Clearly if we discover that *power to do what is good, righteous and holy is the essence of masculinity*, then Lewis's idea makes sense. In his novel *That Hideous Strength*, one of the characters, Jill, attempts to explain to Ransom, the director, a terrifying mystical encounter with a pagan Venus. Their discussion includes the issue of masculinity and femininity and the masculinity of "what is above and beyond all things."

> "No," said the Director, "there is no escape. If it were a virginal rejection of the male, He would allow it. Such souls can by-pass the male and go on to meet something far more masculine, higher up, to which they must make a yet deeper surrender. . . . The male you could have escaped, for it exists only on the biological level. But the masculine none of us can escape. What is above and beyond all things is so masculine that we are all feminine in relation to it."[7]

We must, however, keep the shared nature of gender in mind constantly. "When a man says, 'God is male,' women have said they feel they have no right to pray," notes Robert Bly.[8] And men do say that, not only by their words, but by playing God in the home. Women who have been subject to suffocatingly authoritative fathers have told me repeatedly, "I can pray to Jesus—but not to God the Father. I just can't." God is not male, he is masculine, and also feminine.

As I minister to men and women with various sexual problems, I find again and again that underlying their problems is confusion about their gender identity. Addiction to pornography, the temptation to molest children, to exhibit oneself, to be a peeping Tom, to engage in animal sex, and the ongoing inability to quit masturbation—all can be associated with some degree of gender identity confusion. (I am also convinced that homophobia itself—the fear and hatred of homosexual persons—arises from the unconscious fear of being tarred with the same brush, which itself results from identity confusion.)

And though the victims may not realize it, identity confusion is also associated in married men and women with an inability to relate to their partners in the fullness of their maleness or femaleness. They therefore derive less from their marital experience than God intends for them, so that they search for what is missing in sinful ways, never finding what they seek.

I have a close friend who was married for years believing his sexual relationship with his wife was normal. However, in order to complete intercourse and achieve a satisfactory climax, he had to engage in sexual fantasies. He was unaware that anything was wrong. "I thought all men did that," he said.

Not knowing this, it so happened that I encouraged him to learn to wait in silence upon God and learn to hear him speak. A year later, as he was doing so, memories were brought back to him: memories of a father who, following the son's puberty, had distanced himself from him. He also recovered memories of two forgotten incidents in his teens. Both incidents involved sex acts with another male.

When the sins were dealt with fully (openly with his wife and appropriately before the Lord) and when resentment over his father's inability to affirm him as a man had been dealt with and his father pardoned, there was a radical transformation in every aspect of my friend's relationship with his wife, and of hers with him. The sexual side of the relationship was so different that not only was the need for fantasies gone, but "it was *holy!* It was terrific! It was like we'd never really *had* sex before. God was right in the bedroom!" That was probably not the end of his sexual journey, but a release after one stage in it.

Origins of the Confusion

To explain how sex and gender confusion arise I must talk about our origins, about the relationship between heredity and environment. Do we have gender confusion because we were born with it? Or because of what happened earlier in our experience? Is the confusion inherited or environmental in origin? I suppose geneticists and environmentalists will discuss the matter until doomsday. As a Christian I have to bear both factors in mind. The effects of the Fall come to me genetically. The sins of my early life (certainly sins committed against me) come environmentally. Therefore both factors may play a part in determining my gender confusion or lack of it.

We will have to look at this matter more carefully when we deal with the issue of homosexuality. It is there that the issue has assumed too great a significance. All of us have a vulnerability to particular sins. And our weaknesses differ. You may be tempted to steal or to lie from time to time, whereas my difficulty may be to perpetual drunkenness or bitterness. Whatever the form of the sin, heredity and environment will both play a part. And neither of the two constitutes an excuse. We are responsible for our sin.

Healing can be of help in greatly diminishing the force of temptation. The difference can be like night and day. Healing is merely a part of something greater and more important, our ongoing sanctification. In fact, the less we talk about healing and the more we think in terms of sanctification, the clearer we will be in our minds.

Whatever the term we use, buried memories of incidents when we sinned and were sinned against profoundly influence our behavior. They make us more vulnerable than we need be to temptation.

I have misgivings about some psychoanalytic doctrines. But I am convinced that Sigmund Freud's reemphasis of the *unconscious* is of enormous importance. You have one. I have one. And their contents influence our behavior every day.

I call it *reemphasis* because Freud's idea is a biblical one. "Who can discern his errors?" the bewildered psalmist asks. "Forgive my hidden faults" (Ps 19:12). Jeremiah understands the problem more clearly still. "The heart is deceitful above all things and beyond cure," he cries. "Who can understand it?" And God calls back to him, "I the LORD search the heart and examine the mind" (Jer 17:9-10).

Who can understand the heart? God can. He knows the hidden depths of my heart, even secrets I keep locked so deeply that I do not know them myself, secrets I can no longer remember. I may think I know myself well, know my character accurately. But I am a fool if I think that. My heart is a mass of hidden fears, lusts, hates and passions.

Freud's explanation is that it is our fear—our fear of the buried, hidden mess—that keeps us from knowing. Such are the contents of the unconscious that we dare not lift the lid to peer within. Memories of early events we cannot bear to think about, memories whose implications are utterly unendurable to us, still lie hulking in the dark shadows of our unconscious. And while the unconscious may still exert a powerful, unseen influence on our behavior, only in our dreams do its contents slip out, and then only in disguise.

I can only suppose that the existence of an unconscious mind is also an effect of the Fall. It involves internal, mental deceit, an internal, mental covering up of a host of facts about ourselves and our personalities. It also covers from our awareness *sinful attitudes which grieve God*—attitudes which you would deny indignantly if I were to accuse you of them. Whole tracts of memory have been buried. They were buried furtively in the darkness, and we no longer know where to find them. What we know (or think we know) about ourselves is only the tip of the iceberg.

Pandora's Box

Freud was also right in suggesting that healing from conditions he called neuroses could follow our rediscovery of unconscious material. Healing *can* follow, but it rarely does. For we buried the memories not only in fear but also in sin and bitterness. Often we were sinned against. And as we shall see later, it is only as we pardon those who have sinned against us, entering into an understanding of God's forgiveness to us, that the cure takes place.

In Greek mythology Pandora is the equivalent of Eve, the first woman. There are different versions of her story, but in one Pandora is sent down with a box from the gods to the first man, whose hidden contents intrigue her. At last, her curiosity growing unbearable, she raises the lid. Immediately she discovers her folly as out of the box fly all the plagues and ills that were to beset humanity down the ages. Only hope remained in the box.

We say we have no fear of "opening Pandora's box," of knowing the hidden contents of our unconscious minds. We say, "If there's a hidden secret there, I want to know about it. After all, if it's causing problems, why should I be afraid of it?" But the child inside us, the child that once we were, has not ceased to be terrified. To approach the memory in reality is to become that child again, to know the same terror. So practiced are we—from long-established habit—at avoiding the curtain-enshrouded entrance to the darkness, that we miss it every time we pass it, miss the cowering child that tries to hurry from it, but never can, trembling by the entrance. I have known people to scream in terror when God begins to pull the curtain back.

All this we shall look at later. For now it is only necessary to know that our hearts are dark and deceitful, and that the hidden depths of our hearts contain the keys to things we do not understand about ourselves. But the symptoms I have described and the sins they give rise to can be painful. We tend to be very ashamed of sexual weaknesses. We hate to think of ourselves as kinky. No one wants to be a freak.

Yet all of us are freaks. None of us are what God intended us to be. But we must face what we are and begin right there. Sam Keen says, "The chains that bind us most tightly are those we refuse to acknowledge." Keen, reminding us of the Freudian saying that "a negation [is] as good as an affirmation," illustrates the rule as follows:

"It's not the money—it's the principle." (It's the money.)

"I'm not mad, but . . ." (I'm mad.)

"I don't depend on women, unless . . ." (I depend on women.)

Thank God he will not leave us in this sad state of denial! He is faithful and true. He has plans for all of us.

CHAPTER 11
The Roots
of Inversion

Perhaps . . . demands from within the Church, outrageous as they are,
have done us all a favor. They've pointed quite forcefully
to the fact that the Church as a whole has not known how to minister
to the healing these sufferers need.
LEANNE PAYNE, *THE BROKEN IMAGE*

S am Keen tells us that Paul Tillich used to be fond of saying,
Every serious thinker must ask and answer three fundamental questions:
(1) What is wrong with us? With men? Women?/Society? What is the
nature of our alienation? Our disease? (2) What would we be like if we
were whole? Healed? Actualized? If our potentiality was fulfilled? (3)
How do we move from our position of brokenness to wholeness? What
are the means of healing?[1]
Tillich's statement is a profound one. Sam Keen deals with men and their
search for identity. But the groping among those of us who call ourselves
Christian is in both sexes. For both men and women, negative experiences
with a member of the opposite sex range widely and can produce both hatred
and an exaggerated need for conquest. Common to them all is the absence
of that peace and quiet joy that should characterize an ongoing male-female
relationship.

The most seriously disturbed reaction is the extreme homosexual experience of inversion, the underlying and sometimes unconscious fear and hatred
of both the opposite sex and oneself. Any of the varieties can also be associated with self-hatred.

Self-Hatred

Many, perhaps most, of us have bouts of it. My younger years were plagued with it. Not all the bouts I suffered had to do with problems of sexual identity, but some did.

I lived in the days when sexual naiveté was at its height. I also attended a boys' school. Though we talked a lot about the girls in the nearest girls' school, our contact with the girls was in fact minimal. I liked girls. We didn't know anything about petting in those days, but we talked a lot about inter-course—though we used a different word for it. And that very word seemed wonderful to us. It gripped us as an esoteric and fascinating mystery, as being in some mysterious way a form of rebellion against all adult authority as well as the supreme achievement of manhood. We never grew weary of discussing it. Sex education was unknown.

My father was the first adult ever to raise the issue of sex with me, and he waited until I was in my twenties. By then I had been in the armed forces and knew a great deal about the seamy side of sex, even though I had remained a "technical" virgin (one who had never indulged in intercourse of any kind), and I was studying medicine. All my father did was push an old-fashioned and totally inadequate book into my hands as we passed on the stairway. It was a book with the aim of discouraging masturbation. "Here, read this, son," he said, turning away embarrassed.

It was actually a brave act. I am grateful for my dad's attempt, even though it was too little, the information irrelevant, and too late. It took courage and was a sign that he cared.

During those school days, to be able to masturbate was for all of us the first major accomplishment. It was our initiation into the circle of the elite, and we would share the triumph with pride with our intimate friends. It meant you had graduated; now you were ready for the other thing, when you could "do it properly."

As for sexual intercourse, we thought of it with awe, yet were worried and troubled by the fact that our parents could actually have done anything so wicked. Perhaps they didn't enjoy it, just did it to bring us into the world, and never did it again. What especially troubled the Christians among us was that *we knew we all longed* to do this wicked and vile thing. What kind of person was God? Sex was fascinating, awesome, the greatest mystery of all, a magnet that drew us endlessly but guiltily.

I was determined to be a boy's boy. From the very start of secondary education I strove for school teams, played the British games of rugby, football (American soccer) and cricket, soon became the captain of the junior gymnasium team, and won medals at a county and city level in field days and in swimming. I wanted to grow up to be a real man, and to me, in my ignorance, that was what being manly was all about—playing rugby and winning races. But no amount of medals ever satisfied. There were always the games you lost, the races you didn't win, the medals you still had to compete for.

My distress grew gradually around two or three areas. One was an invitation to walk in the fields with a friend. We talked sex—with girls—of course. We sat down. He showed me his penis and suggested we masturbate. Unwilling to be outshone, I showed him mine. This was big-time stuff. I was being sophisticated, a man of the world. He challenged me to touch his penis and, a little frightened, I did.

I did nothing more because I began to feel sick, nauseated. What we were into ceased at that point to be a grown-up, sophisticated activity for men of the world. It became hateful, disgusting. I stuffed my half-roused organ back inside my British schoolboy shorts and struggled to my feet. "Let's just walk," I said, not knowing what to say or how to bow out gracefully. I remember that I felt loathing toward the guy I had just become friendly with and loathed myself for what I had done. So trivial by today's standards, it was for me a turning point. For a little while, everything to do with sex became sickening.

Neither of us knew the pathway we were on. Nor did we realize the enemy's plans. Our ways became separate, but we were both part of a school system that has produced inversion among men and given its quota as well to become traitors and do espionage. In the hallways at school, where our schoolmasters in billowing academic gowns swept majestically past us, we were always busy watching for the chance to grab a passing boy's crotch. "Gotcha that time!" we would exult. One-upmanship consisted in grabbing without being grabbed. As time went on, however, it became clear that some boys didn't try too hard to avoid grabs. I sure did. No one was going to grab me!

It may seem incredible now, but we had no concept of what we were doing, nor of how our games (which we thought of as manly) could have a very different effect. Most dangerous of all was our game of strip-Jack-naked—not the card game, but a bit of locker-room horseplay. We would say, "Let's strip Smith (or Berringer, or Laporte)." Then the game was on. The object: to remove all the victim's clothing and to have him running round the locker room while anyone and everyone grabbed for his genitals. It was a wild rough-and-tumble in which boys knocked one another down while the fleeing victim dodged and squirmed, leaped over benches to avoid being caught. Truth was, we never caught a victim. At least I never remember our doing so. The nearest we ever got was a giggling, struggling boy who always broke out of the clinch. We didn't really want to do more. The chase was the fun, not the catching. All we wanted was a chance to humiliate the victim by grabbing at his genitals. We wouldn't have known what to do had we caught a victim and sat on him.

For me the game went terribly sour one day. A particular boy, who seemed to like being the victim, was the gym master's son. We picked on him one day, and at one point in the wild scramble he was running naked along the bench where I sat. He tried to leap over me, and I grabbed at him as he passed overhead. I did not succeed (perhaps I didn't want to) but his genitals swept over the back of my hand.

A terrible arrow pierced me, and my heart began to beat. *I liked what had happened.* It was exciting yet totally impersonal. I didn't like the boy, just the sensation of soft male genitals. There was no love, only abstract genital lust. From that day I began to doubt and fear myself and my sexuality. Self-hatred grew in me. I was eleven years old and my life grew dark.

I learned to masturbate soon after that, and my lust became centered on myself. I boasted about the accomplishment, but it was hollow boasting. My self-disgust grew to intolerable proportions. The guilt and the shame were endless. I kept telling myself that I was not a homosexual, but I could not be absolutely sure. The very denial seemed fraught with accusation. No one had heard in those days about sexual identity confusion.

Significantly, my father was away much of this time, busy founding agencies for a French manufacturer of automobiles.

Homosexuality

Is homosexuality acquired, or is it inborn? Do we attribute sexual orientation to heredity or to environment? What is homosexuality? What is its essence?

Where did it come from?

Homosexuality, as we saw in the previous chapter, is one of the results of the Fall, just as every other proclivity to sin is. We and our forebears failed. Homosexuality differs little from any other form of sexual sin. It is sexual identity confusion expressing itself in a particular way. Homosexuals may have more extreme forms of sexual identity confusion; but even so, we are dealing with a difference in degree, not in kind.

I have become convinced that there is no such separate condition as homosexuality—just sinners with different forms of sexual weakness and different degrees of identity confusion. People who adopt a homosexual lifestyle may not like my saying that, wanting us to legitimize their behavior as a special yet natural condition or state—but I believe it is true. Homosexuals are men and women like the rest of us, and *all* of us sinners are either wrestling with or giving in to our particular sexual vulnerabilities.

Inversion

The word *inversion* means opposite, upside down. To invert something means either to turn that something upside down or to make it do the opposite from what was intended. We were all made sexual for two reasons. The first and I believe most basic reason was that we might know intimacy. "It is not good for the man [the prototype human being] to be alone," God muses (Gen 2:18). Intimate relationships are a part of the divine image.

Intimacy, however, glorious as it is and *necessary* as it is, can never be an end in itself. It bursts with onwardness, with creativity, is pregnant with new life. You cannot separate intimacy from life and creation without destroying it. To separate the two transforms intimacy into a death's head. If by our deliberate choice it is not allowed to lead to life, then in the long run it will produce a degree of spiritual dying. Creativity, it is true, can partake of many forms, but in physical human beings it takes the form of children.

Homosexual encounters, therefore, ultimately *invert* both intimacy and sexuality. You cannot understand sex unless you understand both that God created it and that he had purposes in doing so. He planned to multiply his own image in humankind. He planned also to teach us the nature of intimacy with himself, that we might anticipate divine rapture. His still deeper purpose was to show us the connection between intimacy, creation and life. Sex is a marvel in itself. It also serves as a parable, an illustration of the true. It shows in the natural realm what is true in the spiritual.

In homosexual encounters, we seek sexual intimacy with no possibility of procreation. Intimacy of this sort, split from sex and procreation, dies in isolation. So we kill the thing we crave. All we then can do is cover the corpse with wax and make ourselves a mold. If we do not worship the true God, we have to create—often unconsciously—a substitute. From the mold we have made, we may fashion our idol and worship our death mask.

What Has Science to Say?

In August 1991 Simon LeVay, a neurobiologist at the Salk Institute in San Diego, published findings of a small difference in a group of cells in the hypothalamus of homosexual men, as compared with the same group of cells in heterosexual men. He had examined the brains of deceased homosexual men, heterosexual men and a few women. His findings suggest that homosexuals may be born that way.

Previous experiments with mammals had led to LeVay's study. Following mammalian conception, the brains of mammals seem to start their development in the female form—with no "male cells" in the hypothalamus. Roger Gorski of the UCLA School of Medicine had conducted experiments with male rats. The experiments suggested that at a critical juncture in rat development, a small cluster of neurons in the hypothalamus comes into existence, establishing the rats' sexual preferences. Testosterone from the testes of the young rats, immediately before and just after they are born, seems to bring this cluster into existence. On the other hand, castrated newborn male rats, deprived of testosterone, show no interest in females, and they allow males to mount them.

Neither Gorski nor LeVay feels that their findings are conclusive. Gorski states that "humans are so complicated" that environmental factors may also shape a person's identity. In addition, LeVay points out that there could be two explanations of the differences in the brains of homosexual and straight men. It is just as possible that a homosexual lifestyle *produced* the brain changes, which may not have been present from birth. The size of bodily organs can vary with the demands made on them.[2]

These studies are a part of ongoing research which will in the end lead nowhere. It may succeed in showing that there are cases where genetic factors are more important than environmental ones, but it is unlikely even to do that. Both heredity and environment are almost always important when we are considering human behavior. However, if research is designed to justify certain behavior, it is attempting to use science for an end that can never be justified scientifically.

As we have already seen, the heart of the moral question lies elsewhere. It lies in whether God exists and, if he does, what his rights are in relation to our bodies. If he has rights, what had he in mind in giving us the gift of sexuality? Whether a particular tendency is inborn or environmentally produced is morally irrelevant. Neither in the one case nor in the other is sinful behavior excusable. If homosexual behavior is sinful behavior (and the Bible, in spite of attempts to prove otherwise, plainly states that it is), it can be excused neither on environmental nor on genetic grounds. The Bible sees us both as individuals and as a society.

All proclivity to sin is in part inborn. Like David, we, being fallen men and women, are born in sin, "shapen in iniquity" (Ps 51:5 KJV). If the tendency to sin is genetic, then we must all carry "sin genes" of various sorts in the cells of our bodies. (How else would we pass our fallenness on to our children?) Yet according to Scripture this hardly excuses our sinful acts. We share in the guilt of our forebears. Even on those occasions when we truly *can* resist sin, we fail consistently to do so.

What matters to God is behavior. He has compassion on our weakness, whatever form that weakness takes. David compounded adultery with murder, yet he met only compassion *when he acknowledged and repented of his sin.* In Scripture there is no such being as *a homosexual.* There is only homosexual behavior. It differs in no significant way from any other form of sinful behavior. Its rapid increase both in society and in the church is one form of God's judgment on us all, judgment for our failure to treat him as truly God.

> Because of this, *God gave them over to shameful lusts.* Even their women exchanged natural relations for unnatural ones. In the same way the men also abandoned natural relations with women and were inflamed with lust for one another. Men committed indecent acts with other men, and received in themselves the due penalty for their perversion. (Rom 1:26-27)

AIDS and those behaviors with which AIDS is associated are not so much a judgment on drug addicts and homosexuals as on society and the church. In any case, AIDS has now spread more widely than addicts and homosexuals. God judges the world. He also judges the church. His judgment is to remove his protection: to *give the world and the church over to* sinful sexual behavior and its consequences. Why? Because in neither the world nor even the church do we truly acknowledge him as God. In the church we may declare his deity, but we ourselves run the corporation, expecting him to bless us as we do so.

If we wish to be helpful, especially about a homosexual orientation, we must ask whether there is any way of relieving its pain. Is there a release from it? And the answer most certainly is yes. I know that now.

It was this question that most troubled me when I wrote the book *Eros Defiled.*[3] Most of the material in it I still approve of heartily, but there was one answer I sought in vain. I had at that time many homosexual patients, most of whom professed to be Christians. It was their pain that got to me. I had then no answer for it. I said then, "When I learned of the monthly gay banquet attended by hundreds of gay men and women in my home city, my spirit was crushed and my heart bowed low in prayer. I felt no anger. Only a yearning possessed me, a yearning that cried to God over the misery of people who call themselves gay."[4]

I still experience the same pain, the same yearning. The hate and mutual hostility that exist between homosexuals and those who disapprove of homosexual behavior have increased since I wrote *Eros Defiled.* The social picture is distorted by widespread fear and misunderstanding which, since the discovery of AIDS, grow ever deeper. Those who are progay tend to view the rest of us as homophobic, whether we are in fact so or not. Those who are truly homophobic see homosexuals and their liberal-minded supporters as a diabolical menace to the whole of society, and with rare exceptions lack compassion either for the dilemma of the homosexual orientation or for the fate of men and women who are HIV-positive. Some of these victims are wives and husbands and children, innocent of homosexuality or drug abuse.

The Day I Discovered the Truth
My eyes were opened while I was in California doing research for the book *When the Spirit Comes with Power.* I heard one day of a Los Angeles conference for homosexuals, organized by a local group, Desert Stream. I arrived for the tail end of the conference, where at which about seventy men and women had gathered to listen to the teaching of Leanne Payne. I heard the

last part of the last lecture, drank coffee with young people in their twenties and thirties, then attended a time of prayer.

Leanne prayed. If I am not mistaken she prayed audibly but quietly for about forty-five minutes. She seemed to cover a great deal of theological and biblical ground in her prayer. I sensed the presence of the Holy Spirit. Young men and women began to fall on their knees, a few on the floor. Some were weeping.

I cannot remember all that followed, but I had arranged to have supper in a restaurant with the organizers of the conference, all staff members of the Desert Stream ministry. All of them were former members of the gay community, having been free of immoral sexual behavior for up to a period of seven years. I questioned them closely, one by one, taking careful note of their stories. While none claimed total immunity from temptation, all testified to a profound difference in their sexual feelings. Some were by that time married with children. Others contemplated marriage, having discovered heterosexual attraction.

The difference was illustrated powerfully a year or two later when I served as a keynote speaker at a conference of Exodus International.[5] During one session I listened to the testimony of a young lawyer, formerly a member of the gay community. His conversion had resulted in a conviction that he must cease from homosexual activity. He was able to quit the lifestyle "through gritted teeth." The experience had been a grim and painful one—until he had discovered God's pathway of deliverance. His face shone with joy and enthusiasm as he described the relief and freedom that progressively followed. He had not merely reformed his life. He had been *transformed* by the healing life of Another.

The Environmental Roots of Inversion

The discovery of a major root of sexual identity confusion is recent. We owe it partly to the research of Dr. Elizabeth Moberly,[6] and partly to the practical work of Mrs. Leanne Payne[7] and other Christians whose ministry sees men and women changed in their sexual orientation.

Sexual problems may have many subsidiary causes, but it now seems likely that one root cause has unusual importance. Even though the pattern of events may vary from person to person, the root cause is probably the same. *Where the bond linking a child with the parent of the same sex has suffered damage, sexual identity problems are likely to occur.*

Psychologist-theologian Moberly reexamined the psychoanalytic literature on homosexuality. As she did so, she discovered a clue she thought might have been missed. Lionel Ovessey, in classic studies dealing with the cause of homosexuality, noted that in all his cases a smothering, overprotective mother was present. He concluded on the basis of this evidence that possessive mothers were the root cause of male homosexuality.[8]

The clue Moberly picked up was in Ovessey's own cases. Not all the boys with overprotective mothers became homosexual. Where the father was active, present and had a good relationship with the boy, that boy did not need to struggle against a homosexual preference. He was "straight." In her researches, Dr. Moberly began to ask whether the bonding with a member of one's own sex was the key to a homosexual orientation. If it were, could that bonding be repaired?

While not everyone agrees, I suspect that Moberly is right, especially in the case of male homosexuality. More research is needed on the issue of female homosexuality, as anecdotal evidence points to some lesbianism developing as a result of damage some women have endured at the hands of men (such as incest and rape). There may also be many subsidiary causes of sexual identity confusion.

Soon after the incidents I described at the beginning of the chapter, I was sexually molested by a male Christian worker. Even as a young boy, the breasts of women displayed in pictures of primitive people had aroused me sexually. Following my molestation I noticed the same thing about pictures of male nudity. Curiously, in my case it was pictures and statues that aroused me, not the physical presence of naked boys or men. There was little chance of my ever adopting a homosexual lifestyle, but as I grew older I was aware that I could if I so chose. I kept fantasies at bay with relatively little effort, but I sensed within myself that all was not well. In the locker room in the men's health club at the "Y," my reactions at being naked among men had no trace of erotic arousal. It was simply good to be a man among men. To be sure, I sometimes wished that my penis was as large as one of the more magnificent specimens—but my reaction was less erotic than of fallacious envy, a mistaken acceptance of male inferiority. I wanted a bigger one myself.

No, the nature of my own identity confusion lay deeper. The trauma of having to suffer my molester's shame-arousing, rage-producing advances (I was unable to tell my parents why I was so reluctant to see him) undoubtedly contributed to it, but an earlier incident was more basic.

An incident when I was three had destroyed my trust in my father. He had played a somewhat innocent joke on me that had the effect of filling me with fear and rage. (I relate the story fully in chapter eighteen when I discuss healing of inner wounds.) Suffice it to say for the moment that the result was that trust was never fully restored between us, even after the incident had been forgotten and buried in my subconscious for decades.

Sometimes the term *bonding* is used to describe the relationship between two people. Bonding between children and their parents is important. Bonding with the parent of the same sex has a powerful bearing on sexual preferences. Bonding is that process by which the child *identifies with* one parent more than another. It is the process by which the little girl hangs around Mommy when she is helping others move into an apartment, or by which the little boy says, "I wanna work with computers like Daddy—an' get to use all kinds of neat stuff."

I am not, of course, discussing male or female roles, except insofar as a child's desire for those roles is a result of attachment to a person. It is the latter that seems to determine later sexual preferences and orientation. Roles are partly interchangeable. Women can do police work and fly fighter planes, and men can cook. It is not roles that determine sexual orientation, but the identification of a girl with a womanly mother and a boy with a manly father.

Ruptured Bonds

Bonds may be impaired in many ways. The damage usually has to do with traumatic experiences of one kind or another. They can occur at any level in the child's development. Damage to a young child will cause more harm than damage to an older child. Again, the more severe the trauma, the worse the damage.

In chapter nine I mentioned a man who had confessed his masturbation to his pastor (to whom he felt a strong bond) only to be rebuked by the pastor and then further humiliated when the pastor referred to the encounter in his sermon the following Sunday. In addition, he had been a foster child. He had no recollection of his natural father. His foster father abused the boy sexually, beat him frequently, mocked him repeatedly. Understandably he grew up confused about men and about his sexual identity.

The trauma can be much milder. Bill had a father who became distant and awkward when Bill reached puberty. Of course, this is a stage at which it is important that the boy receive warm reassurance from his father. "Hey, your body's developing! Welcome to manhood! You may feel a bit strange from time to time, but you're becoming like the rest of us!" Coming with a hug from a good father who has always maintained a warm relationship with the boy, such a remark can have powerful affirming effects about his developing sexuality, and can open the way to conversations that would never otherwise take place.

Because puberty is a critical time in a boy's development, the effect on Bill of his father's withdrawal was moderately severe. (Bill's grandfather had died at a time when Bill's father was himself just beginning puberty. Thus he had no model for how a father is to affirm a pubescent boy.)

The trauma, mild or severe, can occur through no fault of the parent. Parents can be ill, can have mental breakdowns, can be away for long periods in wartime—and there are other unavoidable reasons. Again, the child may completely misunderstand the intent of the parent, or the parent may fail to perceive a need in the child. A misunderstanding can interrupt effective communication for a lifetime.

Sometimes the serious illness of another sibling can have profound effects. One couple I know has six children—five girls and a boy. The boy was the third in the succession and was followed by triplets—three sisters when he himself was only thirteen months old. His mother was severely ill and was hospitalized for several weeks following the birth of triplets, then subsequently a second time with a severe renal infection. The couple was living in a small Asian country at the time and in an area where medical facilities were poor. The triplets were premature, and there were inadequate facilities for their care. No family members were nearby.

The father was given time off his job to care for them, and there was a maid in the house who could keep house and cook, but the father was still run off his feet feeding, changing and diapering three premature little girls plus his thirteen-month-old son. Even when his wife returned home, the precarious thread by which the little girls clung to life meant that inordinate amounts of time were spent caring for them. After three months, one of them died—there was a funeral and, understandably, grief.

In all the preoccupation with the triplets, the other children suffered neglect. The child who suffered most was the little boy. Until the arrival of the triplets he had been the center of attention of the rest of the family, and particularly the delight of his father. With the pressure of caring for the triplets, his father could no longer spend the kind of time he had once spent with him. The boy became attached to the maid. Later, when he was able to talk, he was heard to say, "Mommy and Daddy like girls. They don't like boys." He grew up with clear signs of sexual identity confusion.

Homophobia

I have no doubt that some degree of sexual identity confusion is virtually universal. How could it be otherwise when none of us receive perfect parenting, and when all of us as we grow up misinterpret even the best and kindest actions of our parents? Some degrees of identity confusion, especially in more severe cases, lead to the exclusive preferences for persons of the same sex. But all of us are tarred by it to some degree, and the forms of sexual temptation to which we are drawn will vary enormously.

Satan's joke is that our varieties of temptation determine to some extent the pet hates with which we regard one another. Yet all of us are victims, and few of us are pure in our inmost thoughts. C. S. Lewis put it this way: "The old Christian rule is, 'Either marriage, with complete faithfulness to your partner, or else total abstinence.' Now this is so difficult and so contrary to our instincts, that either Christianity is wrong or our sexual instinct, as it now is, has gone wrong. One or the other."[9]

We are damaged in our sexuality. And among the most damaged are the biggest prudes. I mention the word *penis* when I talk about sexual issues. One missionary, at a missionary conference where I did so, refused to speak to me personally about it but trembled with indignation as he talked to other men. What was it that upset him? The word had doubtless half-unearthed that which was deepest and darkest in his own soul, hidden where he himself had buried it with the intention of never revisiting it. Again and again it happens.

So what do we say about homophobia? Or about the hatred on the part of some homosexuals for "straights"? We must simply say that on both sides it is naively hypocritical. We are all wounded by satanic arrows, and our sanctification begins when we realize our own woundedness and stop pointing fingers. God's mercy is for all sinners, even though he loathes all forms of sin. Our proclivity to any and every form of sexual sin is a divine judgment.

It is God saying to us, "If you will not let me be to you all I want to be, you will have to face the consequences. I will not force my love on you. I made you in my image, and I must respect the work of my hands. Only turn to me and I will heal all the damage you have suffered at the hands of the enemy. But you must turn with all your heart." Those who declare they have no wounds can sometimes be the most wounded of all, the blindest among us.

More to the point, how are we to be healed, sanctified? If you experience homosexual attraction or have adopted a homosexual lifestyle, how can you find the roots of the problem? And having found them, how can they be uprooted? How can you enter into the fullness of your womanhood or manhood? Can you be healed? Of course you can! You are no different from the rest of us.

It involves a biblical understanding of what it means to be masculine and feminine, what memory is (from both a biblical and a scientific perspective) and how the Holy Spirit can work to heal, sanctify and make whole our gender, our memory and our lives. These are the issues I will take up in the following chapters.

CHAPTER 12
Manliness and Womanliness

The tendency today is to stress the equality of men
and women by minimizing the unique significance of our maleness or
femaleness. But this depreciation of male and female
personhood is a great loss.
JOHN PIPER

The physical differences between the man and the woman are a parable
of psychical and spiritual differences of a more ultimate nature.
EMIL BRUNNER

*J*esus was male. As a male, he is (among other things) a model for manhood. When we ask the question, "What would a truly manly man look like?" we find the answer in the Jesus of the Gospels. It is in his manhood that Jesus is a model for men. Men and women were equally created in the divine image and in Christ are equally restored to it. Within the Trinity itself there are masculine and feminine roles. The Holy Spirit plays a feminine role in relation to the Father, but a masculine role in relation to us. However, the human Jesus is a model for the truly manly man.

In chapter ten I raised the question of manliness and womanliness, without saying much about what I meant by either term.[1] I suggested that women are basically feminine but have significant masculine traits, and that men are basically masculine but have significant feminine traits. I said that identity confusion arises when the full development of either masculinity in a man or femininity in a woman has been frustrated. I also made it clear that a macho man without feminine traits has not reached full manhood. Nor has a woman reached full womanhood while the masculine side of her is re-pressed.

We nonetheless need models of womanhood and manhood, people we can look at as standards of womanliness and manliness. For women I suggested that the woman in Proverbs 31 should be complemented by the submissive courage before God of Mary, the mother of our Lord. For men I suggested that the man Christ Jesus is the model. Let me now make what may be a provocative statement.

If men were the sort of man that Jesus was, women would have no difficulty in accepting the idea of male authority or male courage to face danger. By male authority I do not mean male *power* or anything that contributes to the sort of patrimony that women struggle against. All I am saying is that if a wife saw in her husband the character of Jesus, she would automatically respond to *what was there* in him. Unfortunately, most Christian men are not at all like Jesus.

Women would even be attracted by that which is *wild* in man—not savage, or crude, so much as *untamed,* wild in the sense that Lewis's Christ figure, Aslan, "is not a *tame* lion." Aslan is not *safe.* To be wild in this sense, a boy needs a "wild" instructor. No woman can teach him wildness of the kind I speak of. I am not talking about "cigarettes and whiskey and wild, wild women," but about a deeper and more fundamental wildness, without which no true godliness can exist either in men or in women.

The Holy Spirit himself is not "safe." When he is poured out in revival, strange things frequently happen. We think of revival with nostalgia for books in which we have read about it. Real revival is messy and frightening. The powers of darkness do not take flight in an orderly and decent fashion, but uttering screeches and creating havoc.

In Search of a Real Man

I say masculinity is male, meaning it is meant to be more male than female. Men are currently disheartened and confused. Feminist reactions to male violence, to male irresponsibility, to male shiftlessness and to male exploi-tation of women are all rooted in justice, even though the underlying fem-inist philosophy is, I believe, neither valid nor godly. In the face of women's understandable protests and the male bashing of feminist-oriented literature (which currently greatly exceeds literature about how to be helpful to men), men are uncertain what they are supposed to be. Gordon Dalbey quotes cartoonist Lynda Barry's amusing series of frames about the "sensitive" man.

Man: Tonight? It's up to you, Angel.

Woman: Why do *I* end up making all the decisions in this relationship, Bill?

M: Because I want to treat you equally, Dear. The last thing I want to be is a dominant male, Honey.

W: I don't have anything to worry about.

M: I want this relationship to *work*. More wine?

W: Look, Bill, I realize you are trying to be sensitive to my needs, but do you have to be such a *wimp* about it?

M: I resent that, my Darling.

W: OK, Bill, Listen. I want *you* to make all the decisions tonight, all right?

M: Whatever you say, Dear. But what if I make decisions which oppress you? Or, what if I start being macho by *accident*? What if I *like* it? Are you sure you can handle being confronted by my powerful masculinity, Honey? I mean, maybe you should think this over.[2]

Bill is a washout. He has been tamed—but is now *too* tame. He's also more than a trifle manipulative. Faced with a choice of being either wimp or Rambo, which are men to choose? Men are unhappy in both roles, finding fulfillment in neither. Women, likewise, find neither role satisfactory, unless they are the sort of women who enjoy keeping a man as a pet. And those are no more real women than their "men" are real men.

Poet Robert Bly has blistering words for male passivity, which he also sees as utterly naive. "If his wife or girl friend, furious, shouts that he is 'chauvinist,' a 'sexist,' a 'man,' he doesn't fight back but just takes it. He opens his shirt so that she can see more clearly where to put the lances. He ends up with three or four javelins sticking out of his body, and blood running all over the floor."[3]

Sam Keen addresses the grief suffered both by men and by many women who have faced the injustices men have inflicted on women, yet still long to understand one another. He quotes from one woman who reflected the feelings of many women present at a men's conference as "flies on the wall." The conference dealt, among other things, with the terrors the men had experienced in battle. I wept when I read the quote.

I have been married twice, and had several other relationships that ended badly. Like most women I have always "listened" to men, but until today I never heard them. I have never heard men talk to other men with such depth and love. And I never imagined what it was like for men to live with the knowledge that they must be prepared to kill, or with the actual horror of battle. This weekend I feel I have been in a room with giants. I thank you for letting me listen.[4]

The One Who Teaches Wildness

Bly tells the ancient story of Iron John, using it as his core illustration about manhood. A young man who is ready for any adventure offers his services to a king. The king sends him to solve the mystery of a forest near his palace, where hunters keep disappearing. Accompanied only by his dog, the man goes out. He stops near a pond. A hand reaches out of the water, grabs the dog by the leg and pulls it down. Clearly this must be the place to solve the mystery. Bly sees the pond as the human unconscious, the wildness deep in the male psyche.

To "get to the bottom" of the mystery the young man, assisted by a small bucket brigade from the palace, empties the pond bucket by bucket. In the mud at the bottom they find a huge wild man covered with red hair, and so he is called Iron John. They capture him and lock him in an iron cage in the palace grounds.

One day the eight-year-old prince is playing in the grounds with a golden ball, symbolizing the creativity, the spontaneity, the vision of completeness in the mind of children. Bly quotes Freud's remark, "What a distressing contrast there is between the radiant intelligence of the child and the feeble mentality of the average adult."[5]

The prince's ball rolls into the wild man's cage, and fearfully he asks Iron John to return it. The wild man says he will if the prince will let him out of the cage, but the prince hurries away, scared.

To get in touch with the wild man in the depths of ourselves is a frightening and lengthy business. It involves meditation and hard work. He is not safe at the bottom of the pond, however, and still not entirely safe captured and caged.

The boy returns the next day to ask again, but the wild man wants out.

That will be the only condition of returning the golden ball. Again the boy hurries away. On the third day, however, when Iron John insists on his demand of being set free, the boy says he doesn't know where the key is. The wild man tells him his father has given it to his mother, and that it now lies beneath his mother's pillow. He must *steal* it from her.

He must steal it, not ask for it. The story is speaking of the day when every boy or man emerges from the control of his mother, the day when she discovers she has "lost" him. At this point he becomes truly part of the world of men. To some mothers this is a joy mingled with the pain of nostalgia, to others a tragedy against which they fight bitterly. The boy cannot *ask* his mother for the key, for that is not to take control, but to allow her to retain control. For then she has the power to retain, or to give conditionally. He has to *take* it. He has to take it to let the wild man out. As long as he yells at his mother or is rude to her, he is still not free from her, still cannot relate to her as a man. Only the wild man can teach him how to be a man.

The prince steals the key and releases the wild man, who, at the prince's request, takes him on his shoulders and off into the woods. Here, with further counsel from the wild man, he enters into his true self, saves a distant kingdom from its dangerous enemies and wins the hand of the princess of that country. Bly treats the story throughout his book as a key to the understanding of the nature of manhood.

My Own Wild and Hairy Man

I had to decide in a hurry to get married—and not for the usual reason! The woman I wanted as my wife was on her way back to the Philippines as a missionary. It would be five years before I would see her again. Both of us were getting older. I had just turned thirty-one and Lorrie was twenty-six. Five years was too long to wait. I wanted children and so did she. Lorrie was beautiful and powerful. There seemed to be nothing she would not face. If I were to marry her, I would find myself riding an unbroken filly. Was I up to it? Disturbed, I prayed and asked God.

I prayed alone in the chapel of the missionary "boot camp" where we then were, pleading for understanding. Suddenly I had the curious impression that the Holy Spirit was standing behind my left shoulder, and that he was about fourteen feet tall. Very clearly he said, "Is not my name Counselor?"

The Holy Spirit has been my wild man every since. As a counselor he has had some frightening instructions for me.

That evening as we sat by the river I told Lorrie about what I felt God had said. Immediately she burst into tears. When she could speak she said, "All my life I've been longing for a man I really could count on." Lorrie is a woman. She had faced danger, taken initiative, knew her own mind, made decisions. I still have a healthy respect for those qualities and have learned to treasure them. I did not have to "break" her. Nor would I ever want to. I'm too fond of her.

Yet, deeper than her strengths, a longing existed for a man she "really could count on." Ever since the afternoon in the chapel, I have slowly been learning to be a man. With some of us it takes a lifetime. My teacher has been the Holy Spirit, my wild man.

When Adam Flunked a Man's Supreme Test

When a man can't be counted on, when he sacrifices his integrity, when he chooses to go along with what he knows is not of God, he sins against God and against the woman. In particular, he fails the woman *as a man*. Women can, of course, fail men in precisely the same way. But I suspect men do it more frequently. A man who does so acts in an unmanly way.

This is what happened in Eden. First, Eve bought the serpent's line. She listened to darkness and did what the serpent suggested. Then when she approached Adam, he let her down badly. Unwilling to lose what was "bone of [his] bones and flesh of [his] flesh" (Gen 2:23) and what had become precious to him, he did the very thing that God had charged him personally (though not the woman) never to do. He "wimped out."

Faced with a disagreement with the women they love, many, if not most, men choose between wimping and brutality. They may gratify themselves sexually in some other way, may agree to avoid trouble (both of which reflect wimping out)—or they may resort to brutality in their fear of woman, on the principle that what cannot be controlled must be subdued and overcome. Men may beat women because they still want their own way, but, more important, wife-beaters do so because they *fear* their wives.[6]

Adam was, I believe, more to blame than Eve in his choice. He knew what the score was, for God had charged him, not Eve, personally. He had, in the somewhat sententious words of a great aunt of mine, "sinned against known light," presumably in order to hang on to his woman. This is why Paul says,

"As in *Adam* all die" (1 Cor 15:22). On the male is placed the ultimate responsibility for the Fall. The redeemer is likewise a male: "For as in Adam all die, so in Christ all will be made alive."

Unhappily, throughout all history we men, having inherited Adam's sinful tendency, have compounded our sin by abusing the male prerogatives and strengths God gave us. Secular feminists are correct to point out male abuses. Christian men must repent, accepting our identity with that sin which brought the Fall. As males, we especially are to become like Christ.

I suspect that the philosophical basis of feminism is a rationalization of its aims. Few of us have an honest grasp of our motives. Feminists covet the prizes which men have wrongly sought and in pursuit of which men have injured women. They seek their own rightful share of power and wealth, to be presidents of countries or companies—and so on. Yet *wealth and power bring no happiness.*

The hope of happiness through power is an illusion. Lust for wealth and power is folly both in men and in women—equally wrong and equally a mockery. Men (males) have never found peace that way, nor will women. Why do men die sooner than women? Because all that they have reaped in achieving patriarchy is a shortened life span. You don't correct a wrong by competing for the prizes won by doing the wrong. All you get is a headache and a shorter life.

God's Kind of Authority

Jesus made it plain to his disciples that the kind of authority he taught differed radically from worldly authority:

> Jesus called them together and said, "You know that those who are re-garded as rulers of the Gentiles lord it over them, and their high officials exercise authority over them. Not so with you. Instead, whoever wants to become great among you must be your servant, and whoever wants to be first must be slave of all. For even the Son of Man did not come to be served, but to serve, and to give his life as a ransom for many." (Mk 10:42-45)

Where could we find a more total reversal of the common concept of au-thority than in Jesus' own words? The common view is that authority is invested in an office of some kind. You are appointed to the office, often on a competitive basis, because you have met society's qualifications for the office. Holding the office (in church, state or business) affords both status and the right to expect your instructions to be carried out. If they are not carried out, you have the right to know why.

Power differs from authority, and the relation between the two is complex. It is too simple to say that a gun (force) represents the world's power and a badge its authority. Nevertheless, there is some truth in the analogy. You don't have any authority unless you are backed by a few guns. Such is the nature of worldly authority. It is the antithesis of godliness.

In contrast, godly people have the kind of authority that comes when others find themselves automatically following their views and advice. If you have this sort of authority you will need great humility lest you become a tyrant or a guru. It can go to your head just as easily as being appointed to some office or other.

The essence of authority in Jesus' teaching is servanthood. In serving, I lead. By my becoming a servant to others, giving my life to serve them as Christ served his followers, an invisible mantle of authority begins to settle on my shoulders. As a result, people begin to trust me. People respond quickly when I speak. So long as I can maintain my determination to serve others for Christ's sake, my mantle of authority continues to be effective. But quickly I can begin to despise those who look to me as an authority. Compassion can quickly become contempt. The moment I start to "lord it over" others I not only begin to lose that mantle, I take the first step toward becoming a tyrant. This is what happened to King Saul. True authority comes from spending time in God's loving presence and responding to his authority.

Creation or Fall: Paul the Woman Hater?

Men and women need one another *as* men and women. They need real men and women, *healed* men and women. And the day has come for manliness and womanliness to be restored. Yet I shall talk more about manliness than about womanliness. Why? Because I believe that when men are men, women will find much less difficulty entering into their own identity.

The fault has been more of a male fault all along. Men's and women's natures, the nature of manliness and womanliness, were determined at creation, damaged at the Fall, redeemed at the cross. Christ restored and still restores what sin so seriously damages, on the basis of his sacrifice and supreme victory. In restoring our natures, he also restores in practice the equality of men and women.

Paul's theology is the first century's supreme interpretation of this theme. It focuses on the equality: "Now that faith has come, we are no longer under the supervision of the law. You are all sons of God through faith in Christ Jesus, for all of you who were baptized into Christ have clothed yourselves with Christ. There is neither Jew nor Greek, slave nor free, male nor female, for you are all one in Christ Jesus" (Gal 3:25-28).

Paul does *seem* to contradict himself elsewhere, however. He says, "A woman should learn in quietness and full submission. I do not permit a woman to teach or to have authority over a man; she must be silent. For Adam was formed first, then Eve. And Adam was not the one deceived; it was the woman who was deceived and became a sinner. But women will be saved through childbearing—if they continue in faith, love and holiness with propriety" (1 Tim 2:11-15).

Earth Mother Cults

Paul is not blaming the woman for the Fall. The context has to do with teaching. He appears to be defending his practice of not allowing women to teach authoritatively in the churches he founded, by arguing that Eve was—and therefore women in general are—more easily deceived by Satan. But at this point we are stuck with a serious problem of interpretation. Perhaps Paul *is* defending his own practice of not allowing women to teach. On the other hand, he may be doing something entirely different.

Paul is part of the world of the New Testament, the sort of world our own is rapidly becoming. It is a world of idolatry.[7] Earth Mother cults were part of the scene. Just as Satan seduced Israel into believing that pagan deities would make a better contribution to the multiplication of their crops, so in the world of the New Testament he fooled men and women into believing they needed initiation into the mysteries of creation. In both cases the come-on was sex.

One such cult flourishing in the Ephesus of Paul's day taught that a female goddess was not only the originator of men but of God himself. Mystic knowledge about him could be obtained by having sexual relations with a priestess of the cult. In *I Suffer Not a Woman*, Richard and Catherine Clark Kroeger point out that one word critical to correct translation is used only on this occasion in the entire New Testament.[8] *Authentein* had several uses, of which to have or usurp authority is only one. The word is also used to mean to originate, to murder someone (often in a sexual context), and, falsely, to claim ownership of something. The verse could in that case mean, "I do not permit a woman to teach or to represent herself as the originator of man"[9]—which was exactly what priestesses in that cult taught. Not only so, but mysticism involving worship is again linked with the power of our sexuality. Men are once again being hooked into the satanic strategy as Satan reaches for their genitals. It is his favorite opening move in controlling fallen men and women.

Certainly the Kroegers' translation fits Genesis 2 and 3 better. Eve was deceived. She was deceived by Satan, who told her that in eating the fruit she would become like God, "knowing good and evil." *She would be initiated into the mystery known only to God.* But the serpent was not telling the truth. As I have already pointed out, she would know evil only by doing evil, not as God knows it. Pagan religions of New Guinea and a number of the Pacific Islands, including ancient Hawaii, reserve the mysteries of religion to men. The gospel opens them to women as well.

Authority and Power
However, even if the Kroegers' suggestion is not the correct one, we are dealing with Paul's practice. If he is saying "I do not permit," he is not necessarily giving us revealed doctrine.

On at least one other occasion he distinguishes clearly between what the Lord says and his own opinion (1 Cor 7:10-12).

Yet, even majoring (in my view) on male-female equality on the basis of creation and atonement, Paul seems to make strong statements that men are somehow to be superior. We have that impression because of the emotional loading of words like *authority* and *power* and our confusion as to what they mean.

The semantic confusion is seen, for instance, in Roy McCloughry's *Men and Masculinity.* He gives a superb review of the arguments on both sides of the theological debate about men and women, yet says, "I cannot see how we can talk of a man's authority over a woman being 'natural' since there is nothing natural about a distorted relationship which came about through disobedience. If we persist in sanctifying the pervasiveness of male power in our world we turn the outcome of our fall into the norm, enshrining that which is evil with sacred power. Genesis 3:16 is a prediction of the effects of the fall rather than a prescription of God's ideal order."[10]

Curiously, following the statement, McCloughry gives a clear exposition of the nature of biblical authority. Yet in the statement above he uses the word *authority* in the worldly sense. The moment you add the word *over* to the word *authority,* you make it almost synonymous with the word *power.* McCloughry himself goes on to talk about "male power in our world," using the word *power* as though it meant the word *authority.* We have authority *over* the enemy and his works, but we submit to one another. The godlier a person is, the easier it is to submit to that person. But we are to be the judges of what is godly, and not to submit to what is ungodly.

Other Ways Men Fail

How can I express the difference between men and women without raising the specter of patriarchy? The Scripture does make it clear that what I would call the mantle of authority (that to which people tend to respond) rests more easily on the shoulders of a man—not because men are superior, but because they are more often called on by God to assume responsibility, *and because theirs is the primary fault.* Tragically, it is in taking authority that we men fail. This may be why McCloughry makes statements about enshrining evil when he refers to male authority.

Men fail in the area where responsibility matters most—in the home. Christian men fail there particularly. A visit from a friend recently reminded me of that.

Jackie Pullinger To has become known throughout the world for her work in the Walled City, for many years an administrative no man's land, neglected by both Hong Kong and China. It became a ramshackle center of crime and neglect, a base of operations for the triads (the Chinese "mafia") and for drug addiction and prostitution. Eventually Jackie won the respect of triad leaders. She saw many triad members who had fallen foul of drugs cleaned up and converted. The Hong Kong authorities, noting that her "program" was at least as effective as their own, helped her to establish camps and centers where men could be withdrawn from drugs. In the end Queen Elizabeth awarded her the M. B. E. (Member of the British Empire).

The last time she stayed with us in Canada, our family had a conversation with her that went on into the night. As nearly as I can remember Jackie said, "I'm beginning to dread seeing some of the ex-triad members get married. What happens when they do is that very soon they start coming to more Christian meetings than they did before they were married. They end up neglecting their wives and children. They don't know how to be men.

"I'm a woman. I can preach the gospel to them, can be used by God to deliver them from addiction, *but I can't make men out of them. It takes a man to do that.* They don't know how to be a husband to a woman or a father to children."

(I thought, "No, nor do many of us in the West.")

Men do not fail in the home because they are too busy outside it. The business organization, the club, the pub, even Christian service, are too commonly excuses that enable us to escape and to do what we prefer to do. To escape is to fail in one's manhood. Men fail to be true men in relation to women and to children. If a man fails in the home, he is not a man but something less than a man. To take responsibility in man-dominated organizations can be to play the world's authority game, not Christ's.

What is authority? Here McCloughry is on firm ground. We must examine both the teaching and the practice of Jesus. This is how I hope to support my statement that if men were real men and in fact displayed the sort of manliness Jesus displayed and taught, then women would have no difficulty in accepting male authority. However, while biblical authority may or not be understood by Christians, *few Christian men practice biblical authority.* Only remember, as we saw above, it is Paul who finds the source of greater male authority in the creation, and not in the sin that led to the Fall.

Perhaps it is time to look at Christ. It is in Christ as a male that the model for men is to be found. How was Christ's manhood expressed? How was his authority reflected in his earthly life?

CHAPTER 13
Christ,
Model of
Manliness

We are more profoundly united by our common humanity
than separated by gender. . . . The most hopeful thing we can do to end
the war between the sexes is merely to witness to each
other, tell our stories, and listen quietly.
SAM KEEN

Christ practiced what he preached. But what did he practice in relation to his authority? (I am using the word in the way I defined it in the previous chapter.) How did he exercise his authority on earth? The question has great importance. For as he is in relation to us, so we all must be in relation to others, and so we men must be in relation to women. So, also, church leaders must be in relation to members of the congregation. In this chapter, primarily for men, I will look at how Jesus provided a model of manhood. We shall consider especially the last days of his life.

Washing Feet
I notice one thing about Jesus' relationship to women. He may rebuke a woman as he rebuked Martha over her lack of faith and over her resentment of Mary's sitting at his feet. But he never patronizes a woman, nor does he ever say, "Look, I'm not going to say it again. Either you obey me, or else . . ." As far as his earthly example is concerned, he shows us both how

to serve and in what way to exercise authority. He repeatedly curses the Pharisees for the way they misuse their positions of leadership (Mt 23:13-36), warning the crowds against their teaching. He does so *in the presence of those Pharisees,* knowing they will plot against him and bring about his death. Yet he never forces them to accept his will.

Nor does he do so now. He forces no man or woman to see things his way. He may go a long way to shake some of us out of our blindness, illuminating our hearts with such strong light that we *have* to see the truth. But we can still choose not to.

The most striking example of Jesus' approach to leadership, in contrast to the Pharisees, is seen at the Last Supper when he washes his disciples feet.

> Jesus knew that the Father had put all things under his power, and that he had come from God and was returning to God; so he got up from the meal, took off his outer clothing, and wrapped a towel around his waist. After that, he poured water into a basin and began to wash his disciples' feet, drying them with the towel that was wrapped around him. (Jn 13:3-5)

Jesus knew he was God the Son. He had come from God and was returning to God. He knew that after the cross, the throne awaited him. He knew he was the teacher and the Lord of his followers. Yet he washed their feet.

> When he had finished washing their feet, he put on his clothes and returned to his place. "Do you understand what I have done for you?" he asked them. "You call me 'Teacher' and 'Lord,' and rightly so, for that is what I am. Now that I, your Lord and Teacher, have washed your feet, you also should wash one another's feet. (Jn 13:12-14)

In washing their feet, Jesus did something far more profound than giving a mere teaching demonstration. His action arose out of genuine compassion. You trust someone who washes your feet, because he cares for you. Jesus had no false notions about his dignity or his position. He was not afraid of losing face. He got partially undressed, as a servant washing feet would. He assumed "work clothes," so to speak.

In this he could be compared with a Christian leader who donned painting gear or steel-toe boots, jeans and a hard hat. (Politicians also dress down—but their motive is often far from a true spirit of service.) Christ had compassion on the discomfort, both emotional and physical, that came from having dusty feet at what may have been an embarrassing moment.

Authorized by Being Served

But how can we become like that? The "how" has to do with a process that is deeply mysterious, touching the depths of our souls. We get a hint of it in Peter's response.

> He came to Simon Peter, who said to him, "Lord, are you going to wash my feet?"
>
> Jesus replied, "You do not realize now what I am doing, but later you will understand."
>
> "No," said Peter, "you shall never wash my feet."
>
> Jesus answered, "Unless I wash you, you have no part with me." (Jn 13:6-8)

Most of us would resist as Peter did. Our thinking is, "I wish a servant were here to do our feet, but it's not *my* place to do anything." If we were to see Jesus half-naked, stooping to wash our own dirty feet, it might bother us. His interest would be in our discomfort, and the discomfort, on an occasion like that, would have two elements.

Picture it. Pretend you are Peter, and that you have watched him washing the others' feet. Now it is your turn. Or picture your entrance into the room. The realization of your own discomfort troubles you. First, there is your embarrassment, your unwillingness to take the initiative and stoop. Why you, rather than one of the others? In addition, there is the discomfort of the dirt. However, Jesus should not be the one to do it. The thought is inconceivable. You prefer to see Jesus enthroned, which is his right, or else out there in the front, leading the charge into battle. But first you must come to trust him as a leader and to receive from him in a different way.

We become like Jesus by allowing him to serve us, to wash, so to speak, our own feet. We have to know what it is in our experience *to let him love us, to let him minister to our intimate needs.* But we are too proud. We need to let him show us the sin we hide even from ourselves and restore our family relationship with him. We do not lose his righteousness when we sin, but we do lose fellowship with him. Time and again we need to experience the mysterious way in which he reveals a sin, never to condemn us, but only to release us from it. Only thus do we adopt his servant role. Only thus can we become like him.

Jesus: Model of Manliness

Though he was both divine and human, the impression one gets from reading the Gospels is that Jesus operated primarily in his humanity on earth. While in his atoning death it was essential that he be God *and* man, in most of his earthly acts he seems to act as *man empowered by the Spirit of God*. That is why Paul refers to him as the second man or last Adam (1 Cor 15:45, 47). The fact is of incalculable importance. It means he performed his miracles, gave his teaching, not as God, but *as a human being filled with the Spirit*. He did not cease to be God, but his *mode* was human. How else was he tempted? You can't tempt God. Why else did he need to be anointed and filled with the Holy Spirit? *You don't fill God with the Spirit!*

Please understand what I am saying. I am *not* asserting that his divinity played no part in our redemption. We needed a Savior who was and is fully God and fully man.[1] I stress the fullness of his human experience because it is the one less taken into account. We can do the same works he did only if he did them not as God, but as man. We cannot and must not play God, but we can follow Jesus and walk in his Spirit. But it is of his maleness that I most want to speak.

Rambo, Jock and Wimp

Two basic models characterize men's behavior. First, there is the supermale, the jock, Rambo. Then there is the wimp. Jesus is neither a wimp nor a Rambo. Though he is God, he is yet a man. Rambos, jocks and wimps are not fully men but caricatures. Their manhood is deficient.

On the other hand, Jesus is the last Adam. Where Adam failed both morally and as a man, Jesus did not. In his triumph he opens the way to true manhood and true womanhood. At the heart of the human nature of Christ lies what is in God's own heart. For he is God the Son. Servanthood lies at the heart of his relationship with others, and servanthood is seen supremely in his redeeming death. As he said, "Whoever wants to be first must be your slave—just as the Son of Man did not come to be served, but to serve, and to give his life as a ransom for many" (Mt 20:27-28).

True servanthood is not wimping out. It includes speaking frankly, honestly and openly, yet not in petulant anger or needless truculence. Jesus loved the very people who roused his anger. Why else would he eat with Pharisees, for example?

Jesus displayed manliness in standing up to Pharisees, Sadducees and teachers of the law. He was in no way cowed by their learning or their pseudoauthority. Some of the passages in John 8 and in Matthew 23 make John the Baptist's outburst sound mild. Yet while Jesus was enraged at their abuse of power, he still loved the Pharisees, as he loved the Jewish nation in entirety. He would hardly have eaten with them had he hated them. In his manhood he can show both stern anger and tenderness. He moves from Matthew 23:33 ("You snakes! You brood of vipers! How will you escape being condemned to hell?") to Matthew 23:37 ("O Jerusalem . . . I have longed to gather your children together, as a hen gathers her chicks").

The Last Adam, a True Man

Throughout his life Jesus displayed the capacity to initiate, to lead in new ways that bucked the whole society. He was fearless in his initiating. While he used the rabbinical teaching method, his disciples were men who had been trained in the hurly-burly of life. They would hardly be the training material preferred by most rabbis. Because he always spoke the truth, even when it hurt, many of his disciples took offense and left him (Jn 6:66).

He also bucked society by presenting a view of God that was hardly in vogue, teaching about *Abba,* the Aramaic equivalent of *Daddy.* Rambo has no need of *Daddy.* He might have no use at all for a father. If he has, he might call his father Pop, or Dad. He might call him anything, but definitely not *Daddy. Daddy* is for children, and for those who are willing to become like children.

Many men prefer the company of other men because they feel uncomfortable when exposed for too long to the company of women and children. Jesus loved children and rebuked his disciples for attempting to hinder their access to him. His love and his sense of responsibility also caused him to seek out and to stand up for the poor and the oppressed. He had the capacity to stick with anything he was called by God to do, whatever the consequences might be and however great the cost to him.

As for his feminine side, it may be less obvious, but I have already cited Christ's use of the picture of a hen gathering her brood under her wings. There are also examples of his capacity to feel and display tenderness. At the grave of Lazarus, he wept for the hopelessness experienced by those who did not believe, their hopelessness before the Grim Reaper.

A yet more moving example is seen at the crucifixion. In great pain and in a physical state of shock, Jesus is still able to think of the needs of others.

(Women are better at bearing pain and still caring for dependents than men are. The trait is a feminine trait. A mother needs it.) Agonized though he is on the cross, Jesus still has his mother's needs on his heart. He knows John will look after her more conscientiously than his own brothers will. So he calls first to his mother, then to John, "Woman, behold your Son. . . . [Son], behold your mother" (Jn 19:26-27 NKJV). Feminine traits are not wimpy traits. It takes enormous strength to take action in the life of another when your body is screaming its protests.

But, *does a real man ever show weakness?* Does a real man turn to friends and tell them he's reached his limit? Does he say, "Please stick around, guys. I really need your support right now. I'm not sure if I can take what's coming to me"? Is that not a sign of unmanly weakness? For some it may be, but not for Jesus. He shared his own need for human contact—with men with whom he shared his heart. Right before he was arrested and crucified, "He took Peter and the two sons of Zebedee along with him, and he began to be sorrowful and troubled. Then he said to them, 'My soul is overwhelmed with sorrow to the point of death. Stay here and keep watch with me' " (Mt 26:37-38).

What was his need? It was that he knew what was coming to him, the stark horror of that death that was to be like no other human death. He needed a time of prayer so that he could wrestle through to peace in his soul. Yet if God was his help, why the need also for male human beings? Was God the Father not enough? The fact was that the Father God seemed a long way away right then to the man Jesus. What ought we to tell him? Keep a stiff upper lip? "Just have faith, Jesus!"

No. He needed Peter, James and John around, *because he was human.* He was facing the most horrendous test of his human experience, for he was to suffer as a man. And as a man he craved the physical proximity of those dear to him. He was not ashamed to ask for it.

How does a real man face arrest? How would you feel, yourself? To be arrested is disturbing, frightening, bewildering for most people. Jesus was arrested by a rabble of soldiers, priestly officials and Pharisees, bearing torches, lamps and weapons. They meant to use force if it proved necessary. An armed but disorganized rabble can be even more intimidating than a couple of policemen, especially at night. Yet there is a strange contrast between Christ's behavior and that of either the disciples or the rabble.

So Judas came to the grove, guiding a detachment of soldiers and some officials from the chief priests and Pharisees. They were carrying torches, lanterns and weapons. Jesus, knowing all that was going to happen to him, went out and asked them, "Who is it you want?"

"Jesus of Nazareth," they replied.

"I am he," Jesus said. . . . When Jesus said, "I am he," they drew back and fell to the ground.

Again he asked them, "Who is it you want?"

And they said, "Jesus of Nazareth."

"I told you that I am he," Jesus answered. "If you are looking for me, then let these men go." (Jn 18:3-8)

The disciples displayed a mixture of truculence and cowardice. Peter swung his sword and cut off the ear of the high priest's servant. But as the situation developed, "all the disciples deserted him and fled" (Mt 26:56). Even Peter's action strikes me as being counterphobic, an action to convince yourself you are a real man. It was as futile as it was impulsive. We have compassion both on Peter and on the rest because we would probably do no better ourselves. We men, too, need to learn to be men.

The rabble was just as weak. Armed, more numerous than the apostles and backed by authority, they still did not show manly courage.

Jesus towers above them all in his poise, his assurance, his lack of ambivalence. While the rabble fall, backing into one another, tripping over one another in their haste not to get too close, and tumbling like precariously balanced dominos, he alone behaves like a man. He has resolved the problem that plagued him in the garden. He is sure now that what awaits him is according to the will of the Father, and he is ready to embrace it. His reaction is neither passive nor fatalistic. He is ready to "drink the cup the Father" has given him (Jn 18:11). He knows who his true enemy is, and he is ready to face him in combat. The arrest is of little consequence to him in comparison with the real issues at stake.

How does a real man react in a public trial under abusive interrogation? A real man acts as a mature human being; otherwise he is a boy rather than a man. The interrogation begins with an interview with a former high priest, Annas, who asks Jesus about his teaching. The question is absurd. Annas wishes to find a way to trap Jesus in his speech.

"I have spoken openly to the world," Jesus replied. "I always taught in synagogues or at the temple, where all the Jews come together. I said nothing in secret. Why question me? Ask those who heard me. Surely they know what I said."

When Jesus said this, one of the officials nearby struck him in the face. "Is this the way you answer the high priest?" he demanded.

"If I said something wrong," Jesus replied, "testify as to what is wrong. But if I spoke the truth, why did you strike me?" (Jn 18:20-23)

When the overzealous official strikes Jesus across the face, he reacts with dignity, with the singular maturity of the man Jesus. He displays no petulance, no belligerence.

Jesus is then dispatched to Caiaphas (the high priest at the time) and the formal public trial. The interview with Annas may have been for the purpose of advising Caiaphas, since Annas was his father-in-law.

The trial before Caiaphas is a contrived affair. It is another attempt to trap Jesus. It represents a charade, an empty going-through-the-motions. It is a legal fiction in search of legality. Matthew and Mark both make this clear. Jesus listens to the series of false and conflicting accusations without responding in any way.

Like Annas, his father-in-law, Caiaphas well knows what Jesus has been teaching. Like Jesus, he listens to the witnesses, knowing that the testimony is useless. He is playing for bigger stakes than the mere fate of one man. What bothers Caiaphas is that only days before the arrest, Jesus had raised Lazarus from the dead. By so doing he had (in Caiaphas's view) threatened the "peace" of Roman tyranny. Caiaphas had previously made his own attitude clear to the Jewish leadership. An accomplished player of political games, he was out to nail Jesus. Only thus could he save his own skin and secure the continued existence of the Jewish hierarchy. Immediately following the miracle of Lazarus:

The chief priests and the Pharisees called a meeting of the Sanhedrin. "What are we accomplishing?" they asked. "Here is this man performing many miraculous signs. If we let him go on like this, everyone will believe in him, *and then the Romans will come and take away both our place and our nation."*

Then one of them, named Caiaphas, who was high priest that year, spoke up, "You know nothing at all! You do not realize that it is better for you that one man die for the people than that the whole nation perish." (Jn 11:47-50)

Then, as one of the witnesses reminds him of a remark Jesus once made about the temple, he sees and seizes his chance. If only he can get Jesus to admit his claim to divinity! He attempts to get Jesus to answer the charge of the latest witnesses, but Jesus does not respond. He is waiting for a better opportunity to establish the real cause of the official opposition to him. Caiaphas impatiently plays into his hands and charges him under oath to say whether he is God or not. Unknown to Caiaphas, this is the moment Jesus has been waiting for. He replies, in effect, "Yes, that is exactly who I am."

Caiaphas, blind to the significance of Christ's words, acts as though he is shocked and enraged. With the excitement of triumph he acts the part of a distraught man, tearing his garments. His objective has been accomplished. But so has Christ's. He has known all along that it must come to this. For history, his divinity is the real issue. Christianity has no meaning otherwise. The history of the church and of the Jewish nation is bound up in the question. They will one day be united on the basis of the question.

Christ's maturity as a man is seen in his behavior. Though he is God, in the trial he functions *as a man*. Probably very weary, he waits quietly. His calm refusal to do anything but wait until the right question is asked, and in a situation most men would find fraught with anxiety, displays not only his maturity but his incredible strength.

How does a real man take a flogging? A flogging tests any person's humanity. For one thing, you are stripped, usually completely. You feel very vulnerable that way—all defenses gone. There are spectators. The Roman flogging was with leather whips, the multiple ends tipped with either small lumps of lead or small fragments of bone. Either way your skin would be flayed and your back raw, bleeding and oozing. You would be in shock and would also have a painful back to rub against your cross, for the flogging is the preliminary stage of the crucifixion.

No comment is made on Christ's behavior at that point. Presumably friendly witnesses were around to record events, for the mockery that followed is described in detail. If his cry on the cross is recorded, we would expect any cries at the flogging also to be. The absence of any comment seems to indicate that he endured the flogging with wordless dignity.

What followed was barbaric. *How does a real man respond to a vicious hazing?* Following the flogging he was evidently dressed again before being handed over to the soldiers responsible for the crucifixion. Once in their hands, he was again stripped, dressed up as a mock king in a scarlet robe and crown of thorns, blindfolded and given a staff to hold as a mock scepter. The soldiers' fun was to play "subjects bowing before the king." Then, before long, they snatched the staff out of his hand and played "prophet" with him. ("Who hit you that time, prophet?") "They spit on him . . . and struck him on the head again and again" (Mt 27:30).

I am being neither morbid nor cynical. I have wept over the passage more than once. On one occasion I cried out to God in anger, "*That* was not necessary to secure my redemption! Why did you allow it?" The reply was immediate: "Do not pity my Son! Your pity is inappropriate. He endured the cross, despising its shame—because of *joys beyond it.*" Jesus behaved like a man because he saw beyond time and space with eyes of faith (Heb 12:2).

When you are blindfolded, you are unable to dodge either other people's sputum or cracks on the head. You can't even cringe. If you do, they'll wait till you stop cringing before delivering the next blow. But their victim was a manly man. Weary, in shock, in pain, he was manly enough to keep his eyes on the goal. That was what mattered to him. *He despised what he went through, counting the prize well worth what he was enduring.*

So how do we get to be like him? So stunning is the manhood we see that we recognize at once the vast difference that separates us. And though he has "made us nigh" by his atoning death, the difference in our respective characters is appalling. If this is manhood, do we have any hope of becoming men?

Well, there are ways in which we may become progressively more and more like him, especially as we gaze upon him. Part three has the "how" in mind. But we must not forget that the fears and shames we have buried in our unconscious minds will have to be exhumed. We buried them before they were dead. To have the Spirit dig them up again will involve fear, shame, pain. Only he can do it for us. He is sensitive, and when he probes, his fingers will be gentle. He will not make the process more difficult than we can bear. That is the topic of the next chapter.

PART III
Redemption from Distorted Sexuality

If I define healing as a return toward wholeness, toward the restoration of the damaged image of God in men and women, then healing and sanctification are both going on at the same time. Healing and sanctification are two aspects of the same process, two sides of the same coin. Sin is a moral evil (one side of the coin). Sin hurts (the other side). Sin is rebellion against God, rebellion he deals with so that he sometimes cries, "Why should you be beaten anymore? Why do you persist in rebellion? Your whole head is injured, your whole heart afflicted" (Is 1:5). Sin wounds. It calls for the reestablishment of wholeness.

The moral categories are the more basic, therefore the more important. I like to keep the coin "moral side up" so that I do not forget this. Nevertheless pain—damaged spirits, damaged emotions, damaged functioning (both behavioral and physical)—and sin are always associated.

What does sin do? It alienates us from one another and (more importantly) from God. What does sexual sin do? It does the same as any other sin, alienating us from one another and from God. Healing means restoration of relationships, with God and with one another. While his judgments are appallingly severe, God's heart is still for human beings. As we draw near to him we share his heart and draw closer to other human beings. Sin, woundedness, alienation from God and others—all are bound together. Therefore, we see at once that the cure for sexual sin does not differ from the cure for any other sin.

In parts one and two of this book, I have dealt extensively with both the subjective and objective sides of sanctification as it relates to sexual sin. I feel strongly about both sides. Sanctification is both a subjective and objective process, involving both pain and joy. It is also a long process.

Living as we do in a world that offers instant solutions, we want the same in our religious life. Miracles are great. Each time your wounds are miraculously healed you will marvel. What you will slowly discover is that your sexual healing is a far greater and more extensive work than you had realized. In its totality it will take a lifetime. Each miracle will lay the groundwork for the next.

Most important of all, you must take part in your own healing. As an apprentice surgeon I operated on anesthetized patients, who played no part in their healing, but lay passive and unconscious under the ministrations of doctors and nurses. Sexual healing is different. There will be times when the doctors and nurses are present in the form of other members of the Christian church. But you will be conscious—and often in pain. At other times you will be alone with God. And whether alone or with others, your own decisions, your own participation in what is happening will be crucial.

I want to stress both that for your personal healing your own active involvement is necessary, and that your times alone with God are more important than times with a prayer team. While I am profoundly grateful for the times when others have "prayed on" me,[1] and for the changes that occurred in me when they did so, most of my healing has come through my time alone with God. God is the one who heals. We need one another in the church, and we must learn mutual dependence. Nevertheless, other people are not meant to solve all, or even most, of our problems for us.

Because so much of the healing and reorientation of practitioners of homosexuality, as of other people enslaved to sexual sin, involves delving into early memories, chapter fourteen is devoted to a discussion of normal memory formation and of what are now referred to as *traumatic* memories.

Chapter fifteen examines attempts to heal victims of early incest and sexual molestation, and the problems that can arise in a society that has lost its sense of the importance of the family. The dilemma that arises is one that defies any social or scientific solution.

In this section I also reflect on what older evangelicals used to refer to as the means of grace, thinking in particular about three means of grace: repentance, prayer and the church. Chapter sixteen discusses how we collaborate with the Holy Spirit in repentance. The church itself seems largely to have forgotten the place of repentance in sexual healing, and the human sciences ignore repentance altogether. Chapter seventeen discusses the place of waiting on God in our sexual healing, that is, of prayer as a means of grace, while chapter eighteen discusses issues that arise as other church members minister to us in prayer. A pattern for conducting a healing session is suggested in chapter nineteen.

Chapter twenty brings the book to a conclusion, as I look at the glorious hope that lies before everyone enslaved by sexual sin, at the strength that lies in weakness, and at God's amazing preference to use the weak and the wounded rather than experts.

CHAPTER 14
Hidden Memories

Who can find a proper grave for the damaged mosaics
of the mind, where they may rest in pieces?
I. L. LANGER

The heart is deceitful above all things and beyond cure.
Who can understand it? I the Lord search the heart and examine the mind.
JEREMIAH 17:9-10

I have been assuming all along that hidden memories can be the key to helping men and women overcome the proclivity to various forms of sexual sin. Many of these hidden memories concern sexual molestation that happened to people when they were children.

The opening case history in Leanne Payne's book *The Broken Image* is a good example. It concerns a twenty-two-year-old medical student, whom Payne refers to as Lisa. Lisa was homosexual in her orientation, had been suicidal and abused drugs. At the root of her problem was a traumatic event, repressed in her memory for nineteen years. After warning Lisa of the danger of embarking lightly on an attempt to uncover and deal with such a memory, Payne describes what took place.

She was three years or perhaps a little older in this memory and her own father was . . . forcing her into acts of fellatio.[1] Her mother walked into the room and in her hysteria, rather than handling the situation with the father and comforting the child, grabbed the little girl and threw her against the wall. Her father's words to her mother then boomed out and resounded once again through her head: "Aw! she'll never remember!"[2] Modern Christian literature has many accounts of this sort, increasing the tension and disagreement between charismatic Christians and their non-charismatic colleagues over the place of subjective experiences, and over whether the rediscovery of a memory can help release us from a sinful tendency.

What does the Bible teach about memory? What scientific evidence exists that memories remain in pure form? Can pseudomemories be implanted among our true memories? Let me begin with science (even though I cling to the old-fashioned notion that theology is the queen of the sciences and should precede a discussion of scientific evidence).

The Science of Memory

A good deal of the investigation of memory[3] reveals how fluid the process of remembering is. An event we have forgotten, even completely, is part of the normal working of memory. Therefore, I must begin by explaining the working of normal memory.

We remember best whatever we can understand, whatever *makes sense* to us. That is, we attach our memories to the way we understand the world around us, automatically revising our memories from time to time. Behavioral psychology thinks in terms of learning, of learning to do things—to play the piano, for instance. And behavioral learning affects what we might call narrative memories, or what we might think of as videotapes of the stored memories in our brains.

If there are chemical videotapes in the temporal lobes (or wherever) in our brains, then they are subject to ongoing editing. They are modified by behavioral learning—learning how to do things, learning by experience.

Have you ever noticed the number of arguments that arise when one person describes an incident to others who were there at the time? The arguments can be heated. Psychologists call the memories they are discussing *narrative memories*. Such memories change because behavioral learning affects the way we remember things.

For instance, as I grow from childhood I learn about time partly from repeatedly experiencing time's passage and partly by learning to tell time. Think about small children on a long drive who ask for the twenty-third time, "When *are* we going to get there, Daddy?" The expression *five hours* does not have the same meaning to a child as it does to an adult or teenager.

New experiences can be understood only in the light of prior memories. Because behavioral learning affects the way I remember, at some point as I recount to a friend an experience from my past I may be a little puzzled. I pause and say, "No, it *couldn't have been that way,* it must have been"—another way. The manner in which I understand the world around me has changed what I remember, changed it either toward reality or away from it. In this and other ways arguments arise between family members about "the way it really was." Therefore, the events subject to recall are not always reliable.

Sometimes we remember things that never happened to us. A parent may have described an incident that took place in our childhood, such as how we reacted when we got a dog as a present. Over many years we may have talked about the event so often that we no longer remember the actual event but only the retelling of the event by someone else. So vividly has the scene been imprinted on our minds that we feel we can remember "really being there."

I must not exaggerate the problem or suggest that our memories of past events are entirely erroneous. I suppose most have a lot of truth in them. Yet they are far from being entirely trustworthy.

The History of Traumatic Memories

Disagreements arise over what are called *traumatic memories,* an area in which both the neurosciences and the psychologies are becoming more interested. Recent work among victims of the Holocaust has also awakened interest. Interest is likewise increasing in the work of Pierre Janet.

Janet (not Freud) was the originator of the idea of traumatic memories. He declared that these memories were stored differently from other memories, and recent work in the neurosciences confirms this. Janet was a French neurologist and psychologist who was for a period in charge of the psychological laboratory at the famous hospital of Salpetriere in France. It was he who originated the idea of memories that were sealed off from other kinds of learning, retaining their purer, more accurate form.

While Janet was in Salpetriere, he described a case which exemplified the kind of memory he attempted to explain. Irene, a twenty-three-year-old single woman, attended her mother during her last illness. Irene was deeply attached to her mother, her father being a cruelly abusive alcoholic. Whatever money she had earned that could be kept from her father (which was little enough) was spent on food. When her mother died, Irene, her sole attendant during the final illness, had known little sleep for sixty days. Her father, as was the case so very often, was drunk when Irene's mother died. In her exhausted and confused state, Irene could not grasp the fact of the death. She continued to treat her mother as though she were alive, finally pulling the corpse on to the floor in an attempt to get her to straighten out her legs.

Unable to understand what was going on, Irene laughed at the funeral and denied that her mother had died. Her aunt brought her to Salpetriere. On admission she said, "If you insist on it, I will tell you: 'My mother is dead.' They tell me that it is so all day long, and I simply agree with them to get them off my back. But if you want my opinion, I don't believe it. And I have excellent reasons for it." The first excellent reason was that she would grieve deeply if her mother were really dead, and the second, that she loved her mother dearly—and would therefore know.

Now comes the hub of the matter. Though Irene had no memory of the death, she reenacted it repeatedly. The reenactment would recur when she saw a bed that seemed to trigger the memory. As in a trance, she would go through the actions of giving a drink to an imaginary person on the bed, and then a mouth wash, talking to the imaginary person as she did so. For three or four hours a stereotyped behavior would continue, following an exact sequence during which she would not respond to real people who addressed her. The sequence represented that final three or four hours of her mother's life.

Janet noted that the repetitions of the reenactment always followed the exact same sequence, lasting the same amount of time. At other times Irene seemed perfectly normal, except for the fact that she appeared to have no memory of her mother's death. Her "sanity" was touched in only these two ways.

Characteristics of a Traumatic Memory

Pierre Janet characterized the symptoms of a traumatic memory as follows:

1. The memory is maladaptive. It wastes time without restoring the memory to the person who experienced it. Irene would have no recollection of the stereotypical behavior. Other patients with the syndrome might have nightmares or frightening flashbacks not recognizable as memories.

2. There is no social component. The memory Irene reenacted was shared with no one. It was not available for sharing in the way narrative memory is.

3. The memory is evoked under particular conditions.

4. If the memory is dealt with as Irene dealt with hers (rather than through flashbacks or nightmares), then once one element is triggered, the other stereotyped elements automatically follow. This is not true of ordinary memory, where one is free to select a part of the memory from the whole.

Why the trance state? Does one part of her not know what the other part of her is doing? If so, how can the difficulty be resolved (as it eventually was)?

Freud, Janet and Recent Findings

Freud adopted the views expressed and taught at Salpetriere after visiting Janet in 1885, acknowledging the debt in his book *Studies in Hysteria* in 1895. He differed somewhat in that he thought of memory in terms of depth. Dissociated (traumatic) memories were pushed down below the level of consciousness, to emerge in dreams, verbal faux pas, word associations, and so on. Janet, on the other hand, had a kind of side-by-side model of memory. He thought of traumatic memories as *split off from the normal learning process.*

Often the terms *repression* and *dissociation* are used synonymously. It is the latter term that reflects the side-by-side model as well as the recent idea of an *alternate stream of consciousness.* A distant memory can be forgotten easily enough, but not split off into an alternate stream of consciousness. Most of the things we have forgotten are of this kind. They have not been "split off," but simply forgotten. There have to be extraordinarily traumatic circumstances surrounding the memory for the splitting to take place.

For a time Janet enjoyed greater respect than Freud. Later the popularity of Freudian psychoanalysis obscured Janet's findings. He was rescued from obscurity in 1970 by Henri Ellenberger in his book *The Discovery of the Unconscious* and by developments in the neurosciences in the 1970s and 1980s. For many years previously, both "depth" and descriptive psychiatry ignored the fact that actual memories can continue to exert their influence on current behavior because of dissociation.

Van der Kolk and van der Hart state,

Contemporary research has shown that dissociation of a traumatic experience occurs as the trauma is occurring (Putnam 1989). There is little evidence for an active process of pushing away of the overwhelming experience; the uncoupling seems to have other mechanisms. Many trauma survivors report that they automatically are removed from the scene; they look at it from a distance or disappear altogether, leaving other parts of their personality to suffer and store the overwhelming experience. "I moved up to the ceiling from where I saw this little girl being molested and I felt sorry for her" is a common description of incest survivors.[4]

Notice—the dissociation occurs *as the trauma is going on*. Tragically, there are some victims of traumatic events who can never resolve the trauma. Many Holocaust victims are among them. Kolk and Hart report:

Many traumatized persons . . . experience long periods of time in which they live, as it were, in two different worlds. This is most eloquently described by Langer (1991) in his study on oral testimonies by holocaust survivors who never succeed in bridging their existence in the death camps and their lives before and after. "It can . . . never be joined in the world he inhabits now. . . . He switches from one to the other without synchronization because he is reporting not a sequence but a simultaneity" (95).[5]

Unresolved differences remain between the Freudian view and Janet's view. Many psychologists and psychiatrists seem unaware of the volume of recent work both in neurology and with trauma victims.

To summarize up to this point, two types of memory seem to exist in human beings. One we call traumatic, the other ordinary. Yet some of the memories which we remember clearly, which we have never forgotten, continue to have power over us, changing our behavior. These also need to be healed. It is just that we may not have remembered them accurately. The tattered version is all we have. And all we need to be healed from.

As I said above, Payne stressed the need for a thorough grasp of what one is getting into. To deal with traumatic memories is no light matter. It has the possibility of disaster.

Janet used hypnosis (though this is not the way many of us recommend) with Irene to help move the traumatic memory into the realm of ordinary memory. Even so, Kolk and Hart noted,

Whenever [Janet] returned to this subject [of her mother's last hours] Irene started to cry and said, "Don't remind me of those terrible things.

It was a horrible thing that happened in our apartment that night in July. My mother was dead, my father completely drunk, doing only horrible things to me. I had to take care of the deceased and all night long I did a lot of silly things in order to try to revive her."[6]

Was Irene cured? Was she well? What *is* cure? She had reincorporated the memory into her current experience, but she was still full of pain and distress, unable to stand the pain the memory had now burdened her with. No, she was not healed.

Only the experience of a loving Christ can *heal* such a memory. And this is why I insist on the church's role in such healings. It is also why I declare that healing is a sanctifying process. For Irene was yet to face her resentment against a cruel, selfish and heartless father. She had to know in her experience the love and forgiveness of God her heavenly Father (Mt 6:14-15) and to impart that forgiveness to her own father.

The Trauma of a Remembered Past

David Seamands records a healing of a memory which was certainly traumatic, but not traumatic enough to bring about a split in a stream of consciousness. It was a memory of a humiliation.[7]

A forty-year-old pastor recalled being humiliated his first day at school. His teacher had asked if anyone could write his or her name. Proudly he had raised his hand to indicate he knew how. The teacher, however, had insisted that the name Stanley be spelled with a *d*, as *Standley*. Knowing no other way to write his name, he twice wrote it as Stanley, thus subjecting himself to a barrage of mockery from the teacher, which caused the other children (who at that age have a tendency both to be cruel and to side with the teacher) to laugh at him. In the end he was forced to write his name with the misspelling. In Seamands's words, "his spirit was crushed." The mockery had reached him with all the power of a curse, with damage from which he still suffered at the age of forty. The first day at school is traumatic enough for some children, even without public ridicule.

The pastor's subsequent experience is interesting. "That scene seems stamped on my mind forever. I cringe and hurt inside every time I think of how the class laughed when she told them how stupid I was. And, worst of all, I accepted her evaluation."[8] His accomplishments, which were many, never convinced him that he was not stupid. He could see and appreciate them, but his logic and his feelings about himself were incongruous, irreconcilable.

Was his memory accurate? He would have said so. But does that matter? His perceptions of the incident mattered more than the memory's accuracy. Perhaps the teacher was not ignorant and malicious. The point is that his first day at school had been ruined. I have no doubt that he went home mortified, crushed. That being the case, the memory *as Stanley remembered it* called for healing, whatever inaccuracies it might have accumulated subsequently. It was the effect of the memory that mattered—its results in his subsequent experience.

The Trauma of Sexual Humiliation

What could be a traumatic memory for me might not be the same for you. Everything depends on a person's ability to tolerate a given experience. I believe I may have recorded the following incident in another book, but I have failed to find it (and am loath to trust my memory). Nevertheless, the essential detail is correct, illustrating as it does the matter of splitting from reality.

During my psychiatric days we admitted to the hospital a soldier who had gone AWOL (absent without leave). He was complaining of memory loss. His last memory was of being in a bar. He "woke up" to find himself on a bus "going home to Mom." In the bar he had been egged on to leave with a prostitute, but he had no memory of what happened subsequently. Several days were missing. The army wanted to know whether his loss of memory was real, admitting that the circumstances were very puzzling.

We gave him intravenous amytal in a dose large enough to calm his anxiety, to relax him to near sleep but not let him sleep. He was relaxed enough to talk, peaceful enough to remember without much pain, but not aware enough to evade our questions.

He had indeed left the bar with the prostitute, accompanying her to her room. His previous habit of boasting about amorous adventures overseas did not hold up. He was impotent when the supreme test of "manhood" was upon him. The prostitute was not the legendary golden-hearted whore. She had laughed at him, ridiculing him to scorn. At some point during the encounter he had split, unable to bear the humiliation. He "came to" on the way home to where his real security lay—to his mother.

We had not healed him. He had his memory back, but his head hung low and he was profoundly ashamed, not of going to a prostitute for sex, but of not being able to perform once he got there. As in the case of Irene, the restoration of the memory did not relieve his pain—it added to it. Only an experience of loving acceptance could relieve it. For loving acceptance he had, in his split condition, eventually turned toward the person most likely to provide it—his mother. He did not know our loving God, the real source of security and acceptance.

The human sciences are helpful, but not helpful enough. They cannot do what God alone can do—provide love that knows no limit. Nor do they deal with the issues of morality. The soldier would need to know sin and forgiveness; he would need also to forgive.

Scripture and the Root of Sin
Remember again Jeremiah's words about our hearts being very deceitful. He reminds us too that a God who is the soul of justice searches its secret depths: "I the LORD search the heart and examine the mind, to reward a man according to his conduct" (Jer 17:10). God alone knows the depths where secrets lie buried—including split-off experiences we could not face. Therefore, Paul describes himself as doing actions for which he had no explanation, "I do not understand what I do. For what I want to do I do not do, but what I hate I do" (Rom 7:15).

The existence of the unconscious goes back to the Fall of mankind, when our hearts became deceitful. Who can penetrate their secrets? Only God. Our actions are not the only clue to our conduct. God takes into account the motive—often hidden, even from ourselves. Therefore, the psalmist is forced to cry out in desperation, "Search me, O God, and know my heart; test me and know my anxious thoughts. See if there is any offensive way in me, and lead me in the way everlasting" (Ps 139:23-24).

David knows perfectly well what his anxious thoughts are. However, he is unaware of the reason for them. He knows what he is anxious *about*, but he does not know *why* he is so anxious. His question is, "Why am I like this? Could I have offended you? What hidden offense lies buried in my heart to make me like this?" The idea, the principle, has been known for thousands of years. Janet rediscovered or seized on an ancient biblical idea.

Paul wrote, "My conscience is clear, but that does not make me innocent.

It is the Lord who judges me. Therefore judge nothing before the appointed time; wait till the Lord comes. He will bring to light what is hidden in darkness and will expose the motives of men's hearts. At that time each will receive his praise from God" (1 Cor 4:4-5).

In response to the question "Does the unconscious exist?" John Smelzer says, "The most significant biblical passage concerning the unconscious, 1 Corinthians 4:1-5, suggests that it does. While Paul is not conscious of anything against himself, he is not acquitted (v. 4). The word 'conscious' is the Greek word 'sunoida.' It means 'to know together with' (someone or something)."[9]

You only truly know something when you know it with and in God. We all are thoroughly "messed up." The Fall affected our reasoning powers, our emotions, our consciences, so that none of these can be our guide. Therefore Paul, even having a clear conscience, is still not acquitted. God has to examine his heart for things of which he is not conscious. If he is not conscious of something, he must be *unconscious* of that something. As Smelzer expresses it, "It follows therefore that he must have an unconscious part of his brain which performs without his awareness."[10]

We forget some things so completely that we no longer have access to them until the Holy Spirit moves in and shows us the "split-off" portion of our psyches. When that happens it can be devastating. I remember one woman who screamed at what she saw as a split-off memory returned while fellow Christians were praying with her. The memory was of her father holding a knife to her throat during his attempt to rape her during her childhood. There was not only the terrible, burning pain of his attempts to penetrate her immature introitus, but the look on his face, and the knife at her throat. For years her fear of him had puzzled her, often causing her, even when other people were present, to leave a room if her father entered.

Only God has fully tabulated the mysterious dumping ground of fearful memories in some people's brains. Who of us can be sure of their access to the bank of memories stored chemically in our brains? No one. Only God knows them. Only God can heal them. And he longs to do just that.

CHAPTER 15
Forgiving Family Sin

The family was ordained of God that children might be trained
up for himself; it was before the church, or rather the
first form of church on earth.
POPE LEO XIII

For a son dishonors his father, a daughter rises up against her mother . . .
a man's enemies are the members of his own household.
MICAH 7:6

The family is more sacred than the state, and men are begotten
not for the earth and for time, but for Heaven and eternity.
POPE PIUS XI

*F*amily is more important than we think. It has a greater impact on our lives—for good and for ill—than we imagine. Both society and the church lack this understanding because they lack God's perspective. In this chapter I will consider how the state (and sometimes the church) can set children against parents in a destructive fashion when parents have wronged their children. Then I will look at how Christians have failed to understand the full extent of the effect of sin from one generation to the next.

Confrontation

There are times when abuse victims need to confront their abusers, especially when the abuser is an incestuous parent. Of the many means of grace we have focused on, memory healing is unique in the family and it raises unique social issues. We must therefore look at these.

I say it is *sometimes* necessary to confront, because as we shall see, a less assertive stance is in other cases preferable. But let me begin with an example in which assertive confrontation was needed.

Jim was a twenty-year-old male prostitute whose parents were into porn parties. He lived in a North American city. From his earliest childhood, Jim and his only sister, along with other young children, attended regular social get-togethers where they were paraded naked. They were left in a room where adults could come and admire them, fondle them, play with them, photograph them. This was supposed to be "fun" for both the children and the adults. As they grew older, Jim and his sister were repeatedly involved in sex acts with their own parents. Such relationships continued through their teenage years.

Jim professed to resent what his parents had done and saw himself as their victim. He felt they had shamelessly exploited him, and he sought our prayers, longing, he said, to quit the life he was leading. But he also noted that whenever he visited his parents he would automatically slip into an incestuous relationship with his mother. "I still have a need to please her. I don't like hurting her." He seemed to have no backbone, and he wanted us magically to give him one.

There is no doubt that Jim's parents were guilty of great wrong. *But Jim was still going along with that wrong.* He did not seem to have a sense of guilt, only a resentment toward a demanding mother. He would acknowledge his actions were sinful actions but was blind to the horror of them. Resentful and self-pitying, he was more concerned with the wrong done to him than with his own sin and his collusion with his parents as an adult. A professing Christian, his heart was unrepentant.

Clearly at some point his healing and sanctification would demand a confrontation with his parents, not in order to put them down, but to make his own standards and intentions clear. It would have to be, "Mom, what we have been doing all these years is very wrong. I see it now. It's got to stop. My relationship with you is a sick one. You know what it leads to whenever you start talking a certain way, or start touching me. From here on in, I'm not going to let you. Since I have found Christ, I see how wrong it is. That business will end—or I'll have to stay away from you until it does."

If his relationship with Christ is genuine, then he also owes his mother an explanation of the change in him. At present Jim seems to be resisting the process of change, so that his claims of wanting out of prostitution are not real enough for him to face his family members as they should be faced. Jim does not want help so much as magic.

The Place of Law

Another problem can arise with relation to confrontation. Jim's parents were still into porn parties, even though their own children were grown. They were busy having fun by destroying the lives of other children. What is Jim's duty to those children and to society? In much of North America, the law demands that this kind of activity be reported to the police. Jim must be prepared to testify in court about his parents' activities so that the law can deal with them, sending them to jail if necessary.

Police and social workers in some areas are anxious to stamp out a great evil, and they are often frustrated by the reluctance of children to testify in a court of law against their own parents. In Jim's case the matter is clear. What needs to be removed from society is a ring of child molesters involving many families.

In other more limited or less severe cases, there may be different considerations. To testify against one's parents in a court of law may have value in stamping out a vile social evil, but it may at the same time be destructive to family life, and I am going to argue that there are times when *even a bad family is better than no family*.

Two values clash. One is a healthy sexual environment for the child; the other is the importance of family as a basic building block in society. We do not face a simple issue of right vs. wrong; we live in a fallen society where we must frequently choose between the lesser of two evil choices. Divorce statistics tell us that the integrity of the family is valued little, even by Christians. Divorce, for all the pain of the experience, seems an easier or more attractive option than sorting the marriage out.

The critical question about incest is: At what point do we see a family as having irrevocably destroyed itself? Can incestuous parents be cured? Can they be healed enough to be able to live with their children again? Apparent cures are often followed by a return to the destructive behavior. Nevertheless, if we abandon the family too readily, we allow society to continue rushing downhill on a self-destructive path.

We can afford to abandon the family only when we absolutely must. In Jim's case, many families were involved in practices which were themselves destructive to society at large, not only damaging youngsters now but turning scores of potential future child-molesters into the world. Clearly, civil action by society and its appointed representatives is needed to prevent anything of this sort. And yet we must recognize that there are limits to what law can do in reforming society.

Police and judges are themselves sometimes involved in vile practices. As I write, Canadians are shocked by yet another child-molesting baby-sitting service in the sleepy little town of Martensville, Saskatchewan. Among those arrested are five police officers, two of them former chiefs of police in the community. In some areas social workers are being charged with child molestation. Judges in certain city centers are reported by witchcraft victims to be involved in the practice, being themselves Satanists. The practice is endemic throughout the whole of society, either as an expression of Satanism or merely as a pathetic human weakness. As long as it remains so, efforts to deal with the matter by law will never totally succeed.

There is another danger: The state can be set over and above the family in a destructive fashion. If the law is applied too vigorously, if children are unnecessarily called on to side with the state against their parents (when there is hope for correction or cure), worse damage may be done to the children and to society. Our continued failure to recognize the high value of family will end in destroying society itself, will create chaos—an even greater evil—in an attempt to control the evil we all want to oppose.

God invented family. It arises out of the being and nature of God. Because of this, it is something Satan has always yearned to destroy. Commentators argue about Paul's meaning in Ephesians 3:15, where he talks about the Father "from whom his whole family in heaven and on earth derives its name." I believe Francis Foulkes is right when, after careful examination of the Greek text, he says, "God is not only Father, but he is also the One from whom alone all the fatherhood that there is derives its meaning. . . . In effect the apostle is saying, think of any 'father-headed group' . . . *in heaven and earth*. Each one is named from Him. From Him it derives its existence and its concept and experience of fatherhood."[1]

I would add that a family's experience of motherhood also derives its existence and its concept and experience from God. All parenthood arises in him—and will therefore be a target for Satan.

The mission of John the Baptist had an aspect we rarely speak about. It reflected something dear to the heart of God: the restoration of the relationships in the family, of children and their parents. "And he will go on before the Lord, in the spirit and power of Elijah, to turn the hearts of the fathers to their children . . . to make ready a people prepared for the Lord" (Lk 1:17). We still look forward to a day of restored family relationships. It is something Christ paid for by his blood.

Positive Family Confrontation

Let me get back for a moment to the issue of confronting another family member. A group of Christians prayed for a woman I will call Janette. While they were praying, Janette recalled a long-forgotten conversation with her mother. She was shocked by the restored memory. The two had been close, and Janette, then a teenager, remembered she had been sharing with her mother the anxieties she experienced when she touched her own genitalia. The mother sought to be reassuring. But at that point there came a turn in the memory. In the daughter's memory the mother exposed her own body to Janette and asked her to touch what she was exposing.

According to Janette, the counselors had told her that the incident explained sexual difficulties she was experiencing, and instructed her to confront her mother with what may well have taken place. When Janette, fresh with the recovered memory and rejoicing in a healing she professed to have received, broached the subject, her mother at once denied that any such thing had taken place. The conversation, yes, she remembered clearly. She also remembered Janette's anxiety about dawning sexual feelings. But she could not relate to the account of her own exposure, much less her request that her daughter touch her (the mother's) private parts.

Janette's mother recounted the matter to me. It was obvious to me that if Janette's memory was a valid memory in its entirety, *the mother herself did not share it.* When I saw her, she was not acting a part but was quite bewildered by her daughter's story, so troubled and bewildered that she had sought me out. Either the exposure was totally blotted from the mother's memory, or else the daughter's memory was a memory containing other ingredients. But if the mother had not exposed herself, how had the "memory" arisen?

Sometimes there is no way of knowing, but in this case there was a very real possibility. The mother described to me the great difficulty she and her husband had experienced during a number of years. They had once lived in a small house, too small for their growing family. One room of the house was occupied by the woman's mother-in-law, who was senile. The senile grandmother was aware enough to dote on Janette, then only a small child. The friendship was disturbing to the parents, because the old lady perpetually left her door open and occasionally exposed herself, masturbating. They never saw the child with the grandmother on such occasions, but since the child frequently ran into the grandmother's room, and since the grandmother often called to the child and gave her candies, the mother was anxious. The father tended to pooh-pooh the idea that harm could come, which added to a certain tension between husband and wife over the mother-in-law's taking up a room in their little house.

The mother's question was simple. Could her daughter now be confusing two incidents, bringing the two together as one? I had to admit that, yes, that was perfectly possible. It happens all the time.

Let us be clear about two things. First, that God is a revealer of secrets. He reveals accurately and clearly. Second, that visions, words of knowledge, pictures in our minds, even memories come through the filter of our fallen personalities. God is faithful, and will always clarify things when confusion arises. The revelation of a memory under the influence of the Spirit is a communication from God, and as Thomas Keating expresses it, "One can get into all kinds of trouble. There is no guarantee that any particular communication to an individual is actually coming from God. Even if it is, it is almost certain to be distorted by one's imagination, preconceived ideas or emotional programming, any one of which can modify or subtly change the communication."[2]

Already we have discussed the issue. Recovered memories are not Holy Writ. They do not have the infallibility of Scripture. But let us suppose the memory was a real one, not a traumatic one, and that the mother had repressed it. What should she do? Or her daughter? An embarrassing impasse has been created. Mother and daughter stand on either side of a wall that neither of them enjoys and that neither of them wishes to vault. Neither can be certain of the truth.

We must remember who is behind the destruction of family life, and who is the true source of it. The widespread disintegration of Western families, whatever social and legal forces may contribute to it, has a satanic source. If it is to be overcome, it must be by means of an outpouring of the Holy Spirit in revival. And if mother and daughter come together, then it must be by biblical principles. Both must recognize that at present no certainty is possible.

If the mother has repressed a memory, then God can reveal that memory. Nothing will be resolved by an accusatory shouting match.

Or, if the daughter's recovered memory has been polluted by other elements, God can also make that clear. He is in the business of reconciliation. But it may take time. God has his own timetable in our sanctification and healing. We do not know his timetable with either mother or daughter.

It is for the mother to say, "Darling, I'm glad that this memory helps you. But I really have no memory of parts of it, though I could be wrong. At any rate, I am sorry for any way in which I ever did hurt you, because I love you and don't want to see you unhappy."

It is for Janette to say, "Mom, Satan is in the business of breaking up families, and you mean a lot to me. I believe what you say—you really *don't* remember what I think *I* remember. But God still reveals hidden things. Why don't we pray together that God will sort this out for us, and that he will help us resist the temptation to resent each other."

And both should think twice before sharing the matter any more widely, even in the family. The mother wouldn't want to, unless it were to win support against false accusation. The daughter, on the other hand, could be spreading a false accusation.

I think of three other families that have recently come to me with similar problems. I know that this sort of thing is going to happen more and more, for the underlying problems are common and widespread, and counselors and churches are getting in at the deep end in dealing with it. I admit that the scenario I paint with mother and daughter would take a lot of grace. But God is into grace. We are to be on his side where incest, possible incest and other family abuse are concerned. We want healed families where possible, not fragmented ones.

The issue is important, especially where the church is involved. Church discipline arises out of a gospel of reconciliation. It is above all things a reconciliatory procedure, a healing of alienation. To be such, the heart of the offended person, the victim, must itself be so drunk with the glory of Christ's forgiveness that it cannot spare one cubic millimeter of space for the proud and self-righteous stance of resentment.

The Family of Love

Not long ago I watched a television program featuring a mother's rescue of her children from their father. The father, who lived with the children in an Asian country, was a member of the cult known as the Family of Love, once called the Children of God. The movement, beginning as an evangelical entity, deteriorated over the years to something very evil. One of its evils concerned teaching children "to share their love." By instruction in the family, by the use of frankly pornographic comic books portraying parent-child sex acts (in fact giving instruction in erotic behavior), parents and children of the movement give themselves to evil.

The quintessence of the evil is that children are taught that evil is good. They are taught to see evil acts as holy acts. (What else is new? We have already seen that this was precisely the evil of the pagan fertility religions.) But children in the Family of Love are also instructed never to show the comic books to anyone outside the movement or to mention what takes place in the home. During the program, as the mother and a TV interviewer questioned the children, the younger ones freely admitted what was going on. But when in the interview the comic book was displayed, an older girl cried out in obvious distress, "People are not supposed to see that! It's not for showing to everyone!" Her face, her gestures, her distress came through powerfully. It was as though she were being the "good girl," standing up for what was upright in the face of an evil mockery of holy things. What picture, we may well ask, did that girl have of God?

In *Eros Defiled* I described my own molestation by a Christian worker who, to my parents' joy, took me on holiday with him to his own home. They told me (not realizing what they were saying) to be a good boy, and to do "whatever Mr. X tells you to do." What followed was embarrassing, horrifying, shameful. Most humiliating was the discovery that my pajama pants had disappeared. I felt very strange, naked from the buttocks down ("Oh, come on! A boy your age doesn't need pajama pants!"), kneeling beside the bed with Mr X's arm around my shoulder as we "prayed" together. It was a bed where we were also to sleep together. His wife used the guest room.

Long after he had finished, I lay in bed awake while he slept. God, I had discovered, dwelt in darkness. Perhaps there was no God. I could not find him for a long time after that. At times I thought I must be very evil. Paul was right. Children have a deep knowledge about what is sexually evil. Paul is correct as he writes to the Corinthians about sex and gender issues. As he puts it, "Does not the very nature of things teach you . . . ?"

Yes, children know. The girl who protested about the display of the "sacred" comic books could be rescued. Beneath the wrong standards that she had slowly come to accept as right (in her need to please her father and "be a good girl") there lies a deeper knowledge, implanted by her heavenly Father. But nothing would be gained by teaching her to deny or hate her father. The unlearning and relearning that she faced would take years. She must learn to be loved truly, learn forgiveness and cleanness, learn to respect herself, and from the firm basis of knowing love, forgiveness and cleansing, then learn compassion for a deceived man.

Parents and children may need to separate at times, but parent-child bonds are made in heaven, and we must be cautious about teaching a child to consider a parent to be an enemy. Certainly in the case of the Family of Love, the father is a sinner and may need to be separated from his children. But that does not end the relationship, and it does not mean he cannot receive the forgiveness of God and his family.

The Nature of Mercy

How did the community in Saskatchewan react to the public officials' involvement in molestation? With pain, with horror and dismay, but also with deep anger. Arrested police had to be shipped to Regina for their own safety. We have no place in our human hearts for the molester. Contempt, disgust, rejection and even hatred are the molester's lot. It is what they deserve, you say. Yes, but so do you. So do I.

Instead, Christ offered us mercy. We all owe a persistent offer of mercy to molested children and even to their molesters. But for molesters it must always be *the mercy of deliverance, and on the evidence of true repentance.* Our debt is to Christ himself, and he asks us to pay it to both sides, to the victims and to their offenders—who were so often victimized themselves in childhood, becoming victims of the malice of fallen angels, victims of darkness and of the forces of darkness, the spiritual hosts of wickedness in heavenly places. Powerless because of the sin in our midst, it is against those spiritual hosts we wrestle so feebly when we preach.

We must walk in forgiveness and teach it. Our model is God the Father. His heart never stops reaching out to the sinner. He is patient, longsuffering, "plenteous in mercy." He waits on the rooftop, scanning the horizon for the prodigal's return. Once he is sure who is coming, he rushes to meet him. His prime concern is not the precise degree of repentance. Look at the text of the parable in Luke 15. If you compare what the son planned to say with what he got time to say, you will notice a difference. The father seems to cut off the confession speech before the son finishes speaking, in the overwhelming joy of feeling his son's body, chest to chest, in his arms again (Lk 15:18-22).

The evil of parents who abuse their children in porn parties, the evil of families engaged in witchcraft, the evil of movements like the Family of Love are at least straightforward. Evil is evil. Sooner or later children must resolve their own stance and face their parents. But there are murkier cases, especially when we are dealing with the recovery of forgotten memories involving isolated incidents.

So What Can We Be Sure Of?

You can be sure whether you yourself truly know God's forgiveness. Knowing verses about God's forgiveness does not necessarily mean you really know it in the depths of your being. You can measure your apprehension of God's forgiveness to you *by the ease with which you can forgive others.* Often I hear the words, "Oh, yes! I know God has forgiven me," when the actions and attitudes in the person speaking represent a denial of their words. The speakers know forgiveness by intellectual conviction only. They have not experienced its depths with their whole person.

I have taken the trouble to examine this question in detail because I know it will become more and more important as more and more Christians come to terms with memories of past incest. Some already, wrongly instructed by would-be counselors, refuse to have fellowship with their parents, because the parents will not or simply cannot remember and acknowledge what their son or daughter claims happened in the past. Yet healing is possible even if my parent does not acknowledge the wrong that I say (possibly mistakenly) that he or she did to me. The idea that I cannot forgive (in the sense of experiencing a tender, forgiving attitude) until the person who hurt me has repented is also unbiblical. Only God has that prerogative. It is painful to face an unresolved issue between my parent and myself, but it does not have to be the end of all communication or all expressions of affection.

Healing Hereditary Traits

In discussing sin and forgiveness, we have already moved into the second area in which the importance of the family is not realized, this time by the church.

Many believe that nothing can be done about inherited traits, that one just has to struggle against them with God's help. Already I have pointed out that *both* environment and heredity are sources of your sexual sins and struggles. What is a Christian and biblical understanding of heredity?

I inherited sin. It came to me in my parents' seed. But to understand what this means, we must understand the doctrine of the seed as it is developed in the Old Testament. It is the view adopted by orthodox Jews. According to this view, my seed does not merely refer to the first generation of my children, but also includes the descendants that will follow them hundreds of years from now. It also means that my own seed carries sins from my remote ancestors.

Chaim Potok refers to this in his very moving and perceptive novel *My Name Is Asher Lev*. Asher, his hero, is a member of an orthodox Jewish sect, born and reared in New York. It is the story of the progressive misunderstanding he meets from other members of the sect as he pursues a career as an artist, even though he remains faithful to the sect. It is the story also of his struggle to be accepted by his father.

Early on in the book the father, who travels on secret missions rescuing fellow Jews from behind the Iron Curtain, is commenting on the treatment of Jews under communism. He seems both distressed and bewildered. "They kill people the way they kill mosquitos. What kind of human being kills another human being that way? To kill a human being is to kill the children and children's children that might have come from him down all through the generations."[3]

God is the God of families. We think of the earth's inhabitants in terms of nations, of peoples, forgetting that the original human way of looking at them was by generation. Seed has to do with descendants, and descendants with spreading families. God blesses families. The King James version of God's promise should not be forgotten: "and in thee and in thy seed shall all the families of the earth be blessed" (Gen 28:14).

Your weaknesses to sin have a particular pattern. Stealing may cause you no major temptation, but you may have to struggle against the urge to fool with your little daughter sexually. You've never done it, but you've come near it at times. Jim, on the other hand, finds himself slipping his arm around the waist of every woman he meets, while Mary's struggle is against bitter jealousy. People differ in what tempts them most. People of one ancient city will have a tendency to be more inclined to drunkenness, whereas another city may display a greater tendency to homosexuality. Scots are said to be more prone to resentment and suspicion, Welshmen to depression and self-pity, Jews and Chinese to too great a love of money. There is more than a grain of truth in such generalizations. The patterns come not only from wounds in a people's past (sins against them by others), but from the failures and sins of their forebears.

God decreed that this would be so. "The LORD is slow to anger, abounding in love and forgiving sin and rebellion. Yet he does not leave the guilty unpunished; he punishes the children for the sin of the fathers to the third and fourth generation" (Num 14:18).

God's ways may seem unjust to us. We have been indoctrinated with the world's point of view—and have mistaken it for God's. We have lost our sense of corporate responsibility, in spite of the confused web of genetic links that binds us. God punishes in two ways, first by certain inevitable consequences that follow a man's or a woman's sin—the loss of a fortune, the blame and opprobrium that fall not only on the sinner but also on that sinner's descendants. Second, God punishes by a proclivity in future generations to sin in a particular way. Moabites and Ammonites were known for sexual sin. From whence came the grip that Baal worship had on them? After all, their origin was the incestuous relationship between Lot and his daughters (Gen 19:35-38).

To understand why this is so, and why biological studies now link certain behavioral traits with genetic anomalies, we need to understand Scripture's teaching about the human seed. Covenants and promises concern descendants. Unlike the attitude in modern abortion—a self-centered concern about the immediate consequences of sown seed—Scripture looks wider and deeper, having a concern not only for the child, but for the many future generations that would have come from the child. The child in Scripture is seen as the vessel of the seed, the head of a future line of descendants. The term *murder* minimizes the offense of abortion. To cut off many future generations is even more serious than killing the one child. We are all links in a chain. We pass on who and what we are. Descendants are seen as a God-given right, and God takes the long-down-the-line view.

Thus Isaiah's lament over the death of the Servant-Messiah is a lament also over the descendants who would never be born: "By oppression and judgment he was taken away. *And who can speak of his descendants? For he was cut off from the land of the living;* for the transgression of my people he was stricken" (Is 53:8).

In the same way God weeps over what could have occurred had Israel obeyed him—if they had not followed Baal and Molech, had not needed to be purged by their Babylonian experience of judgment. *God's promise was not fulfilled to Abraham in the degree that it might have and could have been.* Recalling the promise he had made to Abraham, that his seed would be as the stars, he says: "Your descendants *would have been* like the sand, your children like its numberless grains; their name would never be cut off nor destroyed from before me" (Is 48:19).

Now let us talk about the doctrine of original sin. "In Adam all die," Paul tells us (1 Cor 15:22). The doctrine of original sin declares two things: that the consequence of Adam's sin is that I inherit a law or principle of sin inside me, and that it is sin that kills me, makes me mortal. *I* die because *Adam* sinned. My body will rot in a grave because of something Adam did. Thus two things have come down to me through my relationship to Adam: my proclivity to sin and my vulnerability to death. How did those things come down? Clearly through human seed. Sin is in some mysterious fashion passed on from one generation to another by means of infected parents. If this should seem startling to you, it may be that you have never thought through the implications of such biblical doctrines as original sin and the significance of human seed and our essentially bodily nature. So the sins of past generations affect me.

And in just the same way as physical traits from past generations may appear only episodically in a family (great-great-grandfather's nose, great-grandmother's blue eyes), so the proclivity to certain sins will also depend on the particular strains of my heredity that happen to make their appearance in me through what some people call the *blood lines* connecting me with the past.

Often we say, "He's a real musician. It's in his blood." It was in *Vanity Fair* that James Crawley made his famous remark about the "blood, sir, in hosses, dawgs, and men."[4] Shakespeare gets nearer to the point of inherited sin, when he talks of "any taint of vice whose strong corruption inhabits our frail blood."[5]

Confessing the Sins of the Fathers

It would be useless to talk about heredity if no practical gains were to arise from it. Can they? Indeed, yes! To understand how this may be, I need to refer to yet another biblical principle which I have dealt with elsewhere.[6] When godly people intercede for the nation of which they are a part, indeed, whenever we pray about the sins of anyone, *we are to identify ourselves with those sins,* accepting the blame for them as though we ourselves were also to blame.

Study Nehemiah 1, or Daniel 9. You will find that neither Daniel nor Nehemiah, when they mention the sins of their forebears, talk about *their* sins, which *they* sinned. Nehemiah says, "Let your ear be attentive and your eyes open to hear the prayer your servant is praying before you day and night for your servants, the people of Israel. I confess the sins *we* Israelites, *including myself* and my father's house, have committed against you. *We* have acted very wickedly toward you. *We* have not obeyed the commands, decrees and laws you gave your servant Moses" (Neh 1:6-7).

"*We* Israelites, including myself and my father's house, have committed . . ." The sins most discussed in the prophets center around idolatry (and its sexual implications), violent cruelty and oppression—the social consequences of sexual promiscuity. We have no reason to suppose that Nehemiah had ever practiced idolatry, and we can be absolutely sure that Daniel never did. They were not individually guilty, yet because of their links with their forefathers they shared in the corporate guilt. And they both acknowledged this in true repentance, with contrition.

On two recent occasions I have been amazed when, in reference to specific sins on the part of parents, grandparents or more remote ancestors, people have been encouraged to confess those sins, identifying with their forebears and confessing the sins as though they themselves also were guilty—as indeed the Scripture portrays the matter.

One person whom I personally observed said, "Sure!" and proceeded to confess specific ancestral sins which he knew of but was not personally guilty of. No sooner had a few words left his lips than a sudden awareness broke over him of the reality of his guilt. Gone was his easy manner. He began to weep. Before long a look of wonder replaced the expression of grief, as he became aware of changes in his being. Behavioral changes followed in succeeding months, in relation to the problem that the sins of his forebears had given rise to. When such identification-based repentance takes place, the grip of ancestral sin is broken, and Christians have authority to declare the chains broken. Chains of sexual sin, too, can be broken in this way.

After all, this is precisely what Jesus did in breaking the curse over us. At his baptism he identified with us *in our sin and guilt*. (The idea that his baptism was merely "an example" for us to follow cheapens the magnificence of his action.) What else was he doing when he stood in line? What else, but declare, "I have come to be one with you in your sin, to share its guilt"? He was to be baptized with a baptism of *repentance*. What need had he for repentance? Did he not hate and loathe sin? Did not his cousin John, sensing his great virtue, protest the idea of repentance in Jesus? Jesus had nothing to repent *of*, nothing to be released *from*, no chains that needed to be broken. Yet, in order that our chains might be broken, symbolically he repented, identifying with us in our sin, taking our sin on him as a preparation for becoming our sacrifice.[7] It is that very sacrifice by which he wishes to release us from our habitual sexual sin.

CHAPTER 16
Facing Your Repentant Future

The first step is to realize that one is proud. And a biggish step, too.
C. S. LEWIS

Repentance is the ultimate surrender of the self.
CHARLES COLSON

I n Hebrews 11:34 we read of people "whose weakness was turned to strength." Only the weak are granted salvation. There is no salvation for the strong. Therefore, if you are strong in sexual matters, read no further. The rest of this book is not for you. Certainly the rest of the book builds on what has been said already about gender and memory. Certainly psychology has a role to play. But no amount of psychological self-help can be a substitute for our weakness before God.

As for the sexually weak, we must cease from our very struggles, which will only cause us to drown. We must desist from the effort even of trying to yield to God. We are to wait and quietly hope for the salvation of the Lord. We cannot take the kingdom by storm. The violent who storm the kingdom are its enemies and will ultimately be crushed. Like weaned children, we wait quietly for the kingdom's gates to open. Rescuers come from within. Christ's strength, Paul reminds us, is made perfect in (our) weakness (2 Cor 12:9). And weakness waits. It does not cease to hope, even though hope is almost extinguished, can barely be felt or recognized. Weakness feebly hopes. The dawning of hope will be the beginning of a new day.

Christ, as a human being, is himself the model. On the cross he met force with weakness. And by weakness he conquered.

By weakness and defeat, he won the mead and crown,
Trod all his foes beneath his feet by being trodden down.[1]

It is the age-old secret of victory when we are coping with the powers of darkness. We meet our enemies (pride and force) with weakness, trusting a mightier arm than our own to save us.

Repentance

Weakness recognizes it has no hope in its own strength. It confesses none is left. All its efforts have been futile. Augustine began this way when eventually he came to an end of himself. He found he was powerless even to face giving up his sin. Leaving his friend Alypius, he flung himself on the ground beneath a fig tree, weeping and crying out, " 'And Thou, O Lord, how long? . . . How long this "tomorrow and tomorrow"? Why not now? Why not finish this very hour with my uncleanness?' . . . So I spoke, weeping in the bitter contrition of my heart. Suddenly a voice reaches my ears from a nearby house. It is the voice of a boy or a girl (I don't know which) and in a kind of singsong the words are constantly repeated: 'Take it, and read it. Take it, and read it.' "

He decided that God must have been telling him to take some of Paul's writing that he had been reading moments before. He did so, and opening the book at random his eyes fell on the words, "Not in rioting and drunkenness, not in chambering and wantonness, not in strife and envying: but put ye on the Lord Jesus Christ, and make not provision for the flesh in concupiscence." He tells us, "I had no wish to read further; there was no need to. For immediately as I had reached the end of this sentence it was as though my heart was filled with a light of confidence and all the shadows of my doubt were swept away."[2]

The time had arrived for God to go to his rescue. The words in the book came to Augustine loaded with divine power. Until that time arrives we must wait, but we shall not wait forever. When words of that sort come we begin to walk along a pathway of repentance. It is a pathway that ends beyond the grave. It is for life. On this pathway we enjoy a growing awareness of our smallness and sinfulness before a very great and altogether holy God. Yet we also grow aware of the results of his full and loving acceptance of us as we are.

I will never stop repenting. At times the repentance will be deep and very, very painful. But the pain will turn into sweet pain, the painful awareness of how greatly I have wounded him, yet of how tenderly, in spite of this, he loves me. At other times it will be a pathway of wonder and worship.

Charles Colson puts it this way:

But the repentance God requires of us is not just contrition over particular sins; it is also a daily attitude, a perspective.

Repentance is the process by which we see ourselves, day by day, as we really are: sinful, needy, dependent people. It is the process by which we see God as he is: awesome, majestic and holy. It is the essential manifestation of regeneration that sets us straight in our relationship to God and so radically alters our perspective that we begin to see the world through God's eyes, not our own. Repentance is the ultimate surrender of the self.[3]

What *is* repentance? I talk about it at great length in another book,[4] feeling that it is grossly misunderstood and mistaught in some Bible schools and even seminaries. I must be cautious and somewhat tentative in offering a definition, but I would say that *biblical repentance begins with a radically changed view of God and of sin (that can be the painful part) and proceeds with a change in direction—a conversion, always winding up in comfort and joy.*

Two questions arise immediately. First, how did that changed viewpoint come about? Who or what was at the bottom of it? Second, many older accounts are filled with distressed and weeping people. Were people long ago more emotional than we now are? How important is the distress?

Perhaps there is yet another question. Repentance and lifelong sanctification are connected. But you say: I thought repentance was something that happened once, when I was converted. Isn't it?

Life and justification are what are given once. They are given as your faith reaches up to receive them as gifts, as you trust the word of the Living One. But you go on turning, repenting, changing all your life. You will repent about your sexual sins and stupidities—as well as about every other kind— to the end of your life. The conversion I speak of in my definition is not a reference to justification but to a profound change of habit, behavior and attitude toward an aspect of life—in this case toward sexual sin.

David and Bathsheba

Let me go back to the question of a changed viewpoint. How did the change in David's viewpoint come about? David's blindness to his own adultery and murder ended with dramatic suddenness when Nathan, impelled by the Spirit of God, confronted him. Nathan turned David's burning anger (against an imaginary rich man who robbed a poor man of his one sheep) against David himself. Scales were torn from David's own eyes; his soul was searched with remorseless, searing light.

"Then David said to Nathan, 'I have sinned against the Lord' " (2 Sam 12:13). For the first time since he had been daydreaming on the rooftop he saw his sin with a new and disagreeable clarity, saw it in the light of God's holiness.

Repentance begins with a revelation by the Holy Spirit of our sin and of God's love and holiness. A dramatic intervention is only necessary when we are resisting that process. Sometimes God seems to allow our blindness to go on for a while before he deals with us, allowing us to learn by painful consequences before he shows us what we have done. You learn either by consequences or by illumination. And remember, *the painful consequences of David's sin remained to the end of David's life, even though he repented.* But, and this is what matters, he was restored to fellowship with God.

Some of us, however, are already overwhelmed by a sense of guilt, sometimes an unnecessary sense of it. In that case the revelation is more of the pardoning love and grace of God. The key to the process is a tender heart. The heart in Scripture seems to typify the whole of us, not just our emotions. But tenderness means *sensitivity.* A tender portion of your anatomy is a portion that responds very quickly to pain. Many of us harden our hearts. That is, we grow hardened, insensitive to the voice of the Spirit, shielding ourselves from the pain of seeing. Only God can soften a hard heart.

Who Does the Repenting?

You say, "I thought repenting was up to me. You make it sound as though repentance is something that happens, something I can't help, that kind of takes over. Surely it's up to me to face the fact that I'm twisted sexually and to do something about it. After all, when Peter preaches his evangelistic sermon, he talks about repentance as something his hearers must *do.* " Yes, Peter did say that. "Repent and be baptized, every one of you, in the name of Jesus Christ for the forgiveness of your sins. And you will receive the gift of the Holy Spirit" (Acts 2:38).

You must certainly face sexual sin, but as for doing something about it, that is precisely where the difficulty lies, isn't it? You cannot deliver yourself from a tendency to mess up sexually any more than a leopard can change its spots. Then is repentance something I do? Yes and no. After all, in that very passage in Acts, Peter is addressing people *in whom the Holy Spirit has already produced a terrible conviction of sin.* The effect of Peter's words was devastating. "When the people heard this, they were cut to the heart and said to Peter and the other apostles, 'Brothers, what shall we do?' " (Acts 2:37).

The process had to begin with a divine action, a revelation by the Holy Spirit. The same scales have to be torn from your eyes that were torn from David's. You have to *see* sexual sin the way God sees it, and only the Holy Spirit can reveal that to you. Your grasp of theological principles alone is of no help. Repentance is a collaboration with God in what he is trying to do in you. It is God-centered, not you-centered.

Emotion and Repentance

And that is where emotions enter in. Seeing is an experience, and when you see things the way God does, that seeing can be overwhelming. I am against emotionalism, but I must continually bear in mind that God created me an emotional being. Of course, too much emotion is bad. But then, too little can be the sign of approaching insanity. And most well-educated people of northern origins suffer from too little. We are cool customers whose upper lips are stiff—along with our necks.

Charles Finney (many aspects of whose theology leave me disturbed) hits a bull's-eye in his description of the repentant person: "In relation to God, he feels towards sin as it really is, and here is the source of those gushings of sorrow. . . . when he views it in relation to God, then he weeps; the fountains of his sorrow gush forth, and he wants to get right down on his face and pour out a flood of tears over his sins."[5]

I know that the end result of repentance is a change of mind and changed patterns of behavior. But those changes come about in relation to our being awakened to reality. The reality can produce something Paul calls "godly sorrow." Mere weeping is not to be equated with repentance. Paul was very clear about that. "Yet now I am happy, not because you were made sorry, but because your sorrow led you to repentance" (2 Cor 7:9).

Repentant weeping is *godly* weeping. There are two kinds of weeping in Pauline thinking, two kinds of sorrow—godly sorrow and worldly sorrow. Sorrow that leads to repentance is godly sorrow. True emotion is no enemy of faith, only emotion of a wrong kind, or for the wrong reason. Grief, too, comes in two varieties: godly grief and worldly grief. As Paul explains, "For you became sorrowful as God intended and so were not harmed in any way by us. Godly sorrow brings repentance that leads to salvation and leaves no regret, but worldly sorrow brings death" (2 Cor 7:9-10).

Repentance is a note too often missing from the melody of the gospel. *Saving faith can arise only in the context of true repentance.* The depth of emotion that so often accompanies repentance can be a measure of both the reality of understanding and the behavioral changes that follow it. Repentance alone can be enough to secure deliverance from some sexual bondages and addictions.

I am so grateful that Charles Colson (of Watergate fame) has left us an account of the night of August 12, 1973. It has nothing to do with sex, for sex is not what God is dealing with at this point in his life. Rather, Colson is sitting in his car in the dark. He has left politics for law, little dreaming what the future holds. He has just spent time with Tom Phillips, president of Raytheon, the largest employer in New England and one of Colson's clients. Phillips has recounted to Colson the story of a revolution in his life and has read him a chapter from C. S. Lewis's book *Mere Christianity*. Colson records his feelings as he leaves the house.

Outside in the darkness, the iron grip I'd kept on my emotions began to relax. Tears welled up in my eyes as I groped in the darkness for the right key to start my car. Angrily I brushed them away and started the engine. "What kind of weakness is this?" I said to nobody.

The tears spilled over and suddenly I knew I had to go back into the house and pray with Tom. I turned off the motor, got out of the car. As I did, the kitchen light went out, then the light in the dining room. Through the hall window I saw Tom stand aside as Gert started up the stairs ahead of him. Now the hall was in darkness. It was too late. I stood for a moment staring at the darkened house, only one light burning now in an upstairs bedroom. Why hadn't I prayed when he gave me a chance? I wanted to so badly. Now I was alone, really alone.

As I drove out of Tom's driveway, the tears were flowing uncontrollably. There were no street lights, no moonlight. The car headlights were flooding illumination before my eyes, but I was crying so hard it was like trying to swim underwater. I pulled to the side of the road not more than a hundred yards from the entrance to Tom's driveway, the tires sinking into soft mounds of pine needles.

I remember hoping that Tom and Gert wouldn't hear my sobbing, the only sound other than the chirping of crickets penetrating the still of the night. With my face cupped in my hands, head leaning forward against the wheel, I forgot about machismo, about pretenses, about fears of being weak. And as I did, I began to experience a wonderful feeling of being released. Then came the strange sensation that water was not only running down my cheeks, but surging through my whole body as well, cleansing and cooling as it went. They weren't tears of sadness or remorse, nor of joy—but somehow tears of relief.

And then I prayed my first real prayer. "God, I don't know how to find You, but I'm going to try! I'm not much the way I am now, but somehow I want to give myself to You." I didn't know how to say more, so I repeated over and over the words: *Take me.*

I had not "accepted" Christ—I still didn't know who He was. My mind told me it was important to find that out first, to be sure that I knew what I was doing, that I meant it and would stay with it. Only, that night, something inside me was urging me to surrender—to what or whom I did not know.

I stayed there in the car, wet-eyed, praying, thinking, for perhaps half an hour, perhaps longer, alone in the quiet of the dark night. Yet for the first time in my life I was not alone at all.[6]

The Supremacy of Grace

What happened to Chuck Colson happened because of grace. The grace that God gave him on that occasion was what theologians call *prevenient* grace, grace that comes to us *before* we find Christ, and without which we will never find him at all. You will notice that in the account above he makes that absolutely clear: "I had not 'accepted' Christ—I still didn't know who He was." We need the grace of God all our lives. Every time the Spirit shows us things, it is an act of grace.

Grace puts us in touch with reality. Most of us are not in touch with reality at all. We think we are but we're mistaken. To be exposed to the awesome realities of eternity is devastating. Poor old Ezekiel, after seeing the glory of the Lord, tells us, "I sat . . . for seven days—overwhelmed" (Ezek 3:15). We think we know about lost souls. We don't. If we did we would be like Ezekiel—overwhelmed. We think we know the horror of our own sexual sin. But we're wrong. If we once caught a glimpse of it, we'd be just as overwhelmed as Ezekiel.

Only occasionally have I seen glimpses of what lies beyond. It is more than I personally can handle. For three seconds (I would guess) I once saw the coming judgments of God on Canada. The vision was sudden. I struggled out of the armchair I was sitting in and yelled, "No, God, No! You mustn't do that! Stop! STOP!" I found myself with my hand raised and was shocked. Quickly, I sat down, frightened at what I had seen and at my own instinctive reaction. People around me were startled—we were in the middle of a prayer meeting, and I was embarrassed. But I shall never forget what I saw.

No. We do *not* live in reality; we are mercifully shielded from it. God has to let us have small glimpses of our personal reality. He shows us what our sin looks like in small doses. Even his love overwhelms us when he lets us catch a little glimpse of it. Our eyes are opened to reality, by grace, a little at a time.

The Approach to Repentance

You say, "I'm still not satisfied. You tell me the process has to begin with the illumination of the Holy Spirit. How do I get that? How do I make the process start?"

At last we have arrived at the real starting point. *You cannot make it start.* God has to start the process—and he has probably already started. If you doubt that, then your part is simply to ask him to grant you repentance, to soften your hard heart, to open your eyes. He will not necessarily do so the moment you ask, but trust him. If you really mean business, there is no question that he will start at once—assuming that he has not already started.

But do not delay. In the mind of the writer to the Hebrews, sexual immorality is coupled with giving up one's birthright. Notice what Hebrews says: "See that no one is sexually immoral, or is godless like Esau. . . . Afterward, as you know, when he wanted to inherit this blessing, he was rejected. He could bring about no change of mind [RSV, "he found no chance to repent"], though he sought the blessing with tears" (Heb 12:16-17).

Two things are apparent. First, you cannot bring about a change of mind in yourself about sin, sexual or otherwise. You cannot see as God sees unless he opens your eyes. Second, weeping is not at the heart of repentance. You can weep all you want and get nowhere. If God opens your eyes you may weep, or be shocked, or experience merely a gentle moving of the Spirit of God and be filled with wonder and awe. And the experience will be repeated again and again as long as you live and are tender toward him.

Ask God to give you what you need. Ask him to open your eyes. Sooner or later the process will begin. But do not delay to ask. Take the stance of a penitent. Tell him, "Lord, I recognize that my sexual carryings-on displease you. I know they are wrong and that I've grieved you. Help me to see them as you see them."

He may take some time in doing so, but in the end you will not be disappointed.

CHAPTER 17
Prayer: A Means of Grace

In this humanistic age we suppose man is the initiator
and God the responder. But the living Christ within us is the
initiator and we are the responders. God the lover, the accuser,
the revealer of light and darkness presses within us.
WILLIAM KELLY

Do not be deceived: Neither the sexually immoral nor idolaters
nor adulterers nor male prostitutes nor homosexual offenders . . . will
inherit the kingdom of God. And this is what some of you were.
But you were washed, you were sanctified.
1 CORINTHIANS 6:9-11

S exual sin can eventually become to the struggler what the ocean is
to a drowning man. You struggle as if your life depended on it,
alternately struggling and despairing.

I learned about lifesaving as a schoolboy, even winning the silver medallion (the highest award) in a lifesaving contest. I remember that in training we had to learn how to deal with the drowner's struggles, how to break various kinds of holds, the holds with which a desperate struggler would seize us.

Christ seems to have another technique. He waits till the right moment before rescuing. He alone knows when that moment comes. For a drowning person, this can be terrifying. If you cannot do anything else, you can and must struggle, must fight to keep your head above the surface. You battle

despairingly to resist terrible forces pulling you down. To give up is unthinkable. In fact you are not thinking at all. A deeper instinct has taken over—
one which you are powerless to resist.

Augustine (as mentioned in the previous chapter) had gotten to that stage.
There had been a time when he simply gave way to his sins of "wantonness
and chambering," but as he faced the claims of Christ he saw two things.
First, that Christ's way was the right way, the only way Augustine could
receive him; second, that he had not the strength to deal with the terrible
lust that gripped him. It was too much a part of him. To quit would be the
equivalent of tearing out his own intestines, his lungs, his heart. Sexual sin
and sins of other sorts were part of himself. Overwhelmed, he lay under the
fig tree, weeping bitterly. To Augustine it seemed like an impasse.

There is a form of prayer that expresses this kind of despair.

It waits before God in silence. The author of the book of Lamentations
speaks of it. "It is good to wait quietly for the salvation of the LORD. . . .
Let him sit alone in silence, for the LORD has laid it on him. . . . For men
are not cast off by the LORD forever" (Lam 3:26, 28, 31).

So we wait. Despairingly. *Before God.* And this waiting is not only a beginning. It is to become a way of life, a life that recognizes its own weakness,
its own powerlessness, its utter hopelessness. Even prayer—any prayer—
must be impregnated with this understanding. Prayer is nothing if not the
admission of my helplessness before God. Yet when I speak of prayer, I am
thinking about a particular aspect of prayer, the kind of prayer in which we
learn to hear God speak.

Two Kinds of Prayer

It is that form of prayer, above all others, that God is able to use to deal
with our sexual struggles—if only we will have the patience to learn it. Do
you trust him? Do you believe that he knows the miserable grip that sex has
on your life and that he already has a plan specifically for you? He knows
about all of your sin, all of your struggles, and whether or not he immediately does exactly what you want him to, he will get around to it in his own
good time.

All prayer is an expression of helplessness. Yet when we talk about prayer
we distinguish not two, but many, varieties, talking about petitions, suppli-
cations, intercession, confession, worship and so on. All must be character-

ized by the awareness of our weakness. Yet all of them can be divided into two basic varieties which Andrew Murray calls the *family* and *business* varieties.

> If I am in a strange land, in the interests of the business which my father owns, I would certainly write two different sorts of letters. There will be family letters giving expression to all the intercourse to which affection prompts; and there will be business letters, containing orders for what I need. And there may be letters in which both are found. The answers will correspond to the letters.[1]

And of the two varieties of prayer, it is the family kind that matters the most. For if the family is broken, what good does it do them that the business is successful? Why should it matter if it fails? Where do our values lie? Certainly, in spiritual matters, a broken church is of much less value to a broken world than a church united at its very heart. That is why, in his high-priestly prayer, Jesus besought the Father for unity, "so that the world may believe that you have sent me" (Jn 17:21). Only the Holy Spirit gives us such a church. And this is how the world comes to faith.

Family prayers are those that have to do with tenderness and love, with the intimate relationship with Christ himself which I rediscover every time God rescues me. The kind of prayers that most characterize this attitude are confession, worship, praise, adoration, the general ability to be silent in God's presence and to hear his word as he speaks to our hearts. Business prayers include supplication and intercession. There are thus two sorts of prayer, each dependent on the other. *For you have to be effective in both if you are to have real "success" in either.*

People who most get answers to prayer are people who hear from God, for in their brokenness they long to hear. The fact that they actually do hear from God becomes evident by the answers they receive. It is the proof that they hear correctly, for prayer is collaboration with God, his strength perfected in our weakness. You may, for instance, claim to hear from God when you are merely listening to your own deceitful heart. If so, you are unlikely to receive answers to your pleading, since answered prayer is prayer that is according to God's will. You have to know his will, both in Scripture and as the Spirit speaks to your heart, if you are to ask things that God will answer. He acts and we respond. *He has the masculine role, we the feminine.*

This sort of prayer can be learned. Impossibly difficult? No, for the Holy

Spirit is a teacher who is anxious to teach you. Ask him to do so. He longs to lead you gently into the ways of effective communion with God, a communion which will revolutionize your Christian experience.

I do not say there will be no times of difficulty, but I do insist that God himself longs to teach you. And sooner or later he will start to get at your sexuality. Once you are ready he will not waste a moment.

God's Voice

I have never heard God through my physical ears. Some people have. Most people have an inner impression, which is my own experience. Sometimes I "hear" actual words in this way, but just as commonly it is a nonverbalized impression. However, with increasing experience I am able to put words to those impressions with growing accuracy. The expressions, "I want you to . . ." and "Would you like to . . . ?" are quite different, and I have experienced both. The distinction is important. Yet with practice it can be discerned. The great evangelist George Whitefield had such impressions, but was persuaded by Jonathan Edwards not to heed them. In my view, this was unfortunate.

The experiences I described in chapter two were part of hearing God's voice. The strange instruction to remove my bathrobe and stand before God naked taught me two things. One was that my body was good, and the other, that the righteousness of Christ covered me. I was taking Sexuality 101— in God's school. I needed those basic lessons before learning others.

The terrible encounter with the naked exposure of Christ on the cross taught me many things. It taught me about myself—about my sinful eyes, about guilt, about the unbearable consequences of my own sin, about Christ's compassionate understanding of my difficulties. You say, "But surely all *that* is already in the Bible. Did you never read it?" Of course I did! I could have told you as much—and more. *But what I learned in prayer under the tutelage of the Holy Spirit was burned far more deeply into my soul.*

John Bunyan emphasizes the point. His own pastor, a man named Gifford, had taught him, "For, when temptation comes strongly upon you, if you have not received these things with evidence from heaven, you will soon find that you do not have that help and strength to resist that you thought you did." Bunyan states:

This was just what my soul needed. I had found out by sad experience the truth of these words. So I prayed to God that in nothing related to his glory and my own eternal happiness would I be without the confirmation from heaven that I needed. I clearly saw the difference between human notions and revelation from God.[2]

The principle is true also of sexual temptation. You cannot resist sexual temptation in an area that the Holy Spirit has not revealed to you personally from Scripture.

I have adopted Bunyan's rule for myself. Though I have read through the Bible more times than I can count and have a good notion of its contents, it is only those portions through which God has spoken to me powerfully that assist me when I grapple with the powers of hell. These have become weapons I can count on.

Positions in Prayer

You may have been taught to kneel rather than sit to pray. I usually begin by sitting. I may later be found kneeling or standing, lying on my face or walking. I may be silent, or anything but silent, may shout or sing. My arms may be raised or at my side. But mostly I sit quietly.

You should note two things about position. First, your mood changes subtly with the position of your body. I do not adopt any of these positions consciously. Only as I reflect afterward do I realize my physical behaviors during prayer. To stand with head up and shoulders back makes for a different mood than lying on your face. Second, and perhaps more important, you express differing emotions by your body posture. To lie on your face says, "I am overwhelmed. How dare I raise my eyes to you?" A time of prayer is a time when you should feel freedom to move.

Transformation

It is still important to grasp that God *wants* to teach you. My own constant battle is to remember that God cares, that he wants to teach *me,* that I do not need to hang back in guilt and shame. Over many years a slow transformation is taking place in me in relation to my sexuality. Looking back, I can now see that it has been God who has been pursuing me, but at the time I thought in my despair that *I* was pursuing *him.* There were times when I would grow discouraged and would neglect times with him. Then I would come across some book or other that would awaken the longing that had begun to grow in me and would start me off again.

Everything began with a commitment on my part—first a commitment to spend time in his presence, then, later, a commitment to learn to listen. Yet from my earliest years I had heard. *I was not consistently faithful to my own commitment,* but God was faithful.

Eventually there came a point when I could no longer tolerate his absence, when the longing for his presence, though it still waxed and waned, would not go away at all. At times it grew almost unbearable and I would cry out. Yet I cannot point to any time or incident when the intolerance began.

At this point in my life I have the faith and the patience to wait on him, knowing that, while I may not be experiencing marvelous raptures, I am always in his presence. Then I hang on, sometimes in stillness, sometimes worshiping quietly, at other times interceding. Slowly, over many years, prayer (the prayer that brings me healing) has been transformed. And when God chooses to draw near (an experience I have no control over), there is no way I can convey the glory. Yet I feel like the merest beginner. I not only feel it. I know it. For all of us are beginners and nothing more than beginners.

How the Process Began

I suspect the beginning of the process of transformation, which took place while I was still a medical student, was my discovery that there were portions of the Bible that made me angry. Usually some action of God in the Old Testament would do this. Before that, a lot of my prayer would amount to religious posturing. I would be busy trying to adopt the correct stance (appropriately respectful and reverent). Finally I allowed myself to get mad: "Lord, why did you do that? I—forgive me, but *I don't like that in you!* It scares me. Why are you like that?"

I would experience the fearful feeling that I didn't like the God I was seeking. But, though I was terrified, I had no other God. There *was* no other. The only true God was the one I was stuck with! Again and again I found myself saying (in fear and bewilderment) "Lord, I'm mad at you! I don't want to be, but I am! I know I've no right to be, but I can't help it."

On many of these occasions he would draw near. He would never explain himself. His very presence was the answer, stilling my heart, humbling me, changing me. If you question the appropriateness of my talking to a holy God like this, I can only say two things. First, to have acted otherwise would have been to add insult to injury. It would have been to pretend, to add a lie to my true, rebellious feelings, even to fool *myself* about my feelings. But I would not have fooled him. In any case, my anger could not damage him.

But there is something else. Read the psalms of David and notice his reactions to God. Notice his reaction at the threshing floor of Nacon (2 Sam 6:6-11). Read Job's terribly bewildered reaction in his grief and pain, in Job 16:7-18. And read Jeremiah 20:7—"O LORD, you deceived me, and I was deceived; you overpowered me and prevailed." This is how Scripture's giants of the faith behaved.

We say, "Come on! How can we compare ourselves with the greats of Scripture?" *Precisely at the point of their simple honesty before God!* As I grew more honest, treating him like a real person rather than a heavenly blob before whom I was "reverent," he became to me that real person.

When God Begins to Speak
In my personal experience, ninety-five percent of what God says has to do with his efforts to change me. Only five percent is for other people, and that five percent is a very frightening five percent.

How would you react, for instance, if you were addressing a group of evangelical Christian leaders and God were to say, "See that man there? He's in an active gay relationship. The man on the second row on your left is also. And the two men sitting with an empty seat between them in the back row have similar problems"? That actually happened to me.

Yes, but you are more advanced at this sort of thing, you may say. *It is not a matter of being advanced, but of being willing to obey.*

When God spoke to me about the homosexuals in the conference, I hated the experience. I was not ready to receive that sort of communication. In any case I am chicken when it comes to embarrassing situations. I didn't want to know whether my prompting came from God or not—not in the middle of an address about something entirely different! I concluded that it was "just my own imagination."

I did nothing about it then, but the next morning I had to. God would not let me wriggle out of it. The result was that seven homosexual relationships came to light.[3] They included those four men, three of them members of a senior committee in a well-known Christian organization. Within another twenty-four hours I was receiving telephone calls from desperate women who were saying, "Look, I've got a sexual problem and I just have to see you." Yes, God opens up ministry through his words to us at times. But remember, I said that ninety-five percent of the words are *for me*, to clean me up sexually.

Is it not possible to be mistaken about God's voice? To think we hear it when we are deceived? Indeed it is. John of the Cross warns us against the dangers. That is why you must *learn* to hear. How can you know when you hear correctly?

Already I have pointed out one way—by the fact that your prayers, prayers that arose from hearing God's voice, are answered. Or by the fact that subsequent events prove you are right. Another golden rule is that since God is self-consistent, what he says in our hearts will never violate Scripture. You just have to be willing to look like a fool. Anyone can make a mistake. It is more important to learn to hear God than not to look like an idiot.

In any case, how could I know "what the Bible said" in the case of the men who were in active homosexual relationships? How could I know that they really were doing what the Spirit told me? The only way I could know was by sticking my neck out, running the risk of looking both very foolish and very unfeeling. I had to forget about my dignity. But I had not been deceived. The men God spoke to me about were among the ones who came to light. It was rather like diving from the ten-meter board when the pool looks empty and discovering that it is full only when you hit the water.

Solitude

To hear what God is saying calls for *solitude* and *silence*. If you are broken enough, desperate enough, you will do anything. Abba Anthony (c. A.D. 251-356) was one of the desert fathers who fled from civilization because he saw it as a corrupt and sinking ship where true Christianity could not flourish. But in the desert he discovered that he had not escaped anything. He had brought the world and its corruptions with him into the desert. He had been molded by them and they were part and parcel of his character.

I remember seeing pictures of the temptations of Saint Anthony in paintings by Hieronymus Bosch (c. 1450-1519). If I understood the paintings aright, Anthony's temptations—at least in the vivid and lurid mind of the painter—included sexual ones. There was a hideous, ghastly beauty about the sexual aspects of the temptations.

Anthony spent twenty years in solitude, wrestling with his own character and with the terrible onslaught of temptations he suffered, determined that Christ would have his way in him. In the words of Henri Nouwen, he returned to civilization after those twenty years "an authentic, 'healthy' man, whole in body, mind and soul," to whom people flocked for counsel and instruction.[4] Commenting on this experience, Nouwen writes, "We must be made aware of the call to let our false, compulsive self be transformed into the new self of Jesus Christ. . . . solitude is the furnace in which this transformation takes place . . . it is from this transformed . . . self that real ministry flows."[5]

Was twenty years necessary? Does this mean we must go to the desert for twenty years if we are to be transformed? What biblical examples are there of solitude of such a magnitude?

Well, there are some, though the time the individuals spent was shorter. Jesus spent forty days in fasting and prayer in the desert. Paul the apostle spent three years in the Arabian desert (Gal 1:17-18) while John the Baptist spent an unspecified number of years there.

Revelation (hearing God) and transformation of character go hand in hand. But the heart of solitude lies within ourselves. It is more important to spend time in silence daily before the living God. Begin with just five minutes. Going into the desert may have value, but it seems to be the call of exceptional people. In previous chapters I have testified to experiences I have had personally which led to character transformation. Each was a learning with my whole self (not with the intellect alone) of lessons that the Holy Spirit taught me in the early mornings.

Will it take you that long? Perhaps longer. Take sexuality alone: it may be that there is only one thing that you think is bugging you. You do not know a quarter of what is wrong with you sexually. Once God starts to work on you, you may be very surprised. I thought there was only one very minor thing wrong with me sexually when I wrote *Eros Defiled*. Was I ever surprised once God started on me! He wanted to make me like Christ.

He wants to do a thorough job on us, to "do it right." Nothing less will content him. He is a perfectionist in the very best sense of the term, one whose standards are perfect, as he alone can be.

Silence and Stillness

Running across the surface of your mind every day is an endless stream of thoughts, of words, a jumble of imaginary conversations, arguments, situations, ideas, hopes, fears and worries—including sexual stuff. Thomas Keating[6] calls the stream the *false self.* The true self, the core of your being, is *you in Christ.* It is not the mere garbage that emerges on the surface of your mind. Prayer involves learning to detach oneself from the unending stream of thoughts on the surface (which is by no means easy) and finding one's way down to the meeting place with God, to the real self-in-Christ.

For you died, and your life is now hidden with Christ in God. (Col 3:3)

We were therefore buried with him through baptism into death in order that, just as Christ was raised from the dead through the glory of the Father, we too may live a new life. (Rom 6:4)

For it is there, in that sanctum where time and eternity meet, that place in your inner being where Christ and you have been made one, that the transforming instructions are given. That is where you must meet him. But you must accept the fact that God's order in delivering you will not necessarily be the order you would choose. Those sexual tendencies that most humiliate you may not be the ones God deals with first. He will get to them when the time is appropriate. It may well be that you have one or two preliminary exercises to learn first. But sooner or later he will get around to what concerns you the most.

For instance, it was passivity that caused me to struggle in silence and growing hatred against the Christian worker who molested me. I failed to shout to attract his wife's attention partly from embarrassment, but also because I was passive. I preferred to conduct my struggle with my molester in silent hate. My passivity was inherited from my father, an expert amateur boxer who was aggressive in the ring but passive in the home. I had overreacted all my life against the passivity in me by being too aggressive. The underlying passivity undermined my manhood, made me both manipulative and unnecessarily aggressive rather than loving—even in a sexual relationship.

One day in the silence, as I waited on him, God spoke. "Why do you not accept your father's passivity? After all, it is in the genetic code of your body."

I was alarmed, and a little angry. I knew I had never accepted it. I did not have the least desire to. I was too busy fighting a tendency I hated and wished to overcome. I asked, "Of what use is my father's passivity to me?"

The words that came back hit me hard. "I cannot deal with something you deny you have. It must first be brought to me."

I thought for a while, knowing that what he said was true. Finally, feeling rather depressed, I said, "Okay. You're right. I accept it."

Immediately, as it were, "through" the back of my head, I could "see" standing behind me a long line of shadows. They were the shades of the men from whom I had descended. A sorry lot. But *they were the route God chose to bring me into this world.* I knew then that you cannot be a man apart from a context, the context of your own male ancestors. Christ can redeem only what is *there* in us and we are willing to bring to him. He cannot (or does not choose to) change our ancestors. But he can and does change us.

But where can we find the time to let him do so? Obviously it takes time. *We already have that time.* We are too enslaved to the world's program of rush and hurry to realize it.

Silence, Stillness and Life's Hectic Pace

We rush because we are enslaved. Anthony Bloom talks about "moments when you have absolutely nothing to do," and finds in such moments one test of our enslavement *to* and *in* time. Let me give you an example.

Frequently I arrive in an airport in a late-arriving plane. I have to hurry to the gate of my connecting airline, and I dodge between people coming from the opposite direction, hoping I will not arrive too late at the gate. I get there—and behold, the ongoing plane is delayed for half an hour with some mechanical difficulty. From long experience I know that the half-hour delay could be extended considerably before the problem is rectified. Suddenly I have been switched from rush and hurry to having an unknown amount of time on my hands.

I struggle to readjust my thinking. Perhaps there is another airline going to my destination? I shake my head, thinking of the fuss involved in finding out and in arranging for my ticket to be changed. I hate rush and fuss, and I want a bit of peace and quiet. However, fighting my native passivity, I check at the desk for information about other airlines.

The clerk is unusually helpful. He doubts whether there are any others for my particular destination, but he will inquire to make sure. I put my briefcase down and sink into boredom as he begins to type into his computer terminal and makes one or two telephone calls. Finally he says, "Yes, there is one, and

I don't think you'll want it. It doesn't leave until ten tonight." I glance at my watch (that little god on my wrist to whom I am enslaved and by whose dictates I regulate my life) and think, "Three and a half hours from now." The clerk is still talking. "It's a milk-run that would get you there at one a.m." I thank him and sit down. I feel unsettled.

Purely from habit, I open my briefcase. Perhaps I will find a solution to my restlessness inside it. I could read a book—preferably one easy to read—or glance through a magazine. Or I could get some files out, because I have work I could do.

What is happening to me at this point? I have time on my hands and I prefer to fill it with work (I am a workaholic) or with some form of distraction (I am lazy). But I know what God calls me to do because I know something about the experience of his presence. I could seek God's face as I sink into the rest of the joy of the eternal silences. I could do so *not as a religious duty,* but as an exercise in learning not to be enslaved to time.

Yet a strange reluctance seizes me. Do so here? My thoughts are all over the place. Won't it be impossible? I shrink from the effort. For some curious reason, I shrink from the very thing I most need: peace and quiet, the sense of the Holy Presence. I'm not in the mood. I am suffering the penalties of my enslavement to time and its corresponding fear of eternity's calm.

Sighing, I start. I remember that the omnipresent God is present even here. I also remember that by his Spirit he dwells in my own body. His whole Person is in me and yet he is, as Creator and Sustainer, all around me. Soon, hope and a smidgen of peace steal into my heart and I murmur, "Oh, thank you, Lord!" My mind fluctuates between my circumstances, fragments of conversation with the clerk . . . and God's presence. From habit, now, I keep letting other thoughts go their way and turning them back to God. A few minutes later and without thinking, I stretch hugely, then sigh contentedly and relax. I murmur with real feeling, "I bless you, Lord!"

Some time later there is another announcement. I do not bother to consult my watch. The loudspeaker asks people who have small children or who need assistance to present themselves. Then, in no time, there is an announcement affecting me. I find myself stretching again before getting to my feet. I am smiling—smiling at the people to whom I give place as they hurry to be first in line. Curiously, I almost love them, aware in my heart that I am loved myself. I am one step nearer to being freed from the bondage of time and the fear of eternity, for, however dimly, I have been drinking a little of its peace in God's presence.

The Inner Sanctum

The sanctum within is a place of silence and stillness, so silence and stillness are what we must seek. It is a quiet, restful place. Stillness and silence make solitude a reality. Solitude, stillness and silence facilitate hearing God's voice. There is a hymn we often sing as a mood song (a bad use of a hymn) without any real anticipation of its request being answered. Or if our hopes do lie in that direction, we confine those hopes to the time of the meeting or church service at which we sing.

> Speak, Lord, in the stillness,
> While I wait on Thee;
> Hushed my heart to listen
> In expectancy.
>
> Speak, O blessed Master,
> In this quiet hour,
> Let me see Thy face, Lord,
> Feel Thy touch of pow'r.[7]

The hymn writer is plainly describing something she herself knew by experience. It is something you can know, too, something God's loving heart longs to share with you. It is for ordinary Christians, not just for advanced mystics. It is the prerogative of every child of God. There are ways of learning how to find it, and in the appendices I have included a list of helpful books. But do not wait until you have read a book. Seek God in the stillness today. Already he seeks for you.

Yet why does the surface of our minds so run with words? What is it about our culture, apart from rush, that makes for such intense difficulty when we seek silence? Henri Nouwen says we are "inundated with words." He tells us that once when he was driving on a Los Angeles freeway, he got the impression he was driving through a large dictionary. "Wherever I looked there were words trying to take my eyes from the road. They said, 'Use me, take me, buy me, drink me, smell me, touch me, kiss me, sleep with me.' In such a world, who can maintain respect for words?"[8]

Sexual temptations especially come through words and the images they conjure up in our minds. *They come even when we seek the silence of God's presence.* Today a Christian woman was telling me, "The time is so short. I feel I must stop fooling around. But my mind is so full of impure thoughts."

I said, "Tell Jesus about them. He knows, anyway! Tell him, 'This is the way I am.' Don't feel so bad about it. Don't resist the thoughts, but rather *let go* of them. Let them float away. Every time they recur, do the same thing. Don't fight them."

Words only acquire deeper significance against a backdrop of silence. We should talk less and listen more—especially to our Creator-Redeemer. His words resound through eternal silences. For the words that matter are not the words I am now writing, but those words God will speak in the silence of your heart.

Focused Prayer

Already I have referred to the stream of words and impressions that sweep across our minds continually. People who successfully learn about silence have learned how to detach themselves from the stream. They tell us that to fight against wandering thoughts is a frustrating waste of time. You will never succeed in stopping that flow of thoughts. Let them pursue their own merry way! Some people tell us such thoughts are like interesting boats drifting past us downstream.

If you find yourself climbing on one of the boats out of interest, remember what your aim is. Let them go, release them, and you may begin to find that God is still there. William Kelly says, "When you catch yourself again, lose no time in self-recriminations, but breathe a silent prayer for forgiveness and begin again, just where you are. Offer *this* broken worship up to Him and say: 'This is what I am except Thou aid me.' Admit no discouragement, but ever return quietly to Him and wait in His Presence."[9]

A year or two ago I was walking in the early morning beside a canal in the English countryside. As I walked I happened to be in touch with the silence and was communing with God. Then something at the edge of the canal attracted my attention, and I turned and stood staring at it. A moment later, I remembered with shame that I was supposed to be walking with God.

Instantly I turned and glanced at—at what? For suddenly I was a tiny child, and the memory of my earthly father came back. We had been walking together when I was distracted by a butterfly and squatted to examine it, absorbed with wonder. Then, remembering Daddy, I turned anxiously . . . to see him standing patiently, smiling as he waited. It was as though my heavenly Father now stood waiting, smiling at his so easily distracted child.

Patient persistence in turning back to him is what prayer is about—day after day, week after week, month after month, year after year. But the rewards far exceed the cost. And it is in this way that most of my own sexuality has been sorted out.

CHAPTER 18
Healing Hidden Wounds Through the Body

Nor can a man with grace his soul inspire,
More than the candles set themselves on fire.
JOHN BUNYAN

By the grace of God *(Dei gratia).*
LATIN PHRASE

God yearns with fatherly yearning to heal you from your proclivity to sexual sin. He wants to make you like Christ. To do this he uses means to that end, means of grace. Already we have looked at two means of grace, repentance (chapter sixteen) and prayer (chapter seventeen). In this chapter I want to look at the grace of God that the people of God have ministered to me. Such people were the *means,* the channel by which God's grace came to me. However, *you have to be willing to receive help from any source God offers.* You cannot afford to be choosy.

The Naaman Factor
Naaman had a lofty position. He was supreme commander of the Aramite forces (2 Kings 5). As such, he was accustomed to relating to people in a certain way. He commanded lesser beings. He understood the concept of hierarchy. He operated through channels and by protocol. Naaman also had a problem. He was a leper. And he was desperate for a cure. One source of

help was to be found in Elisha, the prophet of Israel.

Israel at that time in Old Testament history was in decline, and Aram was a great nation. So Naaman would have to show great humility on two counts: first, for a commander to ask anyone for help, and second, for an Aramite to ask for help from an Israelite, someone from a nation he looked down on.

His pride was battered further when the prophet Elisha refused to see Naaman and merely sent a servant to speak to him. In addition, he was told by the servant to go and wash seven times in the miserable little Jordan River. It was unthinkable! The insults piled on insults incensed him.

The story is often used as children's Sunday-school material. It should really be material for adults, for Naaman's pride and rage are similar to our own. For me to descend from my psychiatric and ministerial pose was not, and is not, easy. To be sure, it was not only a pose. I really did have the kindest feelings toward patients, and also toward members of my congregation. I prayed frequently and individually with both—there in my office or after a church service. But my role was to counsel, to pray for others, to help others. I was a helper, not a "help-ee." I was comfortable in the role I understood. If I were to seek help, it would have to be from someone higher up in the hierarchy of helpers—and there were few people who qualified—or so I thought.

It never occurred to me that someone "lower on the scale" could minister to me. "They" were help*ees*, not help*ers*. My beliefs were orthodox: Of course, the Holy Spirit could use anybody. But he was very unlikely to! That is, I could not conceive of his using younger, less experienced people to help *me*.

It was a big mistake. I began to find that, while experience certainly helps, God seems to be able to use almost anybody. I needed to be humbled, willing to receive help from any quarter, from anybody a sovereign God chose to use for that purpose. It was an enormous step, but a step that is an investment paying rich dividends. I suspect many of us who are counselors or pastors need to learn a lesson here. Ask yourself the question: How comfortable would I be to receive spiritual help from one of my clients—to have our roles reversed?

The Church

The church, the body of Christ, was intended among other things to be precisely a place where anybody can help anybody. John Wimber speaks of the church as being by turns a nursery for the newborn, a training and teaching institution, an army in the battle with the powers of hell, and a hospital for the wounded (whether the battle-wounded or the damaged and wounded newborn). If the local church is to become like this, then everybody in the church has to be mobilized.

Few local churches function in all four areas. Yet I believe all were meant to do so, and there are signs that some churches may be doing so. One reason for the failure of many churches to heal the wounded is that, as we saw very early in the book, many pastors are themselves involved in sexual sin, as are many elders and deacons. In many such churches no one wishes to bring the matter into the open, and in others the church now proclaims that certain forms of sexual sin are not sin at all. Satan has been highly successful in making sexual sin an inroad to other forms of sin!

Nevertheless, God's counteroffensive has begun. I believe it may indicate the "wave of the future." A greater degree of flexibility is returning to some of our relationships in the church. Some help*ees* are becoming occasional help*ers*.

God's People Who Minister Grace

God's grace is being ministered through his people in the area of sexual (and other) sin. What are you likely to encounter from such servants? How do they go about what they do? One thing you will certainly encounter is what I dealt with in chapter fourteen, the area of "split" and forgotten memories as well as other issues already reviewed.

At the moment, there is still a lack of workers proportionate to the need. Their work is confined to various conferences and courses. Some conferences are limited to sexuality. Others have a more general approach, but one that includes sexuality. Prominent among the emphases you will come across as they pray for you will be the grace of God, the place and significance of mental pictures, and issues surrounding forgiveness. In this chapter we will look at these emphases. Already we have explored others.

These helpers may spend much longer praying for you than you might be accustomed to. A healing session may continue for three or four hours. Where there is faith in God and a real sense of his presence, his servants *want* to pray, want to call on him for aid. Inquire when and where such conferences are held. Seek out literature describing methods of healing and sanctification.

(I list the names and addresses of agencies willing to help you, as well as books you can read, in the appendices at the back of the book.)

God's Exceeding Grace

John Bunyan tells us (in the quote that heads this chapter) that you can no more produce the grace of God by your own efforts than a candle could light itself. He says this in a book he wrote for children. Children understand grace, and they never stop pleading for it from their parents. Grace is what God gives you when you deserve nothing but hell. Healing and sanctification come to us by grace, even though we may be totally unaware of that grace, attributing its effects to psychology or whatever. Certainly you cannot inspire your own soul with grace. God has to light your candle for you.

Yet there *is* grace for you if you want and need it. It has come to me along ways I have listed above, including the recovery of sins of the past which I had forgotten completely or whose real nature I had never before seen. And God has similar ways of dealing with sexual sins and occult practices through his people.

A Personal Experience of a Traumatic Memory

One healing I experienced took the form of repentance. But it was a repentance that occurred while others ministered to me. Two people were praying for me, a man and a woman. They told me that many others were praying— and I could tell. There was something about the whole time I spent with Dick and Anne (not their real names) that impressed me deeply. I saw them as more experienced than I in God's healing ways.

They spent quite a while allowing me to share my concerns with them, asking me questions from time to time. My concerns took the form of spiritual problems I struggled with. After a while we broke for coffee, then resumed after about fifteen minutes. They then anointed me with oil, not just because of the passage in James, but to remind us all of our dependence on the Holy Spirit. Immediately a couple of unusual things happened. First, the oil on my forehead produced a strong burning feeling.

"What on earth have you got in that stuff?" I asked.

They both smiled. Dick said, "It's just common anointing oil. People react differently to it. Most people feel nothing. A few people complain as you have about burning, and one or two others develop a swelling where we mark a cross." An allergic response? Perhaps. But I never felt a burning upon subsequent anointings with the same oil.

My second reaction was very significant. Over many years I have slowly learned to discern when an exceptional anointing of the Holy Spirit's power comes on me. One of the ways in which this happens is that I experience a weight, a sense of heaviness.[1] On that occasion, such was the weight that I could hardly move. I am *not* a suggestible person, and several attempts to hypnotize me during my psychiatric residency all failed. I have long since rejected hypnosis.

Immediately also, part of me became three years old while the rest of me remained adult. I cannot explain this, but it was very vivid. I became aware that when I was three I knew Jesus, not perhaps as Savior, but as someone who took care of me and whom I loved. This surprised me. I had no idea of it and had forgotten completely. Yet immediately on the heels of the awareness came bitterness and anger. "Why did you leave me?" the three-year-old part of me cried. "Why did you go away?"

"Did he really go away, John?" Anne asked.

I seemed to be two people at the same time. At once the adult part saw that Jesus could not have abandoned me. *I* had turned my back on *him*. I had stopped trusting him, assuming he had left me. Aware of the fact that I must have grieved him, I began silently to weep. Before long I was telling him how sorry I was that I had grieved him, and was asking his forgiveness. I felt it keenly.

Forgiveness for the "sin" of a child of three? Sin is sin, as deadly in a three-year-old as in an adult. Perhaps more deadly. In this respect it compares with cancer. Cancer is more virulent in young children. Let us be under no delusions about the deadliness of sin. Anything that occasioned the death of the Son of God must be horrendously dangerous.

Lost Pieces in a Jigsaw

One thing I had shared with Dick and Anne concerned a memory that had haunted me for more than sixty years. The memory was a loose piece in the jigsaw puzzle of my life. The space into which it might have fit was missing. Yet it was a memory that was clear and real every time it came.

I was alone in a streetcar at the age of three, staring frantically through the window trying to recognize where I was, so that I would know when we were near my home. As I stared, I would think I recognized a building, but I could never be sure. My desperation grew moment by moment. The memory was like the memory of a nightmare. Yet it was no nightmare but a real memory. What could I have been doing alone on a streetcar at the age of three?

And what of the memory itself? Was the streetcar scene real? I had puzzled over it for years, begging the Lord to tell me its explanation. If it was real, where were my parents? Years before, the mystery had been partially solved. One day, as I asked God about it, he had given me a very vivid picture.

It was of my father, not as I remembered him later, but as he would have been when I was three. He looked to be in his early thirties. I saw him dressed in gray, wearing a gray homburg hat and a pearl gray suit. I have forgotten the color of his tie, but I remember that he had a pearl-topped pin in it. He was carrying yellow pigskin gloves and a neatly furled umbrella, and he wore gray spats over his shoes.

But it was his face that frightened me—not that it should have done so. He was grinning with amusement. Yet when I looked at him my heart had begun to pound with both rage and fear. I realize now that the rage and fear belonged to my three-year-old self.

As I recounted the memory, Anne suddenly said, "I think your father had been playing a joke on you." In a flash I knew what had happened. We had been setting out for home after the "morning meeting" at our Plymouth Brethren assembly in Stockport one Sunday. We rode the streetcar. When it arrived I was the first to get on. The streetcar was a "double decker," but because we always sat downstairs I had marched proudly between the two rows of seats showing that I knew what to do.

Parts of the memory are still missing. I must have turned to look at my parents and found they were not there. But I still do not remember doing so. I can *imagine* the moment of terror when I found myself alone. The streetcar must have begun to move and, doubtless, terror would have overwhelmed me. I was cut off from my parents. A terrifying moment of that sort *must* be registered somewhere.

I can *imagine* what had happened. My father must have nudged my mother, indicating by a toss of his head that they should go upstairs. He would have been grinning as he did so, grinning in the way he was when he later descended, anticipating my relief. No doubt my mother would have protested, but evidently he got his way.

While I do not remember the actual encounter with my parents as they came down from the upper deck, the picture God had shown me of my father was probably the way he looked at that moment when it was time to get off. It was that grin on his face that must have terrified and enraged me. But that is my reconstruction, not a memory.

Certainly, I never trusted my father after that. Long after I forgot its cause, the mistrust itself continued. He was not a cruel man—he had always been surprisingly gentle. I suppose he had assumed I would be as amused by his joke as he was himself. But in that he had seriously miscalculated. As I grew older I resisted his attempts at closeness until I was in my twenties. I never identified with him. Many of the sexual problems that arose in my life had their roots in the incident. I had retained only a portion of the memory because at some point it had been split off—significantly, at the beginning and the ending.

To this day I cannot handle being lost. I go to elaborate pains with maps to make sure I find my way. My mind freezes when I am lost, and I am unable to make myself think the problem through. And I have traveled alone all over the world! There still are occasions of this blind terror.

Nevertheless, the gender healing began as Dick and Anne prayed with me. Its root was dealt with. I now knew what had taken place. As for my father, I could hold no grudge against him. How could I do anything but forgive— not only when I understood the circumstances, but as I experienced the forgiveness of God to me as I wept in repentance when the interview began. Whether I will ever know healing from that infantile terror of lostness I do not know. It is really a small thing to put up with. I record it to illustrate the fact that God can reveal and use—and heal—our memories, even the split-off kind.

Mental Pictures of God

As you seek sexual healing, you may encounter among evangelical Christians different approaches to "seeing" things in your mind. First, let me point out that it is something we all do to some degree. We picture things. "Yes, I can just see him doing that," we may say. Or, "You know, I see her face, but I don't seem to be able to recall her name just now." Or, "Yes, I know that street well. I can just picture it in my mind."

Certainly God's people down the ages have seen some pretty vivid pictures. When John saw the risen Christ in Revelation 1 (before being invited "up" in Rev 4:1), what was he seeing? *A vision,* you say. And what is a vision but "seeing with the heart"? I know some visions are far more vivid than others, but all experiences of this kind represent a revelation to us of reality, of what is. But reality often has to be coded in a symbolic form. Raw reality is at times more than we can take. In any case, our natural eyes are not adapted to seeing spiritual realities.

When Elisha asked God to open the eyes of his servant, it was his heart's eyes that God opened (see 2 Kings 6:17-20). Our spiritual eyes need to be quickened by the Spirit of God, and then what we see can be seen with our physical eyes either open or shut.

The most dramatic "seeings," I find, come without our asking, totally unbidden. These one could see, I am sure, whether one's eyes were open or not. Mine have always been open when this has happened to me. I've never shut them to validate my theory, because I've been too overwhelmed by what (or whom) I see to worry about theories. But quieter and less obtrusive pictures are best perceived with eyes shut. All pictures are "seeing with the heart" as it is quickened by the Spirit.

Instructing People to "See" Jesus

"But we see Jesus," says the writer to the Hebrews. He also exhorts us with the words, "looking unto Jesus." Is he not using metaphorical language? Yes, of course. But where do metaphors come from? How does a writer produce one? *He or she sees a picture in the mind* and says, "Yes, that's it!" A picture elaborates itself so easily and quickly that writers may not even be consciously aware what of they are doing. Many of us do it all the time. This is a God-created function which God gave us when he created our brains, devoting the right hemisphere to what we mistakenly call intuitive processes. Those of us who are "right-brain" people will function more easily in this area, while "left-brainers" will tend to be more at home with discursive logic.

I remind someone who has had a certain cruelty or bewildering event take place in the past that *Christ by his Spirit was there.* He is omnipresent, always and everywhere present, whether perceived or not. This is reality. However, it is a reality that surprises the people when they think of the horrendous thing that happened to them.

Then I pray that God will enable the person to see what Jesus did, or wanted to do, on that occasion. I have been astounded again and again at what happens. Solutions I could not have conceived become apparent. The Holy Spirit, who alone knows the needs of each heart, ministers to it according to its needs. Often the person weeps for joy and wonder. I, for my part, realize over again that my role in the whole affair is negligible, that God and only God is doing the real work.

I have some misgivings about asking people to see Jesus, because of some experiences I have had with people with an occultic background. It has not happened frequently, but the Jesus they see may not be Jesus at all.

The Struggle with Forgiveness

In chapters ten and eleven we saw that many of our sexual struggles have their roots in confusion about our gender identity. The healing process includes this but, even more importantly, our sanctification as well. We see that forgiveness plays a critical role here, and that our own ability to forgive is related to how real God's forgiveness is to us.

I cannot exaggerate the importance of forgiveness toward those who have wronged us. You will find talk about it wherever people discuss healing. And when you encounter such talk you usually are standing on holy ground. Saving faith is faith of the heart, not just of the intellect. Demons believe—and tremble. Paul makes the matter plain: "If you confess with your mouth, 'Jesus is Lord,' and believe in your heart that God raised him from the dead, you will be saved. For it is with your heart that you believe and are justified" (Rom 10:9-10).

Why my emphasis on heart? It is because Western education overemphasizes intellect, assuming that an intelligent grasp of something makes all the difference. Not so the Bible. B. O. Banwell notes,

> The Hebrews thought in terms of subjective experience rather than objective scientific observation, and thereby avoided the modern error of over-departmentalization. It was essentially the whole man, with all his attributes, physical, psychological and emotional, of which the Hebrews thought and spoke, and the heart was conceived of as the governing centre

for all of these. . . . There is no suggestion in the Bible that the brain is the centre of consciousness, thought or will. It is the heart which is so regarded. . . . It is the heart that makes a man or a beast what he is, and governs all his actions.[2]

Therefore, forgiveness must be heart-forgiveness; the knowledge of forgiveness, a heart-knowledge; and faith itself, heart faith. Such faith brings a subjective awareness to the whole person. It is my subjective awareness with every part of my being that I am forgiven. Only the Holy Spirit can impart such a knowledge of forgiveness. And as we have already seen, it is such an experience of being forgiven that makes a person's forgiveness of others very much easier.

Leanne Payne mentions three barriers to the healing, sanctifying process. They are failure to forgive others, failure to receive forgiveness for ourselves and failure to accept ourselves.[3] The three are linked. The failure to forgive others and the failure to receive forgiveness for ourselves are clearly connected. As Jesus taught in the Lord's Prayer, we are able to receive God's forgiveness to the same degree to which we forgive others. Just as an experience of being forgiven makes it easier to forgive, so a lack of willingness to forgive may be the cause of an absence of any sense of being forgiven.

In addition, failure to accept ourselves cannot be discussed properly unless it is based on an awareness of my being forgiven and accepted by God. I begin to like myself when I know in my heart what God thinks about me.

Let me take the matter of giving forgiveness a step further. If you say, "I'd like to forgive, but I just can't," you stand on perilous ground, not on holy ground. What you may be saying is that to forgive is too painful. Up to now I have only discussed the amazing thing that happens when the Holy Spirit reveals to my heart God's forgiveness toward me. Suppose this has not ever taken place. Am I excused from forgiving because of the pain it causes me to forgive? Certainly not!

The pain of forgiving is no excuse. Sometimes forgiveness may have to begin with an exercise of the will. I may have to assert again and again, every time bitter feelings surge up in me, "I *do*, I *will* forgive." I have already described my own struggle on one occasion, and how it ended. I must not give in to my pain, or I may never know God's loving, forgiving acceptance in my experience.

The Murder I Never Committed

As I waited on God one day, I began thinking about the man who once molested me. Then God's word came to me. "Have you forgiven him?" he asked. "You know that you must."

"Sure. It's no problem. It doesn't mean anything to me now."

Back came another word, "How old would he be?"

"Oh—I don't know. I would guess at least ninety."

Without any conscious intention, I began to picture him in my mind, sitting opposite me as he would be if he were still alive—bald, obese, a little greasy, smiling coyly. Suddenly, aware of the man I pictured, I was filled with rage. Everything that I had pushed down below the level of awareness rose up in me. My hands also rose up, reaching for his neck to throttle him. Yet all this time I had been convinced that I had forgiven him. *Obviously, I had not forgiven.* It was just that I had put it away from me into the distant past. I needed to forgive him, and I did.

I forgave with my will. And I confessed my sin. I resolved never again to allow any scorn of that man to enter my mind. Many nights later I woke thinking about the man again. Would I actually have tried to strangle him if I had met him? Had I forgiven him after all? I could imagine his face reddening as I would have clutched his throat, and as he tore at my hands to free himself. Then I knew with absolute certainty that I could never have followed through.

I recorded the whole thing in my journal the next morning. As I did so, I saw that he was no longer a threat to me. When I was a boy of eleven, his manner, his laughing confidence, had overwhelmed me. His gentle mockery of my embarrassment and fear, my passivity, yet my inability to go along with what he did had dumbfounded me. Worse still, his ability to skillfully awaken erotic feelings in me had awakened something else—disgust, hatred of him and hatred above all of myself.

Now I saw him differently. The old man I had visualized (I doubt that he is alive; I have long since lost track of him) was nothing like the laughing, mocking memory of my boyhood. He was a pathetic object. I experienced a profound but gentle pity for his wretchedness. Forgive him? How could I *not* forgive him?

The issue was resolved. It can be like this always. First comes the action of one's will. One decides to forgive, pain or no pain. One struggles against any thoughts that arise, any lack of a forgiving posture. Then, as the Holy Spirit continues to minister, there comes a resolution, a time when by one means or another all struggling ceases and the very need to struggle is gone. Thank God it is so.

CHAPTER 19
The Healing Session

But for you who revere my name, the sun of righteousness
will rise with healing in its wings. And you will go out and leap
like calves released from the stall.
MALACHI 4:2

Healing is simply the practical application of the basic
Christian message of salvation, a belief that Jesus means to liberate
us from personal sin and from emotional and physical sickness.
FRANCIS MACNUTT

*L*et us say that you have tried to prepare yourself for the task of breaking the bondage that sexual sin has over a person. Let us say that you are as prepared as you know how to be. There are one or two others with you, a small, prayerful team of helpers. There is plenty of time to do what you came to do. How do you start?

There is no set procedure, for we are to be led by the Holy Spirit. The principle key to what you will be doing is to hear what God is saying. It is always good, however, to begin by uniting in prayer in order to be in accord as a group, as both those who minister and those who receive ministry. And what better way to still our hearts so that we can listen to the Spirit's voice? In prayer we invoke God's presence. He *is* present, but when we make it clear that we want him, acknowledge his presence, and start both to count on it and to praise him for it, we enter into partnership both with infinite power and infinite wisdom. At the same time we set our sails because to pray is also to listen and watch for the wind of the Spirit.

Collaboration on the Team

While one member should lead the group (whether it consists of only two persons or more than two), all should contribute. The working relationship of team members is crucial. They should know one another well, love one another, trust one another, have no hidden feelings of resentment toward one another. Therefore, they must pray together frequently and must keep short accounts with one another. Only in this way will they enjoy a good working relationship when they minister together.

Even so, tensions may arise during the course of the ministry. There may be a difference of opinion about the direction the Holy Spirit is leading. The leader should ask, from time to time, what other team members may have seen or heard from the Lord. Should the leader fail to do so, a member who is not leading may wish to suggest something. At a suitable moment the assistant may say, "I think the Lord has been saying to me . . ." or, "I keep getting the impression that . . ." or, "I wonder if you would mind if I . . ." The more people have worked together and the more mature they are as Christians, the more truly they love and trust one another, the better they will work as a unit under the direction of the Spirit.

Where to Begin

Many Christians begin by asserting their authority over the powers of darkness, demanding the departure of demonic presences. Already we have discussed this, and I have no objection to the practice, provided we do not thereby assume that all demons have obeyed. Remember also where our emphasis should lie. We are to focus on light more than on darkness, on Christ more than Satan, on angelic presences more than on the demonic.

But we should be cautious about doing this, or anything else by routine. Since demons make their appearances during the course of the ministry from time to time, it is clear that not all demons heed every order we may give. Christ's authority, even when it is rightly claimed by Christians, is at times resisted, even disputed. It can, therefore, be naive to assume that by means of a command we routinely give we can be sure of no demonic interference.

Nevertheless we do not back off. There can be value in stating the obvious aloud. We bear the authority of the king. The greatest value of such commands lies in declaring from the start where the authority lines are drawn. No darkness can continue to resist the authority of the King of Light indefinitely. It is important to remind ourselves that this is so. Too great a focus on the dark powers, on the other hand, is to be avoided.

Another place to start is with anointing with oil. This is a symbolic act with a long biblical history. Kings and priests were anointed (Ex 28:41, 1 Kings 19:15-16). James suggests that when elders are called, prayer for healing the sick be accompanied by anointing (Jas 5:14). The symbolism is that of the anointing by the Holy Spirit. The ideas are linked in Scripture. Saul's anointing for kingship was in fact followed very soon afterward by the Holy Spirit's anointing. "Then Samuel took a flask of oil and poured it on Saul's head and kissed him, saying, 'Has not the LORD anointed you leader over his inheritance?' " (1 Sam 10:1). And "when they arrived at Gibeah, a procession of prophets met him; the Spirit of God came upon him in power, and he joined in their prophesying" (1 Sam 10:10).

It does not always happen like that, but on one occasion in which I was anointed with oil (though it was the last thing I was expecting just then), the Holy Spirit came very heavily upon me. Still, there is nothing to say that anointing with oil is mandatory. Jesus never used oil when he healed people. In the vast majority of the healings of every variety that I have observed, oil has not been used. The practice is a biblical practice. It reminds us graphically of the need for, and our dependence on, the Holy Spirit's anointing, but must not itself become the center or main focus.

The Healing Interview

What follows next would in most cases be a healing interview with the person being ministered to. John Wimber describes five essential steps.

Step 1: The Interview
Step 2: The Diagnostic Decision
Step 3: The Prayer Selection
Step 4: The Prayer Engagement
Step 5: Postprayer Directions[1]

Most experienced workers, while not always following the precise order that Wimber describes, would accept that these five steps, as Wimber describes them in the book *Power Healing,* are essential. Some might add one or two more steps. Let me deal first with the interview.

Step 1: The Interview

Unlike the situation in a large meeting or seminar, time for taking a history is less of a problem when you pray by appointment for a person. In spite of this, you must take your time and resist the temptation to hurry. Inner stillness is necessary if we are to hear well.

We are all inclined to try to feel spiritual when doing something "Christian," and to assume a posture of intensity. Many people are totally unaware of the way they slip on their Christian Service *persona* like a mask. Being spiritual and feeling spiritual are not the same thing. To slow down, to stop being artificially intense, to know what it is to be still in God's presence commonly means we are better able to focus on what God may be saying. Intensity is usually carnal religiosity. It militates against the Spirit's work.

Let us suppose we are trying to help a person we will call Jerry. Having the time to do so, we take advantage of it. We do not hurry. We listen to Jerry, watching him carefully as we do so. We watch his facial expressions, his bodily movements. All the time we are trusting God to speak, asking those questions that are prompted by what we observe or that the Spirit seems to suggest that we ask. The whole procedure should generally be quiet, tranquil. No hype, no pressure. Apart from any other consideration, this helps Jerry to be calm.

Our object is not to take a complete family and psychological history, so much as to sense the direction in which the Holy Spirit is leading. It is a procedure following heart and spirit rather than doing groundwork for an intellectual analysis of the problem. This is not to suggest that psychological insights we may already have should be ignored, or that we should shut off our brain function and not ask relevant questions. Rather our primary dependence will be on the Holy Spirit's leading. Wimber comments, "I always have the attitude that it is easier to ask questions than think I must receive words of knowledge. But sometimes God reveals that what the person for whom I am praying thinks his or her need is, is not correct."[2]

I shall certainly not triumph by means of an intellectual *tour de force*. Humble dependence on God, listening for his word, should characterize the whole procedure. However, we must not be fearful of asking personal questions of a delicate nature. The embarrassment will be halved if the questioner is not embarrassed. Your embarrassment, your awkwardness, awakens the same in people around you. The best way to ask a delicate question is to use few words and to ask it outright. Picture the following scenario:

You begin to speak by clearing your throat. Then, a little anxious, you mumble at the floor in a low voice, "Do you, er, I mean, have you ever, like, 'um, mastur-"

Jerry says: "I'm sorry. Could you speak up a little? I can't quite catch what you're saying."

"Oh, I'm sorry. I mean—er . . ."

By this time you yourself will be more embarrassed than ever, even a little angry with yourself or with Jerry, so that everyone present will feel awkward. Be deliberate. Look Jerry in the eye and say firmly, clearly, and sympathetically, "Has masturbation been a problem for you?" There is no need to apologize, or to elaborate by saying, for example, "You know, I'm not accusing, only *asking* because it sometimes—er, d'you know?" When you say things like that you are giving way to your own insecurity. Your security comes not from your professional performance, but from trust in God. Experience, of course, brings tranquility, and you will lack experience when you begin. Therefore, be still before God. Be quiet in your spirit, but clear and simple in your speech.

Step 2: Diagnosis—The Problem's Root

The root meaning of the word *diagnosis* is "to know through." It is to be able to see through the surface to what lies beneath. The object you have in mind is to help someone with a problem, a problem that results in sin. You want to find why the sinful habit cannot be overcome, and to correct this. Very gently, but quite directly, you will ask about it, not focusing on the sin, but inquiring what steps have been taken to overcome it, what the person's ideas are of why it is not overcome, and what its roots are.

Jerry may not know the *why* of his problem. The problem itself looms so large that the very question has become a source of bitterness. He has racked his brains, has tortured himself relentlessly with the question why? Therefore, we must try to find the answer together. And since God is in the business of restoring people, we can be sure of his good will in the matter.

We must come to a conclusion, however, about the root of the problem. True, there may be several roots, so that more than one will have to be cut, but usually one is critical. It is at this point that God's willingness to speak is most important. The big question is whether we are listening.

The British and Canadian branches of Wholeness Through Christ, an organization that specializes in healing sexual sin, suggests four areas to keep in mind at this time—sins, emotional wounds and bondages, the occult, and heredity. It is not necessary to raise all four areas or to deal with each in turn. In any case there is a close interrelationship between them. Rather, as I continue to insist, we must allow God the Holy Spirit to lead us. To keep them in mind means that we are less likely to ignore a prompting from the Holy Spirit.

As you gain experience, you will discover how much there is to learn about each area. The more you do this sort of thing, the wider your experience becomes. Take the occult, for instance. I have already made my conviction clear that merely saying to demons we *believe* are there, "I bind you in the name of Jesus," does not mean the demon is necessarily bound. With some I find it to be a personal struggle.

Many differ about how you discern whether a demon is present. All are agreed that the Holy Spirit is the one who gives us illumination about the matter. But many Christians who believe (sometimes mistakenly) that demons are present, say, "I bind you . . ." and then subsequently are not surprised that no demonic manifestation occurs. They assume that their experience confirms the practice even though there is no evidence of such a presence.

My own experience is of two kinds. In some instances I sense God speaking and telling me that a demon is present, even where there is no apparent reason to suppose a demon might be present. Yet as the Holy Spirit leads me to pray for someone, the person suddenly grins and says, "It's gone!" *even though neither of us had talked or thought about demons until that moment.*

The other, and commoner experience, is for me not even to be thinking about demons. I enter a room, or else begin to pray for someone, or begin to preach, and a demon manifests in a noisy, dramatic fashion. Usually it responds to my command to be silent or to quit doing whatever it is doing, but occasionally there is a tussle of wills. Once I had to give up, at least for the time being. (I loathe dealing with demons.) The more I experience, the more I realize how little I know. All I know is that I have authority to cast them out, am commanded to do so, and must obey the word of the living God.

Some of my acquaintances, who seem more sure of their ground than I do, say, "We know our command to bind the demon works because we never get the sort of manifestations you get." Remember, I am referring to a *routine* use of binding (or similar) commands, when there is no particular evidence of their presence. Recently I remembered an old elephant joke. It had to do with the man who walked round constantly snapping his fingers. When asked why he did so, he replied, "To keep elephants away."

His friend objected, "But there *are* no elephants around here," only to be told, "No. Of course not. See how well it works."

During the years I have been dealing with demonized people I have realized that no two demons are the same, no two demonized persons are alike. What worked with one will not necessarily work with another. There are few set rules. The issue with authority is a nonissue. We have authority. I am reduced to two basic principles at the moment, principles which apply to every case I have come across.

One I have been insisting on—the importance of hearing the voice of the Spirit. When *he* says "Do this or that," it is the right thing to do. The other is that I must focus more on the person I am helping than on the demon I am expelling. You don't get involved with, argue with, or allow yourself to be fascinated by the demonic performance. Instead, you command it to quit or to be silent. So I say (in effect), "In Jesus' name, shut up! I'm talking to Susan. Susan, can you hear me?" But always I crave the Spirit's voice. Casting out a demon affects three beings—yourself, the victim and the demon. Only God knows all three of you, and that intimately. Only he can see the best strategy. Hence the importance of hearing his voice.

I have discussed the occult to emphasize that all four areas I mentioned are everexpanding areas. The further we go, the more we discover about the occult, about blood lines, about sin, and about wounds and bondages. We cannot learn them from books any more than we can learn the sufficiency of Christ from books. And if we could, we probably would not use them to the best advantage because we would be relying on our knowledge rather than on the Lord himself. We would tend to think we knew enough—and none of us ever does.

Steps 3 and 4: The Prayer Selection and Engagement.
I shall never tire of repeating that prayer begins with God, not with us. We pray effectively when our prayer coincides with the will of God. We know that will in general through Scripture, but Scripture does not cover every situation. Scripture does not reveal to me the thing that Jerry is trying to

conceal. Only the voice of the Spirit is of help here. And even when I know what Jerry is hiding, and have told him so, I may still not know the best way of resolving the issue. In the same way, Wimber says, "I always ask God how I should pray for a sick person. . . . even when I have a clear understanding of the cause of a condition, I am not sure about how to pray specifically."[3]

He gives several examples of this, talking about *words of command, words of pronouncement, words of rebuke,* all uttered in the context of prayer.[4] It is unwise to assume we always know how to pray. Last night, for instance, some of us were praying for an older married missionary couple. As I prayed for the man I sensed that very real but unknown physical danger lay ahead of him. The time of danger was in the future—perhaps a year or two away. Alarmed, indeed a little frightened, I pleaded with God for him, asking for mercy and protection. Meanwhile my wife, Lorrie, was sitting quietly on the floor and had opened her Bible. As, still bothered, I concluded my prayer, Lorrie said to the man, "I *think* God has given me this psalm for you."

Relief flooded through me as she began to read to him:

He will not let your foot slip—
   he who watches over you will not slumber. . . .
The LORD watches over you—
   the LORD is your shade at your right hand;
the sun will not harm you by day,
   nor the moon by night.
The LORD will keep you from all harm—
   he will watch over your life." (Ps 121:3-7)

Afterward she told me, "While you were praying, God told me to open my Bible. He didn't tell me *where* to open it, just to open it—so I did. Then, when I heard your concern about danger, I happened to glance down at my Bible, and immediately I saw Psalm 121. As I read it I knew I had to read it aloud."

All during my own prayer I had been pausing to look to God and had proceeded with each sentence only as I sensed how God was leading. I was not altogether satisfied with the lack of resolution at the end. Lorrie had in the same way been listening. All she had done was obey the word of the Lord. It was all she had to do. Whether we will ever learn what the danger is and what happens, I do not know.

Lorrie did not have any set procedure. She heard and obeyed. It is not that set procedures are wrong, but they must never become the only means to the end in view. The channels of healing are so many, and God commonly knows how he wants to heal.

This morning I was talking on the telephone to a friend, Henry, who hears from God clearly. He described how a younger Christian, Al, had come into the room where several others were standing. Al had just finished ministering in public and began to talk, anxious (though he never said so) to know what everyone thought of his performance. He was fishing for reassurance from more experienced colleagues.

Perceiving this, and knowing that what people think about us never satisfies, Henry silently asked God what to do—essentially what sort of prayer to pray. "Go kneel in front of him, place his hands together between your own, and ask me to tell Al what *I* think of what he did." Henry followed the instruction carefully and then prayed. Within seconds the look of eager anxiety on Al's face drained away, replaced by gratitude and awe. "He told me he gave me an A+!" Al said wonderingly.

How would you have responded to a man fishing for reassurance, hoping for compliments? You could say, "Al, you did great!" Or knowing his real need, you could say, "You did very well. But you know, your need is to look to God rather than to the rest of us. Why don't we pray together, confessing this to God, and ask him to help you be independent of what the rest of us think." Instead, Henry asked God how to pray. What God told Al both taught him a lesson, and gave him a peace which no amount of compliments could have brought.

Engaging in prayer can (though it need not be) accompanied by many forms of physical manifestation. Once Lorrie and I were praying for a lady who was severely ill, and who "didn't believe in that sort of thing." Nevertheless, she had agreed to let us try. As we prayed, she said, "Oh! My arms and legs want to move about."

We said, "Well, let them!" A series of flailings and jerks followed.

Suddenly the woman began to weep, crying out after a moment, "It's all right, H_____ , I forgive you! It doesn't matter any more!" We never found out what H_____ had done. What was obvious was that the Lord had convicted her of an unforgiving attitude, of harboring resentment against someone who had wronged her. When she rose to leave us, she had been healed of a major physical illness.

I do not commonly see such manifestations when I pray, and they occur mostly when I pray for a physical illness, or for the demonized. When I pray for an emotional condition, weeping is more common.

One man for whom I prayed had cancer. He began to shake, and the shaking became so bad we had to sit him down. It was the first time that this sort of thing had happened to me, and I was awed and excited. I followed my usual practice of listening after each phrase, trying to pray only as the Spirit led. With each phrase it was as though jolts of electricity went through him. Finally he jumped to his feet, crying, "It's done! It's finished!" A large, hard abdominal mass had disappeared, gone.

But something inside me said, "No! It's not finished." However, we terminated the meeting. I laid aside my doubts, excited by what had already taken place. A few years later the cancer returned, ending his life.[5]

Step 5: Postprayer Directions (Follow-up)
Even when there is a dramatic manifestation of the Holy Spirit's intervention, that is not what matters. The key is that the person walk by faith, not by whatever experiences he or she may or may not have had. With the passage of time, memories fade, and with fading memories, the vividness of a particular encounter with God grows too evanescent to count on. You say to yourself, "Did that really happen? Or was it all in my head? Maybe I'm remembering it wrongly. In any case it could be just psychological."

Wholeness Through Christ members talk about "walking out your healing." They emphasize walking by faith, putting on the armor of God, memorizing God's promises in Scripture. It is in the name and character of God that our faith is rooted, in someone who loves us and never mocks us, whose written word is solid as a rock.

Where we are dealing with sexual sin, it is always essential to warn against repeating old sins. The sense of freedom one has at first, and the fading from memory of past events makes it easy for the enemy to tell us a year or two later, "Once will not cause too much damage. You've been under stress. It's not *that* bad. Give way for once."

At that point we need to hear again the words of Jesus, "Go, and sin no more!" I have found from personal experience that deliverance a second time will be far harder than the first time. We should not, like the sow, return to the mire, or like the dog to our own vomit. To do so is to despise Christ's awful darkness and death. And where physical healing is concerned (as I mention in note 5), the consequences can be fatal. When he healed the man at the Pool of Bethesda, Jesus reacted as he did on another occasion. "Later Jesus found him at the temple and said to him, 'See, you are well again. Stop sinning *or something worse may happen to you* ' " (my italics, Jn 5:14).

CHAPTER 20
Your Future

But God chose the foolish things of the world to shame the wise;
God chose the weak things of the world to shame the strong. He chose the
lowly things of this world and the despised things—and the
things that are not—to nullify the things that are, so that
no one may boast before him.
1 CORINTHIANS 1:27-29

P aul the apostle had a weakness, an "infirmity." In 2 Corinthians 12:7-10, he says God *gave* him that weakness, yet he calls it "a messenger of Satan, to torment me." It came from Satan, yet God sent it.

Glorying in Your Weakness

Many arguments have arisen about the nature of that weakness. Some people feel it was a sickness, others that it had to do with the opposition and persecution he faced. My own feeling is that it may have had more to do with the way he handled the opposition (certainly he talks about his weakness in the context of the opposition from the Judaizing party in the early church). Judging by some of his comments in the second Corinthian epistle, he was pretty touchy about their criticisms. However, the precise nature of the "infirmity" is neither here nor there.

Then what is the point in his mentioning it? It is the *purpose* of the weakness that matters, not its nature. Its purpose was to "keep me from becoming conceited." God allowed a weakness to remain in Paul's life, *to keep him from feeling he had "had it made."* That is why I think it may have had to do with how he handled criticism and opposition. He may well have struggled against what we now call defensiveness, resentment, bitterness in the face of the Judaizing party's attacks on him. Defensiveness, resentment and bitterness are satanic in their origin. They are certainly messengers of Satan.

But no matter. Paul was aware of a weakness, a weakness he did not want, yet a weakness *about which he begins to boast.* "Therefore I will boast all the more gladly about my weaknesses, so that Christ's power may rest on me" (2 Cor 12:9).

There are two astonishing aspects to his statement. The first has to do with the relationship between strength and weakness; the second, the idea of actually boasting about a weakness. Let me deal with the second aspect first. The principle Paul talks about is a universal principle, and one that holds good in the case of sexual sins and weaknesses.

Take, for example, the most looked-down-on sexual sin and weakness of all, that of molesting little children. Even if you never gave way to it (many people cannot help themselves), if you found yourself tempted by it from time to time, you would never want to admit the temptation, much less to "glory in" such a character flaw. Weaknesses like that make us ashamed. Yet Paul finds in his weakness a glorying, a boasting, a secret of extraordinary power. It releases the power of the Christ whose strength is made perfect in weakness.

As we return to the relation of strength and weakness, let us imagine, for a moment, what it would feel like to know deliverance from the weakness of molesting children. How would you feel when you were delivered?

I can tell you from my experience of similar deliverances that you would be overwhelmed. You would want to tell people about it. However, that phase might pass fairly soon. Among the changes you would experience would be the gradual assumption that you no longer had any weakness in that direction. Then a day would come when you felt the pull of temptation again. A messenger of Satan would begin to torment you. Messengers of Satan act like worms of death and corruption working inside you. You would cry, "Why, Lord? Why?" You would wonder what had gone wrong.

You had not realized that Christ's strength is made perfect not in your strength but in your weakness. You had assumed that the strength of your deliverance belonged to you *independent of Christ.* It does not. The strength lies in a relationship, in your dependent relationship with him. It is a relationship of trust. The relationship was strengthened at the moment of your greatest weakness—when he delivered you. Feeling your weakness again calls you back to the place where you recognize your weakness, where you hit bottom again and cry out to Christ. Therefore, come to him again and again. It is the only way to keep yourself free from the crawling worms of death.

Accountability

Old habits die hard. The enemy will not leave us alone instantly. Long experience has taught us that we all need one another in the body of Christ. We need someone to be accountable to. It is all very well to assert that we trust in God alone. God has placed us within a body of believers so that we may confess to one another and pray for one another.

You must determine right away that you will, God helping you, find a person who will hold you accountable. It must not be someone with whom you can fall into sin. And it must be a person who really will hold you accountable and will take his or her task seriously.

I have a friend who was once a victim of satyriasis (a word used to describe a man with an insatiable appetite for women). He was known on occasion to use six prostitutes in one day. His enslaving drive to copulate ended his two marriages. He was also a pastor, and his problem (rightly) lost him his churches. God, in mercy, intervened in his life to heal and sanctify him.

God also provided him with a man to whom he was accountable. In his case it was an ideal mentor—a man with insight, who always seemed to know when he began to slip, as he did occasionally. One day his mentor suggested that they drive around to all the places where previous dalliances had occurred. In each place my friend tore down through prayer the "altar to Baal" that he had erected there, and built one to the Lord, his God. What the Holy Spirit had begun a year or two before was completed that day.

Find someone who will hold you accountable. And be honest with that person.

Your New Calling

If, as you have been reading, you have found yourself saying, "I needed this book," pause for a moment. God has more in mind than just you. He is also thinking of and longing for many others like you. He desires not only to heal

266 _____ EROS REDEEMED

(that is, to sanctify) you, but to reach other victims of the old fertility gods through you. Not through this book. Through *you*.

"Oh, no, not through me!" you may say, but I am perfectly serious. What you must grasp is that the weakness in which Paul gloried made him the greatest of all missionary pioneers. God specializes in using the wounded and the broken to heal others. True, your own healing must begin first. But once it begins, God will draw other men and women to you, other wounded who need healing. You are being healed that you might heal them. Your effective service for God is not ending. Your real usefulness is about to begin.

You may be able to create a fellowship group for other strugglers within your church. Together you can covenant to share both triumphs and failures with one another. Together you can pray and minister Christ to one another.

The Importance of Being a Loser

So concerned is God that no flesh should glory in his presence, that his policy throughout history has been one of showing extreme preference for the weak, the wounded, the defeated, the losers, people of no account, the outcasts of the earth. Not only so, they are his favorite soldiers, specially selected as his workers, his army, those who are to do his bidding.

Jesus chose a very odd group of apostles upon which to found the church. They were hardly the cream of religious society. None of them would have been chosen "most likely to succeed." They were, at best, the petit bourgeois of their day. Some of the disciples and the women had a distinctly less salubrious background. One woman dear to the Lord had been a prostitute. But she was forgiven and made whole by and in her relationship with Christ. Therefore, she washed his feet with her tears of gratitude, wiping them with the hairs of her head. Of such is the kingdom of God.

On the other hand, when we want help we prefer that the help be competent, well trained. But the trouble with the well trained is that eventually they may rely on their training rather than on God. Latent within every one of us lies the spirit of phariseeism. Well-trained people are in special danger. They have not always known a sense of desperation and may therefore lack an overwhelming sense of gratitude.

In addition, they are inclined to enjoy the perks that come to the well trained. It is so hard to be highly respected without beginning to respect yourself just a little! I know—I've been there. You gradually forfeit your capacity to sympathize with the world's losers. You fail to see your own weaknesses clearly, and you fail to have the kind of gut-wrenching compassion that Jesus experienced for hurting, sinful people.

In this way the well educated, many of whose grandparents and great-grandparents struggled out of poverty themselves, come under the judgment of the God who brings down the proud and exalts those of low degree.

> Brothers, think of what you were when you were called. Not many of you were wise by human standards; not many were influential; not many were of noble birth. But God chose the foolish things of the world to shame the wise; God chose the weak things of the world to shame the strong. He chose the lowly things of this world and the despised things—and the things that are not—to nullify the things that are, so that no one may boast before him. (1 Cor 1:26-29)

Yet the training itself is valuable. We need theologians and Bible scholars. We need trained and experienced counselors. It is false expectations about training we must beware of.

All healers of others are wounded healers—whether or not we recognize the fact. Healers who know they are wounded are the most effective. But notice my qualification. You must never forget either those wounds that have been healed, or the wounds by which they were healed.

Remembering both kinds of wounds, you who struggle against sexual sin must, as you begin to be healed, also begin to help others. At first you will not be able to help much, but the help you can give will grow. Never allow yourself to be overconfident. Get all the training you can, though your own healing will be the most significant factor in your training. But never run away from the reality of those means of grace by which healing will come to you. Over and over again I must emphasize the importance of getting back to the beginning, of remembering the basics.

Blessed Were the Pharisees

Pharisees are people who know, people who are "in the know," who share a common "in" language. As such they typify many well-trained people, whether the theologically well trained or the trained counselors of various disciplines. Knowledge "puffeth up." It turns some people into balloons, into wordy bags of gas.

The Pharisees may well have begun as faithful servants of God more than two hundred years before Christ. During the reign of the tyrannical Antiochus IV, many Jews chose to risk their lives for their belief in Moses and to study the Scriptures all the more. God honors such men and women. Yet two hundred years later the Pharisees—spiritual descendants of men whom God must have honored—received withering condemnation from Jesus. It is not by any means an unbreakable rule, but it often happens that the grandchildren of today's saints become tomorrow's Pharisees.

Do not become like them. A little knowledge is said to be a dangerous thing. But it becomes a dangerous thing only at the point where we start to overestimate ourselves, where our confidence no longer lies in the Son of God but in how much we know about him. At that point we forget what it was like to be a loser, and we become overconfident and proud. Never forget the bitter pains and struggles of the past. Never forget the times when you hated yourself, when you were in the depths of despair. For the latent spirit of phariseeism lies within all of us, professionals and nonprofessionals, scholars and rank amateurs, theologians and brand new Bible readers, wounded or healed.

Remaining Vulnerable

This morning I had a strange but very wonderful experience as I sought God in prayer. For two or three days, in spite of all our care not to take on too many responsibilities, Lorrie and I have experienced one pressure after another. Then this morning at two a.m., a police officer called at our door asking whether we were willing to accept a man who had stayed with us previously and who was now "very intoxicated." He had been knocking on people's doors in a confused state.

I need not go into the man's history, except to say that he also had a number of sexual problems. Suffice it to say that being dragged to the door by the police at two a.m. seemed the last straw in a series of needless pressures. The timing was all wrong. What was a sovereign God thinking about? The pressure on my wife and myself was almost unbearable.

The officer asked, "Are you willing to receive him?" It was a full minute before I said, "Yes, okay." I was only half-awake and not thinking very clearly. Lorrie was up by then and said, "Put him in my study, John." It was the one place we could use, for Lorrie had two women's Bible studies the next day, one of them with nearly forty women—and we already had three house guests.

The drunk man wanted to talk, and neither of us was in a talking mood. We got him to bed—and then, without thinking of Lorrie, I went to bed myself. I was dog tired, yet I did not sleep. Then I remembered Lorrie's Bible studies. She would need every opportunity for quiet tomorrow, and I had brought in a drunk. She had still not returned to bed. So I got up, went back to where she sat in the den in her favorite chair, almost too weary to move. I prayed with her. Then I kept her company until she herself said, "Let's go back to bed."

In the morning I felt dreadful, waking much later than usual and having no time to shave, shower or spend an adequate amount of time with God. I knew that the reduced prayer time mattered less than at one time I would have thought. Still, I craved what I could not have. I was in a foul mood, tired, selfish, self-pitying. I questioned my motives for admitting the drunk the previous night. I had added to Lorrie's already full program. Did I really care for my wife? Was I a mere legalist, just doing the "spiritual thing"? I allowed cynical thoughts to dominate me.

In that sort of mood I start to think raw sex. I've no idea why—except that it fits in with a mood of general disgust with life. I didn't care. Whether I had a right to or not, I enjoyed my foul and sexy mood. And then the Holy Spirit said quietly, "Go ahead. Complain! Tell me I'm not playing fair, if that's what you think." He was not being indifferent, but genuinely kind. He would have heeded my complaints and answered me.

Instead I realized what a louse I was, how weak, how cowardly and what a fool. At first the awareness brought me no comfort, at least until a new awareness began to dawn. I was a loser. Losers were the very kind of people Jesus received. The fact that I knew myself, that I accepted my loser status meant *that he would not reject me*. Then it happened. Light flooded my night, turning it into day. Profound joy burst out of my heart. "Here I am, Lord! I need you! I'm the worst sort of weakling, yet I know you will receive me. Here I come!"

How can I explain what happened? The whole day has been glorious. I sit here at my computer, itchy, unshaven . . . but joyful. I was vulnerable. I knew and accepted my weakness. I came again to my Savior, aware of my need of him, knowing deeply how glad he would be to receive me. Mine was the same sort of awareness of weakness about which Paul talked in the passage that opened this chapter.

To "hit bottom" is an Alcoholics Anonymous (AA) term describing what happened to me. It is the same thing that I described of Augustine in the previous chapter. But it is not to be a once-in-a-lifetime event. God desires to bring us to that place again and again, not to humiliate us, but because the awareness of our hopelessness releases his power within us. It is to be an ongoing experience, the prelude to a new phase in the sanctifying journey, a new empowering.

Turning Victims into Rescuers

I take my hat off to AA. It is not that their ideas are perfect. (They are accused of weakening and toning down the gospel.) The supreme value of AA is that they turn victims of alcoholism into rescuers. Nobody is more enthused to reach others than an AA member who, having "reached bottom" and seen his or her helplessness, reaches out and discovers there's Someone there.

This is why I salute them. They do more. They minister to, among others, the kind of people who cannot afford to attend expensive programs. They are a volunteer movement, a movement of amateurs helping future amateurs, a movement for recycling survivors to make them rescuers. That is precisely what Jesus did with the twelve apostles and with the seventy-two disciples as well. Through them he changed the first-century world.

In the same way, Exodus International (one or two of whose chapters used to be called Homosexuals Anonymous) turns former homosexuals into men and women who minister to other homosexuals who are seeking a new way of life. Whatever the nature of your sexual problem, and however messed up your life may have been, God wishes to use the very weakness that once ruined you as your most effective area of usefulness. Your weakness can become your greatest strength, the source of your greatest usefulness to God and to your fellow men and women.

The Blessed Ones

Those who will inherit the earth, its future lords, will be ex-losers (Mt 5:5). Knowing and accepting that they are losers, they will find God's answer. It is faith in the power of Christ that turns losers into lords. In the beatitudes Jesus teaches this principle.

The poor in spirit, whom Jesus calls blessed (Mt 5:3), are those people who know they have nothing of value to offer to God except their poor, defeated, weak and worthless selves. They may come from the world's aristocracy, have studied at the best schools and lived in Europe, be fluent in five modern languages as well as in Latin, Greek and Hebrew, yet still be of no value to the kingdom. Only when we are weighed in the divine balance and really see by how much we are found wanting can other things become valuable. The gifts are useful—but they are no credit to us because they were given to us by God. *In our rebellion and sin we are of no worth,* and this fact renders all our talents and achievements as wood, hay and stubble, ready for burning. Paul counted them refuse compared to the excellency of knowing Christ.

Therefore, if your sexual sins and weaknesses make you feel horrible—rejoice! Accept what you are and lay yourself at the feet of the Christ who longs to receive you. Your value lies in the fact that he made you and now longs to redeem you. For in knowing your poverty you begin to fit every category of people the Sermon on the Mount describes. You will mourn and be comforted, be meek and inherit the earth, hunger and thirst for righteousness and be filled. Out of weakness you will be made strong. You will put to flight the powers of darkness.

So rejoice! An unbelievably glorious future lies ahead of you. You are to become the salt of the earth, a powerful preservative in the putrefying society of which you are a part. You will join the ranks of the soldier-saints who do not count their lives dear to themselves, who will be valiant in faith. Your wounds are there to be healed. Your strength lies in your weakness itself, your glory in the One who washes away your shame.

A distant trumpet is blowing. Listen carefully. Can you hear it? It calls you by name. A voice sounds. It calls you by name. A kingdom of glorious power has dawned among us, and you are personally invited to join. You are to be part of an invincible force. Nothing in earth or hell can stop it. No longer is a mere archangel like Michael to lead us, but the King of Glory himself. Your leader is Captain of the hosts of light. His ways are inscrutable and his purposes are unstoppable.

Dawn has broken and the Son will soon arise. Lift up your head! Don't let your hands hang down a moment longer! Quicken your pace! You are about to trample your enemies under your feet.

Appendix A: Organizations to Help You

Organizations That Help with Gender-Identity Confusion

I can recommend two organizations which (1) help homosexuals who wish to leave that lifestyle and experience change in their sexual orientation and (2) offer help with gender-identity confusion:

1. *Pastoral Care Ministries*

This ministry is the result of the work of Leanne Payne and her coworkers, who organize conferences and training courses. They also offer teaching tapes. For catalogs and conference dates, contact

Pastoral Care Ministries
P.O. Box 1313
Wheaton, IL 60189-1313
(708) 510-0487

2. *Exodus International*

This organization offers, among other services, an information package which includes a description of Exodus, its boards and general workings; a book catalog; a list of available tapes; a list of recommended resources; a list of those who minister in Exodus. Address inquiries to:

Exodus International
P.O. Box 2121
San Rafael, CA 94912

Organizations That Help with General Sexual Healing

1. *Vineyard Ministries International*
Vineyard Ministries is a broad renewal movement that ministers healing (both emotional and physical) of many kinds.

> Vineyard Ministries International
> P.O. Box 65004
> Anaheim, CA 92805

2. *Wholeness Through Christ*
This organization specializes in healing prayer for leaders. It exists in many countries, both English-speaking and European. Names for the organization vary from country to country, as may the practices, policies and ethos.

> Wholeness Through Christ
> 792 Sea Drive, R.R. #1
> Brentwood Bay, BC V05 1A0
> Canada

> Wholeness Through Christ
> 11 Arthur Street
> Oswestry, Shropshire SY11 1JN
> England

> Dr. Manfred Engeli
> Christliche Beratungsstella
> Altenberstr. 60, 3013 Bern
> Switzerland

Appendix B: Books to Get You Started

The following books do not represent a comprehensive reading list but constitute a suggested place to begin in three areas *Eros Redeemed* has dealt with: (1) manhood, womanhood and marriage; (2) general sexual healing; and (3) spirituality and prayer.

Books About Manhood, Womanhood and Marriage

Robert Bly. *Iron John*. New York: Vintage Books, 1992.

Gordon Dalbey. *Healing the Masculine Soul*. Dallas: Word Publishing, 1988.

James G. Friesen. *Uncovering the Mystery of MPD*. San Bernardino, Calif.: Here's Life Publishers, 1991.

Sam Keen. *Fire in the Belly*. New York: Bantam Books, 1992.

Kevin Marron. *Ritual Abuse: Canada's Most Infamous Trial on Child Abuse*. Toronto: McClellan-Bantam Seal Books, 1989.

Mike Mason. *The Mystery of Marriage*. Portland, Ore.: Multnomah Press, 1985.

John Piper and Wayne Grudem, eds. *Recovering Biblical Manhood and Womanhood*. Wheaton, Ill.: Crossway Books, 1991. Although this book is addressed to biblical scholars, the preface, foreword and first section are not technical and would repay perusal by people not versed in biblical scholarship.

Books About General and Sexual Healing
The following do not include psychiatric texts.

Elizabeth Moberly. *Homosexuality: A New Christian Ethic.* Cambridge: James Clark and Co., 1983.
Leanne Payne. *The Broken Image.* Westchester, Ill.: Crossway Books, 1981.
Leanne Payne. *Crisis in Masculinity.* Westchester, Ill.: Crossway Books, 1985.
Leanne Payne. *The Healing Presence.* Westchester, Ill.: Crossway Books, 1984.
David A. Seamands. *Healing of Memories.* Wheaton, Ill.: Victor Books, 1985.

Books About Spirituality and Prayer
Books about spirituality vary in their underlying theology. Their aim is usually more practical—to teach methods by which one is better able to hear God's voice. However, no one method fits everybody, and each of us eventually finds how best to do so.

Anthony Bloom. *Beginning to Pray.* New York: Paulist Press, 1970. (Published in Britain by Darton, Longman and Todd, Ltd., under the title *School for Prayer.*)
Richard Foster. *Prayer.* San Francisco: HarperSanFrancisco, 1992.
Joyce Huggett. *The Joy of Listening to God.* Downers Grove, Ill.: InterVarsity Press, 1986.
Thomas S. Keating. *Open Mind, Open Heart.* Rockport, Mass.: Element, 1986.
Brother Lawrence (Frank Laubach, ed.). *Practicing the Presence.* Auburn, Maine: Christian Books, 1973.
Henri Nouwen. *The Way of the Heart.* New York: Ballantine Books, 1981.

Notes

Chapter 1: A Sin-Stained Church in a Sex-Sated Society
[1]"How Common Is Pastoral Indiscretion?" *Leadership* 9, no. 1 (Winter 1988): 12.
[2]Francis Frangipane, *The Three Battlegrounds* (Marion, Iowa: Frangipane, 1989), p. 100.
[3]Quoted by Sam Keen in *Fire in the Belly* (New York: Bantam, 1992), p. 8.
[4]Ibid., p. 9.
[5]For a further treatment, see John White, *Changing on the Inside: The Keys to Spiritual Recovery and Lasting Change* (Ann Arbor, Mich.: Servant, 1991).

Chapter 2: Nakedness: What Went Wrong?
[1]Basil F. C. Atkinson, *Exodus* (Worthing, U.K.: Henry E. Walker, n.d.), p. 323.
[2]C. S. Lewis, *Voyage to Venus* (London: Pan Books, 1960), pp. 123-27.
[3]See Exodus 28:42, Leviticus 16:4, 23. At this point some authors differ from the view I express. The trousers ("breeches" KJV, "undergarments" NIV) were not designed, says Atkinson, as a protection from "peeking." Their purpose was symbolic. Older commentators, noting that in Revelation linen symbolizes the righteousness of the saints, speak of "covering, but not concealing." Yet the context suggests exposure. Why else the warning about ascending steps?

While nakedness in Scripture is most frequently an allusion to genitalia or to sexual activity, this is clearly not always the case. It also symbolizes both guilt and shame at different points. Here, the use could be symbolic, the issue shame and covering, guilt and righteousness.

Basil Atkinson comments, "The imputed righteousness of Christ is not a sham, a concealing of guilt that actually exists beneath, a covering through which God cannot see. Guilt is nakedness. The imputed righteousness of Christ does not conceal but removes the guilt, being a garment put on by one who without it would be naked" *(Exodus, p. 323)*.

[4]John Milton, *Paradise Lost*, in the volume of Milton's poems (Danbury, Conn.:

Grolier, n.d.), p. 254.

[5]C. S. Lewis, *Mere Christianity* (New York: Collier, 1952), p. 53.

[6]Milton, *Paradise Lost*, p. 256.

[7]Ibid.

[8]What I called "the Wizard of Id thing" (the supposed fear that women have of worms and snakes) is not without substance. Women do seem to fear snakes even more than men, and evidence from their dreams has made clear that in some women, at least, the fear is linked with penile fear, far-fetched as the hypothesis might seem at first sight. Some of my female patients who had fears that arose from unconscious and terrifying memories of sexual molestation also suffered from perpetual nightmares of snakes, of wormlike and snakelike creatures.

[9]Lewis, *Mere Christianity*, p. 52.

[10]Ibid. See also John White, *Magnificent Obsession* (Downers Grove, Ill.: InterVarsity Press, 1990), pp. 69-70.

Chapter 3: The Uniqueness of Sexual Sin

[1]Edwin M. Yamauchi, "Gnosticism," in *New Dictionary of Theology*, ed. Sinclair B. Ferguson et al. (Downers Grove, Ill.: InterVarsity Press, 1988), pp. 273-74.

[2]Francis de Sales, *Introduction to the Devout Life* (Garden City, N.Y.: Doubleday/ Image, 1972), p. 229.

[3]Ibid., pp. 228-29. Anticipation of or memory of any pleasure—sensual or spiritual—need not be lust. It can also reflect gratitude and praise for God's goodness. There is a Greek fear of the body, here.

[4]Later, Balaam would receive his punishment for his misdeeds. "The Israelites had put to the sword Balaam son of Beor, who practiced divination" (Josh 13:22).

[5]The sin Ezekiel describes is not sexual sin. Rather, he uses sexual sin as an allegory to represent Israel's unfaithfulness to God in depending on political and military alliances instead of trusting God. However, in the course of the allegory he seems incidentally to be showing the appropriate punishment for sexual unfaithfulness.

[6]G. K. Chesterton, *St. Francis of Assisi* (Garden City, N.Y.: Doubleday/Image, 1957), p. 29.

Chapter 4: Overcoming Idolatry and Sexual Sin

[1]I do not say *the* way, but *one* way, perhaps the most important way. However, virginal men and women throughout history have been able to enter into exquisitely intimate fellowship with God. Clearly, sex is not the only way.

[2]C. S. Lewis, *The Last Battle* (New York: Collier, 1956), pp. 153-57.

[3]G. E. Farley, "Circumcision," in *Pictorial Encyclopedia of the Bible*, ed. Merrill C. Tenney (Grand Rapids, Mich.: Zondervan/Regency, 1975-76), 1:866-68.

Chapter 5: Sexual Sin and Violence

[1]"Confronting the Social Deficit," *U.S. News and World Report*, February 8, 1993, p. 28.

[2]Joseph J. Senna and Larry J. Siegel, *Introduction to Criminal Justice* (Minneapolis: West, 1993), pp. 55-59.

[3]Ibid., p. 57.

[4]Ibid., p. 58.

[5]Charles W. Kegley, ed., *The Long Postwar Peace* (New York: HarperCollins, 1991), pp. 78-79.

[6]Report no. 35 of the Department of Peace and Conflict Research of Uppsala University. A statement in the preface by Peter Wallenstein, professor and head of the department.

Chapter 6: The Question of Satanic Ritual Abuse

[1]Bob and Gretchen Passantino, "Hard Facts About Satanic Ritual Abuse," *Christian Research Journal*, Winter 1992, pp. 20ff.

[2]The particular issue of *The Cult Observer* is uncertain. The general heading lists it as vol. 6, no. 6, November/December 1989. However, at the foot of the same page (p. 2) it is described as the September/October 1989 issue.

[3]"Scholars Find No Evidence of Spreading Occult Cults," *Los Angeles Times*, October 29, 1989, pp. A3, A30.

[4]From the Fort Lauderdale *Sun Sentinel*, September 17, 1989, p. 4E.

[5]"Threat of Satanism Debunked in Study," *The Washington Times*, November 3, 1990, p. B6. Satanism Watch points out that *The Washington Times* is owned by a company in close association with the Unification Church.

[6]Jeffrey S. Victor, "Threats to Civil Liberties," in *Free Inquiry*, Winter 1992/93, p. 52.

[7]Cynthia S. Kisser, "Satanism as a Social Movement," in *Free Inquiry*, Winter 1992/93, p. 55.

[8]By *true believer* the Passantinos mean "someone who is committed to believing the SRA conspiracy world view, and who often is an outspoken proponent, such as a true believer therapist, law enforcement person, parent, adult survivor, and so on." See "Hard Facts About Satanic Ritual Abuse," *Christian Research Journal*, Winter 1992, p. 22.

[9]James G. Friesen, *Uncovering the Mystery of MPD* (San Bernardino, Calif.: Here's Life Publications, 1991), p. 70.

[10]Herbert Butterfield, *Christianity and History* (London: Fontana Books, 1958), p. 20.

[11]Ibid., p. 37.

[12]Quoted by Fred Alan in *Taking the Quantum Leap* (New York: Harper & Row, 1989), p. 116.

[13]Walter Sundberg, "A Primer on the Devil," *First Things*, Winter 1992/93, pp. 15-21.

[14]Mike Warnke's sensational bestseller *The Satan Seller* (Plainfield, N.J.: Logos International, 1972) won him fame and money and assured him of a "ministry." An exposé by Jon Trott and Mike Hertenstein reveals careful research into Warnke's background. It appears in *Cornerstone* 21, no. 98 (June 1992).

[15]Tom Zytaruk, "Coming Out," *Surrey and North Delta NOW*, February 24, 1993, p. A21.

Chapter 7: Satanic Sex

[1]See Susan J. Kelly, "Ritualistic Abuse in Children," *Cultic Studies Journal* 5: 228ff.

See also Judith Spencer, *Suffer the Child* (New York: Simon and Schuster, 1989). This story cannot be verified, since names and other details have been changed to protect the individuals concerned from reprisals.

²Kevin Marron, *Ritual Abuse* (Toronto: McClelland Bantam, 1988), p. 51.

³Ibid., pp. 56-57.

⁴Ken Blue, formerly the pastor of the Delta Vineyard in our area, is currently a pastor in Southern California.

⁵When I speak of a demonic manifestation, I refer to a sudden eruption of a dramatic change in the person's behavior. It may take the form of an outbreak of cursing the name of God or Christ, of writhing like a snake and hissing, of an epileptiform seizure, of feats of extraordinary strength or agility, or even of levitation. I have never seen the latter, but have witnessed all the others I mention, commonly in response to my own preaching, to my approaching someone or to my praying for someone.

⁶"Breeder" is a term given by some witchcraft groups to refer to a girl who is used to produce babies for sacrifice. The sexual act leading to the pregnancy is commonly a ritualized act.

⁷The box in question turned out to be an empty coffin.

⁸The children of Satanists are often taught songs and dances teaching the "evil" and ugliness of Jesus, and the power, goodness and wisdom of the Prince (of darkness).

⁹The views of experienced Christians both in Britain and in North America differ in some details about the treatment of MPD. For instance, Wendy Hoffman writes: "Functions are programmed into victims by cult members. The functions are different from multiple personality in that they are not organic or spontaneous. They do not arise from the survivor's being overwhelmed and using dissociation as a way of coping and enduring. Functions should not be integrated, for they do not come from the survivor's own system of survival" (*Identifying Characteristics of Repressed Satanic Cult Survivors* [available from Box 1898, New York, NY 10025, 212-932-1835], p. 3).

Chapter 8: The Marriage of Sex and Love

¹Sam Keen, *Fire in the Belly* (New York: Bantam, 1992), p. 72.

²Mike Mason, *The Mystery of Marriage* (Portland, Ore.: Multnomah Press, 1985), p. 13.

³Ibid., p. 18.

⁴C. S. Lewis, *The Four Loves* (Glasgow: Collins/Fount, 1989), p. 14.

⁵C. S. Lewis, *The Lion, the Witch and the Wardrobe* (New York: Collier, 1970), p. 29.

⁶Ibid., p. 71.

⁷C. S. Lewis, *That Hideous Strength* (London: Pan Books, 1956), pp. 166-67.

⁸Leanne Payne, *The Healing Presence* (Westchester, Ill.: Crossway, 1989), p. 98.

Chapter 9: Sex for the Castaway

¹Scott O'Dell, *Island of the Blue Dolphins* (New York: Dell, 1960), p. 178.

²The words *in pursuit of an orgasm* are important. Sometimes men and women who

have developed an unwholesome fear of sexuality or of their own bodies are advised to explore their body's sensations. They are counseled in particular to explore their erotogenic areas and not to be afraid of arousing them.

I would add a caution. If the advice is an open invitation to masturbation, it is unfortunate. There is a fine line between *discovery* of the pleasures the body and the *pursuit* of those pleasures. To pursue them for their own sake is to make an idol of them.

[3]John White, *Eros Defiled* (Downers Grove, Ill.: InterVarsity Press, 1977), pp. 33-43.
[4]Charles Williams, *Descent into Hell* (Grand Rapids, Mich.: Eerdmans, 1949), p. 86.
[5]Ibid., p. 87.
[6]Ibid., p. 130.
[7]Ibid., p. 131.
[8]Ibid., p. 130.
[9]Ibid., p. 174.
[10]Thomas R. Kelly, *A Testament of Devotion* (New York: Harper & Row, 1941), p. 62.
[11]Ibid., p. 39.

Chapter 10: Sex and Gender Confusion

[1]Karl Stern, *The Flight from Woman* (New York: Farrar, Straus and Giroux, 1965), p. 39.
[2]The search for male identity is evidenced by the modern men's movement and by such recent books as sociologist Sam Keen's *Fire in the Belly: On Being a Man,* poet Robert Bly's *Iron John* and Gordon Dalbey's *Healing the Masculine Soul.*
[3]C. S. Lewis, *Voyage to Venus* (London: Pan Books, 1956), p. 186.
[4]In some editions, entitled *Perelandra.*
[5]Lewis, *Voyage to Venus,* pp. 184-85.
[6]Leanne Payne, *Crisis in Masculinity* (Westchester, Ill.: Crossway, 1985), p. 49.
[7]C. S. Lewis, *That Hideous Strength* (London: Pan Books, 1956), p. 194.
[8]Robert Bly, *Iron John* (New York: Random House, 1990), p. 43.

Chapter 11: The Roots of Inversion

[1]Sam Keen, *Fire in the Belly* (New York: Bantam, 1992), p. 231.
[2]A helpful summary of these findings can be found in *Discover,* January 1992, p. 29.
[3]John White, *Eros Defiled* (Downers Grove, Ill.: InterVarsity Press, 1977). See chapter six, pp. 105-39.
[4]Ibid., p. 126.
[5]Exodus International is an organization linking together various local groups that devote themselves to assisting homosexuals who want support in overcoming homosexuality. For free information, including a list of ministries throughout North America, contact Exodus International, P.O. Box 2121, San Rafael, CA 94912. Phone: 415-454-1017.
[6]Elizabeth R. Moberly, *Homosexuality: A New Christian Ethic* (Cambridge, U.K.: James Clarke, 1983). Moberly is both a theologian and a research psychologist with

special interest in psychoanalytic research.

[7]Payne, a former lecturer at Wheaton College, is a spiritually gifted woman with an internationally recognized ministry in the deliverance of homosexuals and other men and women with sexual problems. Her books include *The Broken Image* (Westchester, Ill.: Crossway, 1981) and *Crisis in Masculinity* (Westchester, Ill.: Crossway, 1985).

[8]Lionel Ovessey, *Homosexuality and Pseudohomosexuality* (New York: Science House, 1969).

[9]Lewis, *Mere Christianity*, p. 89.

Chapter 12: Manliness and Womanliness

[1]My definition is simple enough, though it raises questions that I hope will be answered in this chapter and the next. Manly men and womanly women are men and women who function as they were intended by God to function when they were first created.

[2]Quoted in Gordon Dalbey, *Healing the Masculine Soul* (Dallas: Word, 1988), p. 70, from Lynda J. Barry, "The Sensitive Male," *Esquire,* July 1984, p. 85.

[3]Robert Bly, *Iron John* (New York: Vintage Books, 1992), p. 63.

[4]Sam Keen, *Fire in the Belly* (New York: Bantam, 1992), p. 9.

[5]Ibid., p. 7.

[6]And please, let us not forget that while men are usually the bullies, some women also physically abuse their men.

[7]See Clinton Arnold's scholarly yet very readable *Powers of Darkness* (Downers Grove, Ill.: InterVarsity Press, 1992). Arnold is an associate professor of New Testament at Talbot School of Theology, Biola University. He deals with the principalities and powers in the Pauline letters, looking at principles relevant for us in our world today, which is rapidly becoming similar to the world of the New Testament.

[8]Richard and Catherine Clark Kroeger, *I Suffer Not a Woman: Rethinking 1 Timothy 2:11-15 in Light of Ancient Evidence* (Grand Rapids, Mich.: Baker Book House, 1992).

[9]Ibid., p. 103.

[10]Roy McCloughry, *Men and Masculinity* (London: Hodder and Stoughton, 1992), p. 65.

Chapter 13: Christ, Model of Manliness

[1]John Owen makes that issue clear. He talks about the *grace of union,* meaning the union of divine and human natures in Christ, pointing out that "the uniting of the natures of God and man in one person made him fit to be a Saviour to the uttermost. He lays his hand upon God, by partaking of his nature, Zech xiii. 7; and he lays his hand upon us, by being partaker of our nature, Heb. ii. 14, 16: and so becomes a days-man, or umpire between both." *The Works of John Owen* (London: Banner of Truth Trust, 1965), 2:51.

Part III: Redemption from Distorted Sexuality

[1]"Praying on" someone, as distinct from praying *for* someone, is a phrase used by

the Vineyard to describe praying in the presence of a person with the full expectation of immediate divine intervention for that person.

Chapter 14: Hidden Memories
[1]In this case, oral incorporation of her father's phallus.
[2]Payne's handling of the woman is a model of good spiritual care and is worth reading in its entirety. See Leanne Payne, *The Broken Image* (Westchester, Ill.: Crossway, 1981), pp. 15-27.
[3]The details are enlarged in a paper by B. A. van der Kolk and Onno van der Hart, "The Intrusive Past: The Flexibility of Memory and the Engraving of Trauma," *American Imago* (Johns Hopkins University Press) 48, no. 4 (1991): 425-54. Much of what follows is taken from this excellent and detailed summary.
[4]Ibid., p. 437.
[5]Ibid., p. 448.
[6]Ibid., p. 429.
[7]David A. Seamands, *The Healing of Memories* (Wheaton, Ill.: Victor Books, 1985), pp. 84-87.
[8]Ibid., p. 85.
[9]From unpublished lecture notes by John Smelzer, who can be contacted though Vineyard Ministries International, P.O. Box 65004, Anaheim, CA 92805. The lecture was given at a Vineyard conference. The questions that I am asking, though my own, were suggested to me as I listened to that lecture.
[10]Ibid.

Chapter 15: Forgiving Family Sin
[1]Francis Foulkes, *The Letter of Paul to the Ephesians,* Tyndale New Testament Commentaries (Grand Rapids, Mich.: Eerdmans, 1989), p. 101.
[2]Thomas Keating, *Open Mind, Open Heart* (Rockport, Mass.: Element, 1991), p. 9.
[3]Chaim Potok, *My Name Is Asher Lev* (New York: Fawcett Crest, 1972), p. 59.
[4]W. M. Thackeray, *Vanity Fair* (New York: Dutton/New American Library, 1962), chap. 35.
[5]William Shakespeare, *Twelfth Night,* act 3, scene 4, line 390.
[6]See John White, *Excellence in Leadership* (Downers Grove, Ill.: InterVarsity Press, 1986), chap. 1.
[7]Ibid., pp. 22-24.

Chapter 16: Facing Your Repentant Future
[1]Samuel W. Gandy, "I Hear the Accuser Roar," in *Believers' Hymn Book* (London: Pickering and Inglis, n.d.), no. 93.
[2]*The Confessions of Saint Augustine,* trans. Rex Warner (New York: Mentor Books, 1963), pp. 182-83.
[3]Charles W. Colson, *Against the Night* (Ann Arbor, Mich.: Vine Books, 1989), p. 140.
[4]John White, *Changing on the Inside* (Ann Arbor, Mich.: Servant, 1991).
[5]Charles G. Finney, *True and False Repentance* (Grand Rapids, Mich.: Kregel), pp. 14-15.

⁶Charles W. Colson, *Born Again* (Old Tappan, N.J.: Revell/Chosen Books, 1976), pp. 116-17.

Chapter 17: Prayer: A Means of Grace
¹Andrew Murray, *With Christ in the School of Prayer* (Westwood, N.J.: Revell, n.d.), p. 76.
²John Bunyan, *Grace Abounding* (Chicago: Moody Press, 1959), pp. 45-46.
³I have changed one or two of the facts in this account to protect the organization concerned. The homosexuality was revealed and dealt with in private. But I note that in one or two New Testament occasions sin is dealt with publicly (Acts 5:1-10; 1 Cor 14:24-45).
⁴Henri J. M. Nouwen, *The Way of the Heart* (New York: Ballantine/Epiphany, 1981), p. 7.
⁵Ibid., p. 8.
⁶Thomas Keating is a former psychiatrist and author of a book about *centering* prayer, *Open Mind, Open Heart* (Rockport, Mass.: Element, 1986).
⁷E. May Grimes, "Speak, Lord, in the Stillness," in *Hymns II* (Downers Grove, Ill.: InterVarsity Press, 1976), no. 140.
⁸Nouwen, *The Way of the Heart,* pp. 31-32.
⁹Thomas R. Kelly, *A Testament of Devotion* (New York: Harper & Row, 1941), p. 62.

Chapter 18: Healing Hidden Wounds Through the Body
¹Such "anointings" take various forms. People's subjective reactions to them vary, as does the language used to describe them in Scripture. I discuss the issue more fully in *When the Spirit Comes with Power* (Downers Grove, Ill.: InterVarsity Press, 1988).
²B. O. Banwell, "Heart," in *New Bible Dictionary,* ed. J. D. Douglas, 2nd ed. (Leicester, U.K.: Inter-Varsity Press, 1984), p. 465.
³Leanne Payne, *Crisis in Masculinity* (Westchester, Ill.: Crossway, 1985), p. 35.

Chapter 19: The Healing Session
¹John Wimber with Kevin Springer, *Power Healing* (San Francisco: Harper & Row, 1987), p. 199.
²Ibid., p. 200.
³Ibid., p. 207.
⁴Ibid., pp. 207-10.
⁵There is always a reason why this happens. Perhaps the commonest reason (not true in his case) is that of a return to a sin that gave rise to the condition in the first place, or of a refusal to repent in those cases where God has revealed the connection between a sin and the sickness. In most cases there is no connection between a specific sin and the sickness.

In this case, witchcraft and a powerful curse were involved. Later when we found out about the curse, partly through the Lord's revelations in the form of words and visions, and confirmed by the discovery of a cardboard box full of correspondence from the warlock who pronounced the curse, we sought to break its power. We thought we had triumphed, and we almost did. But always we had a nagging doubt, which in the long run proved to be true.

Nevertheless God's amazing purposes, both in the man's circle of friends, and in his denomination, were accomplished through the healing.